A COUNTRY CALLED BROOKLYN

A COUNTRY CALLED BROOKLYN

A MEMOIR

HANE SELMANI

SILENT TRUTH PRESS
NEW YORK

For my sister Xharije
Your life brought me joy.
Your death gave me the courage
to overcome the beliefs that enslaved me.

Notes on Language

- My sister's name was Xharije, pronounced jay-REE-yeh. For ease of reading, I spell it Jariyeh.
- When Albanian appears, it reflects a blend of northern Gheg and Kosovar dialects we speak, rather than standard southern Tosk.
- The English spelling of my birthplace is *Kosovo*; in Albanian it is *Kosova* or *Kosovë*. I use Kosova throughout for consistency.
- I use the spelling Moslem, an older English transliteration, throughout.
- Dialogue is in English, though Albanian was spoken in our home.

Names

- Arta *(AHR-tah)*— My niece, Roza's eldest daughter
- Agim (ah-GHEEM) — Mehmet's brother
- Baba (BAH-bah) — My father (also known as Lutfi Feza Alija
- Bekim *(BEH-keem)* — My eldest brother
- Esat *(eh-SAHT)* — Jariyeh's eldest son
- Filanza *(fu-LAHN-zah)* — Jariyeh's mother-in-law
- Gjile *(JEE-leh)* — Saranda's mother
- Jariyeh (jah-REE-yeh) — My older sister, also spelled Xharije
- Kamile *(kah-MEE-leh)* — My sister
- Lata *(LAH-tah)* — Jariyeh's daughter
- Luan *(loo-AHN)* — My youngest brother
- Mehmet *(MEH-met)* — Jariyeh's husband
- Nana (NAH-nah) — My mother, also Nanë
- Perparim *(per-pah-REEM)* — Jariyeh's youngest son
- Roza (ROH-zah) — My eldest sister
- Sam — Saranda's eldest brother
- Saranda *(sa-RAHN-dah)* — My sister-in-law, Bekim's wife
- Selman *(SEL-mahn)* — Jariyeh's father-in-law
- Teze Fatime *(TEH-zeh fah-TEE-meh)* — My maternal aunt
- Vera *(VEH-rah)* — My sister-in-law, Zogu's wife
- Zogu (ZOH-*goo*) — My brother

Preface

———————

I never set out to be a writer. Singing and dancing would have been my profession of choice. Growing up, my sole ambition was to become a good *Nuse*--wife. I was raised to believe that reading was for lazy people, and writing was a senseless act. More important was mastering my chores, so I learned to wash dishes, clean walls, and vacuum in parallel lines.

My writing journey began in my later years, when I shared personal stories with my American friends. Shocked, they would ask:

"In what country was *that?*"

"A country called Brooklyn," I'd joke.

"You should write a book," they'd always say.

Why not, I thought. How hard could it be?

I wasn't allowed to go to college after high school, but did so in my thirties, when I was no longer asking permission. I studied writing at New York University, but the fear of disgracing our family name stopped me in my tracks. After a decade of self-empowerment studies, I found the courage to begin again. But I quickly realized that not being allowed to speak my truth in my early years had left me unable to express myself on the page.

My writing teacher encouraged me to continue.

"It's not that you're a horrible writer," she said. "You just can't write in English."

I laughed. Did she think I could write in another language?

But I persevered because I believed Albanians could do anything, and because the stories demanded to be told. I shared only five pages about the night my sister Jariyeh was murdered, and was ready to move on, but classmates demanded more.

"You need to flesh this out," the teacher agreed. "Your sister's murder was a pivotal moment in your life."

It was true. Jariyeh's death had forced me to question my world. A world I had stitched together with threads of illusion. Illusions of God. Illusions of Honor. Illusions of Female Inferiority—something my sister never accepted.

Jariyeh and I represented two eras of women: the enslaved and the emancipated. Ironically, I was the one who took comfort in my captivity. Jariyeh was the one fighting for her liberation.

But how to write about my sister when I didn't know her story?

"Why are you writing about Jariyeh?" everyone asked, worried that I'd say something I shouldn't.

"Because Jariyeh's death changed my life," I'd reply, which was partly true. I also needed closure.

Though my family was impressed by the accuracy of their portrayals, panic still set in. "Change my name," said one, then another, and another. Then came, "Can't you take that part out?"

At first, I took it out, not wanting my family to think I didn't care about our family name. But the thought of being controlled yet again, in my fifties, made my stomach turn. I asked myself: *Is this what Jariyeh would have wanted?* All her life, she fought to free herself and empower women. She wouldn't have stopped if she hadn't been silenced. I had to honor my sister's life. I had to tell her story, no matter the consequences.

I would be Jariyeh's voice.

For her.

For me.

For all oppressed women.

I. THE FAMILY

Brooklyn Fall of 1970:
17-year-old Jariyeh as a bride, standing with family friends.

ALBANIA, KOSOVA, ITALY & BROOKLYN
1949-1978

Chapter 1

Shattered Illusions

* * *

"Who you marry and when you die is written on your forehead the day you are born," my mother told me when I was little.

I imagined cherubs engraving invisible letters on my temple.

Zot--God was the All-Knowing, the All-Merciful. It was good He made those decisions, I thought. They were much too important to be left up to us to get wrong. All I had to do was be good, and He'd take care of the rest.

I loved God and felt like a dove in His loving hands. I loved being an Albanian girl protected by her fierce traditions. My father and brothers were keepers of the family name—they'd never let anything bad happen to us women.

My world was perfect. My family, flawless. The brainwashing went deep, making it impossible to think otherwise.

Until I was sixteen.

It was 2:33 a.m. on September 18, 1979, in Gravesend, Brooklyn, when my sister Jariyeh was murdered. Her husband Mehmet chased her at gunpoint from their building next door to ours. While she lay downstairs bleeding between the double doors of our vestibule, I lay upstairs asleep in my bed.

"Wake up. Wake up, Hane," I hear a whisper.

Is it morning already? Why did I stay up so late? I open my eyes. My friend Seba is asleep beside me. The room is dark. All I can make out is my sister-in-law Vera's silhouette.

"Jariyeh's dead," her voice trembles. "Mehmet killed her."

It can't be. God wouldn't let that happen. Mehmet was the bad one. If anyone was dead, it had to be him.

Vera walks out of the room.

I sit up and press the back of my head against the wall. Trying to understand. Trying to shift the joyous memories of my sister into a future where she's not there.

Tiny flickers of light flash through pathways inside my brain as I struggle to piece together what is true. Is she alive? Is she dead? Is she alive? Is she dead?

Memories collide and suspend in slow motion, as if in outer space—yet nothing connects.

Jariyeh *has* to be alive. She was going to teach me how to dance. How to sing. How to be loved—just like she was. She made life fun.

The sparks begin to fall and reassemble, and only one clear thought remains: *fun is dead!*

A moan escapes me, an eerie sound I'd never heard before.

The pain is unbearable. I leave my body and am hovering above my head. I watch myself climb over Seba as if I'm watching a character in a movie. I walk into the hallway, then into the bright dining room. My eyes sting. *Nana*--Mom is sitting on the carpet. Rocking back and forth. Crying. I had never seen her cry before.

So, it *is* true.

Jariyeh *is* dead.

I come crashing back into my body and feel the deep sadness waiting inside. Death wasn't supposed to be like this. When Baba died of cancer and was no longer suffering, Nana told me to put on my best dress.

This was different.

I walk into the family room, lie on the carpet and sob quietly, so as not to disturb my mother.

"Go to the apartment," I hear my brother Zogu tell our brother Luan, "because the kids will wake up and be scared when they see only the police and nobody they know."

The kids! *Oh my God, I forgot about the kids.* Who will tell them? There's no way I can. I'm the closest thing they have now to a mother, but I'm useless. Thank God others are here to care for them. I can start tomorrow. Just not tonight. Why had I given Jariyeh such a hard time about babysitting? It can't end like this.

I want one more chance.

Vera walks over. "Mehmet chased Jariyeh from their building to ours. He shot her five times."

I imagine my sister running down her long hallway. Did the bright fluorescent lights make her an easy target? Did Mehmet shoot her there? Did the sound ricochet through the corridor like it did when Jariyeh and I laughed? Why did she have to be so scared in her final moments?

What was God thinking?

Why did He choose Mehmet as her husband, then have him kill her?

Or did God not choose the cause of death?

But she wasn't sick. A car didn't hit her. How else would she have died at that exact moment. Surely God was precise. He must have wanted Mehmet to kill her, I tell myself. But God couldn't be that cruel, myself answers.

Or could He?

Did God exist?

He must.

Someone had to be responsible.

"Jariyeh was ringing our buzzer—" Vera continues my torment.

Our buzzer? We could've saved her? Why didn't I hear it? Why didn't anyone let her in?

"The super saw it and died of a heart attack," Vera adds. "Jariyeh is still downstairs."

Downstairs? I want to go. I want to see my sister one last time—but I'm afraid. I hate my fear. Was Nana expecting me to go? I know she won't stop me. No one would. Albanians are supposed to be tough. This was my chance to prove I was too.

But I don't move.

I can't let that be my last memory of her, I excuse myself, and look over at Nana. Is she disappointed? But for the first time, she doesn't seem to care what I do.

None of it feels real.

I lie on the floor; tears burn down the side of my face and into my hair. No one pays me any mind. The air around me hums, as if alive. Palpable. If I could stand up, I could walk right through it. Everything feels interconnected. But she's not here. How will life go on without her?

Jariyeh had been more alive than anyone I knew, which somehow made her more dead.

Heaving sobs exhaust me into sleep.

I wake up.

How did I get here? What is this heaviness in my chest? What are all these people…

Oh…

I curl into a ball.

My sisters-in-law, Vera and Saranda, walk around like robots. Fulfilling their wifely duties keeps them from losing it altogether. They serve guests bitter Turkish coffee. You never use sugar when someone dies. Sugar is for celebrations. Sugar is sweet. Death is bitter.

I watch the bustle of people coming in and out. Family, friends, and detectives mill around like characters in a play—caught up in their roles. Our apartment is their stage. The same apartment where people once came to sing and dance is now a pit of mourners. Everyone came the moment they heard, not waiting for "an appropriate time." The men try to be strong, but they cry. After all, it was Jariyeh.

Everyone's favorite.

But I'm sure I loved her most.

Saranda's mother couldn't make it. After hearing the news she was hospitalized with a nervous breakdown and would stay five days. "You better cry and get it all out of your stomach," she told her daughter. "Or else you're going to get sick."

Vera's seventy-nine-year-old father walks in already weeping. Jariyeh used to buy him Marlboros whenever he visited. He didn't know what it was about that girl, but he loved Jariyeh as he wished he could have loved his own daughter.

The men are talking in the living room. The women are sitting around the dining room table. My eldest sister Roza sits with them. She doesn't cry. She shakes her head and repeats silently: *I'm in a dream. I'm in a dream. I'll wake up. I'm in a dream.*

Sister Kamile sits on the carpet, weeping softly. Next to her, Nana rocks and moans: *"Shka t'bana moj bi? Shka t'bana moj bi?"*--What have I done to you, my daughter? What have I done to you, my daughter?

Why is she blaming herself?

"Be strong and keep your head," friends say to Nana as they enter.

Later they'd whisper to each other, "They should have known what kind of family they were marrying Jariyeh into."

I close my eyes, needing to get away. If only I could sleep and go back to the place where my sister can still exist.

Jariyeh bursts in wearing her new satin outfit, the colors of the Albanian flag—kuq e zi-- red and black. With hands on hips, eyes straight ahead, and a big smile that proudly displays the gap in her front teeth, she takes long strides in her strappy high heels that should've been left at the door. Like a runway model, she sways her arms, swings her hips, and exaggerates her stride. Her hair flies as she spins, giving the full effect to her flared satin skirt.

Everyone laughs.

"Hajde"--Let's go! she says, eager to get to the nightclub and take over the dance floor.

The memory is drowned out by the sound of bare feet slapping the marble floor, and gunshots reverberating through her long hallway.

She will never dance again.

It's morning. I hear Zogu in the foyer and walk over. He's standing there with a gun. A friend stands beside him. The police and detectives are gone. Now it's our turn. The Kanun allows for the heat of the moment. The first twenty-four hours, while the "blood is hot," are open season on any male member of Mehmet's family. But Zogu wants Mehmet. We all do.

But I'm confused.

The tradition of "blood for blood," which once gave me comfort, now makes no sense. If God had written Jariyeh's death on her forehead, doesn't that make

Mehmet His accomplice? Or is the blood feud also part of God's plan?

Zogu opens the front door.

I'm terrified.

Why doesn't Nana stop him?

Has she no fear of losing another child?

Hasn't Jariyeh's death shown her we're not invincible?

That life isn't fair?

That God can't be trusted?

Please don't go!—I scream inside.

The front door closes.

Chapter 2

The Kanun

* * *

I knew who killed Jariyeh. I knew where she took her final breath. But how did she get there? At sixteen, I was a good girl, and good girls didn't question—they obeyed.

Now, thirty years later, it was time I knew the truth.

My family said the drug dealers made him do it. Mehmet told his children it was an honor killing due to an affair. Each explanation served a purpose. His version shamed our family and made him a hero. Ours preserved our name and reduced him to a liar. What was missing was the evidence. I set out to find the truth, certain it would lead to the drug dealers. Then Jariyeh's children could finally know, and our family name would be cleared.

But where to begin when no one ever spoke of what happened? And if they did, would I be ready to hear it?

I turned to the women first, knowing they'd be more open. They cried as they recalled the memories they'd wanted shut away. I cried along with them, saddened anew by each discovery. Disturbing dreams followed, making me question why I had started this venture in the first place.

"Jariyeh was my best friend. Her death hurt me more than anyone else," each one claimed. Impossible, I'd think—how could that be when her death hurt me most? She was *my* blood. *My* best friend. *My* hero.

The jealousy surprised me.

And their stories revealed how little I had known.

Growing up, no one told me things. I was the baby not worth their while. I thought I was the youngest of seven until my thirties, when I was told I was named after a sister I didn't know existed. She died of dehydration. Nana swore it was the evil eye.

I knew nothing of Albania's history or my family's. All I knew was that my parents were from Albania and that we were *Lumjan*--people of *Lumë*. I later learned Lumë was a river in the northern mountains. My parents had escaped Albania and settled for a time in Kosova, where I was born. I also knew we were proud, but never knew why.

Albanians are an old people of Illyrian descent who speak an ancient Indo-European language.[i] Before Christianity or Islam, we were pagans who worshiped the earth and believed in spirits. Illyria was renamed Albania after the Albanoi tribe in the second century BC. Our land was ruled by many fiefdoms, with two main clans—northern Gheg and southern Tosk. We were a proud people, proud from love of our heritage, not from any wish to conquer or annihilate.

My family had come to America for freedom, not assimilation. That was for the weak. We were *Shqiptarë*--People of the Eagle—Albanians! The greatest of them all. Honor was our aspiration. Shame our tool. More powerful than the guns our men carried. Fear of what "they" might say, silently stripping us of our will—even if we thought ourselves invincible.

Baba--Dad brought us to America for a better life and planned to take us back to our "homeland" once communism fell. Home to me was wherever my family was, and on June 30, 1970, that home was Brooklyn.

I was seven when we landed at New York's JFK Airport. We arrived with luggage filled with tailored clothes, a rug my mother had loomed for her dowry, and my father's two-stringed *çifteli*. We left everything else behind, but kept our traditions intact.

I was in my teens when I asked my mother, "Where did our traditions come from?"

"The Kanun," she said, and walked away.

I'd never seen this Kanun, and from what I could tell, neither had anyone else. But its ways were ingrained in our DNA, dictating our thoughts, feelings, and actions.

In my fifties, I found the *Kanun i Lekë Dukagjinit*--The Canon of Lekë Dukagjin and was shocked to learn that we'd been living according to 500-year-old honor codes—even in Brooklyn. No wonder my life felt so out of place. Another surprise was that Dukagjin was a Roman Catholic prince from the north. I always assumed our traditions had been influenced by Islam.

When the Ottoman Empire occupied Albania in 1479, the intellectual southern Tosk adopted Sharia law, but the Gheg warriors of the north adhered to Dukagjin's Kanun. In the unforgiving mountains, wealth was measured in honor. The Kanun ensured survival and protected our most prized possession—the family name. Once tainted, a name was nearly impossible to cleanse, so keeping it pristine was essential. Reputations took lifetimes to build, yet one shameful act could disgrace a clan for seven generations.

After nearly 450 years of Ottoman rule, most Albanians converted to Islam, including my ancestors—but we would always be Albanians first. Through centuries of occupation and shifting faiths, one thing held: religious tolerance.[ii] "Churches and mosques you shall not heed, the religion of Albania is Albanism." The Kanun had united us forever.

> Kanun Law §19: "The family consists of the people of the house; as these increase, they are divided into brotherhoods, brotherhoods into kinship, kinship groups into clans, clans into banners, and all together constitute one widespread family called a nation, which has one homeland, common blood, a common language, and common customs."

Honor, not heaven, was our reward.

At a time before judges, jurors, and jails, village elders relied on the Kanun to settle disputes and preserve the integrity of their clans. At the heart of it all was *besa*--word of honor: not just a promise, but a sacred obligation. Without it, you were worthless.

In the early 1900s, Dukagjin's oral laws were written into twelve books. Its most sexist decrees were abandoned—yet this remained:

> Section XXIX: "A woman is a sack made to endure as long as she lives in her husband's house...."

I knew women didn't matter, and was now beginning to understand why.

The intellectual Albanians may have moved past these barbaric laws, but not the Kanun-loving Shqiptarë of the mountains. We made our way into the urban streets of the world with the honor codes still burning inside. For my family, those streets were Brooklyn.

I quickly fell in love with Brooklyn and its concrete sidewalks, countless stores, and things called buildings with tiny homes inside. Everyone lived on top of one another—including us. So different from our farm in Kosova. Here, metal cars replaced horse-drawn carriages, toilets replaced outhouses, plumbing replaced wells. Lights turned on with a flick of a finger, and telephones let us speak to people who were far away. America was magic.

Hamit, our visa sponsor, met us at the airport. He took us in for two weeks, then found us an apartment in Boro Park among the Hasidic Jews. News that my father, Lutfi Feza, had arrived in Brooklyn quickly spread, and within weeks the Bicis from the Bronx were at our door. My parents were happy to get visitors in this strange land, but a visit from Selman Bici and his wife was special—they were also *Lumjan* of the north.

Baba and Selman met while serving time in a Yugoslavian prison. Back then, Selman was a tall, strapping man; now he sat in a wheelchair. He was as Baba remembered, a kind, soft-spoken man. His wife Filanza was as Nana remembered, a loud, gossipy woman who spoke in a constant whine. And when Filanza complained, which was often, she wailed. It added to the drama she loved so much.

They came with their twenty-one-year-old son Mehmet in tow, making it clear they had an agenda. While the former inmates reminisced, Filanza and her first-born waited for Jariyeh to reappear from the kitchen. As Jariyeh served them Turkish coffee, Filanza inspected. Did the girl dress modestly? Did she bend low enough when placing the coffee cups before them? Did she avoid eye contact? Qualities that made a girl marriage material. Whether Jariyeh liked Mehmet or not was irrelevant. For honorable Albanians, marriage was never about romance.

> Kanun Law §28: "To be married is to form a household, for the purpose of adding to the workforce and increasing the number of children."

After World War II, Albania's president, Enver Hoxha, outlawed the Kanun hoping to replace traditional law with communist rule. He wrote letters to couples who married for love, but arranged marriages remained.

Like the times of kings and queens, even the poorest villagers, marriages forged alliances between clans and were meant to last forever. There was no divorce, so getting it right was imperative. Parents sought to form connections with families known for bravery, loyalty, and honor. These unions preserved status, ensured survival, and upheld the patriarchal family name. A good breeder was key, so young and healthy wives were coveted. Beauty wasn't supposed to matter. Yet, it mattered.

Selman asked Hamit to be their *Shkus*--Matchmaker. Who better to ask for the daughter of the highly respected Lutfi Feza than his visa sponsor? Matchmakers were chosen for their standing with the girl's family, and no one was better. The Bicis would pay him generously if he could convince my father of their merit as *miq*--friends through marriage. Hamit's job was mostly done. Baba already respected Selman. No one liked his wife, but surely he would keep her in line.

While my family's name ranked higher than the Bicis', that wouldn't matter after marriage. A girl's family held power only during courtship, when they could accept or reject a proposal. Once engaged, authority passed to the boy's family.

My parents said yes to the matchmaker and accepted the bride-price—a gold coin—solidifying the exchange. Jariyeh now belonged to them. Did the engagement happen because Baba respected Selman, or because the pool of suitors was limited? In 1970s Brooklyn, fewer than 3,000 Albanians had settled in New York after World War II.[iii] We knew only a handful.

With the dowry came a wedding date for the following month. We didn't understand the rush, but it wasn't our place to question.

Kamile was still in Italy with her family awaiting their visas, and was sad to miss her sister's wedding—but Jariyeh's in-laws refused to wait.

Jariyeh's new title would be *Nusja Mehmetit*--Bride of Mehmet—though in truth she would belong to his entire family. I hadn't met her fiancé, but that was normal. Even Jariyeh had only seen him once.

Chapter 3

The Sad Nuse

* * *

My first clear memory of Jariyeh was on her wedding day. We were four sisters and three brothers. Of my sisters, seventeen-year-old Jariyeh was the closest to me in age—just ten years older. The other two sisters were more like my mothers. Roza was sixteen years my senior and had four children. Her eldest daughter, Arta, was a year younger than me. Sister Kamile was fourteen years older, and pregnant with her third son.

It was a sunny September day.

On the bed lay a white dress my sister had not chosen. Nana had given Jariyeh's measurements to Filanza, her mother-in-law. She had picked a modest gown, long-sleeved and covered to the neck. Modest meant old-fashioned. Old-fashioned meant honorable. Honorable meant not taking on the "American ways." The dress had come with the groom's dowry, along with evening gowns, shoes, and jewelry, the abundance of which gave credibility to the rumors that the Bicis had left Albania with a trunk of gold. Gold Zogu had seen firsthand.

Fifteen-year-old Zogu was visiting the Bicis when Selman spilled a change bag of gold coins onto a mattress and said, "Take! Take as much as you want." My brother wouldn't take what wasn't his and just stared. Selman gathered the coins and left. That was the first sign that our families were different.

Weddings in America weren't as extravagant as back home. Here, a few immigrants came for Jariyeh's sendoff. There, an entire lamb would be slaughtered to feed the guests, and the uninvited would spill into the courtyard to see the Nuse's transformation.

Becoming a Nuse was the ultimate makeover. The *Telake* tinted Jariyeh's cheeks with the same red lipstick used to color her lips. Good girls began wearing makeup the day they went to their husbands. But my sister was already beautiful. She had almond-shaped eyes and long, wavy brown hair. Even as a teenager, she walked with the air of a goddess. Her constant smile proudly displayed a gap between her two front teeth. When she learned of braces, she joked, "Why mess with perfection?"

But on her wedding day, my sister wasn't smiling. She was sadder than the average Nuse. Girls had to be sad on this day, even if they liked the groom. Otherwise, people would think they were looking forward to having sex. Why else would a girl entering a life of servitude be joyful? All Nuses cried. Some faked it. But Jariyeh's sadness was so authentic it hurt.

Sitting on the daybed, my six-year-old niece Arta and I watched as they placed the veil on my sister. I felt sorry for her, imagining she was upset because she was going to miss us. Never suspecting that there was anything more to her misery. Arta and I would one day be sad, pretty Nuses too, and people would admire us. I didn't know how to feel about it.

Everyone admired my beautiful sister, who stood in the corner covered in gold. Over her white gloves, rings were forced onto every finger. Women took turns standing next to her for a photo. Appropriately, no one smiled.

A gunshot before noon signaled the wedding party's arrival. If they had come later, it would have been bad luck.

"Krushqit kan ardhë,"--The groom's wedding party is here, Roza announced, looking back at us from the window.

Baba and the Matchmaker stood at the front of the receiving line. The lead groomsman walked in first, followed by the wedding party. They were seated at the "head of the room," the place of honor, and we at the "bottom." There was a clear division. Us and them. The girl's side and the boy's side. The "givers" and the "takers." The Bicis had paid a bride-price and come to take what was theirs. Once Jariyeh left our house, we'd have no say. Not that they could kill her without good reason. However, while she was still in our possession, we had power over the wedding party. Unlike guests, who were protected by the laws of hospitality, these visitors were at a disadvantage.

> Law §54: a) "...the bridegroom's men come for the bride, who is considered a slave, like robbers and a band of brigands, not like guests."

They had to be on their best behavior. Even the smallest disrespect was punishable with a higher bride-price, which was why the head groomsman brought extra cash. But Baba would not penalize the Bicis. He knew spitefulness was a favorite Albanian pastime. They could take it out on Jariyeh once she was under their roof. My father wanted peace. He wanted friendship. The saying: *"Ma mirë nji mik, se nji çiflik"*--better a friend through marriage than a rich friend, came from the north, but even southerners knew good in-laws were priceless—especially once your daughter was in their hands.

Sugar water and Turkish Delight were served for a "sweet union," first to the wedding party, then to us. Baba offered Marlboros to the groomsmen with hand-to-heart, showing his gesture was sincere. Respectfully, each man accepted with hand-to-heart. After the Turkish coffee was served, the wedding party placed five-and ten-dollar bills on their saucers. The newest Nuse, from our side, got to keep the money. One of the few perks of being a Nuse.

The head groomsman gave Baba envelopes of cash pre-negotiated by the Matchmaker. One for the Telake. One for the stand-in uncle accepting on behalf of my mother's brother in Albania. One for Baba—money he'd use to cover the cost of feeding our guests. In the old country, the groomsman would have brought a lamb instead. There was no reason for my family to go out of pocket to provide the Bicis with a servant and child-bearer.

It was time to display the Nuse.

The Telake escorted the bride into the living room, and everyone stood. Jariyeh stood at the doorway, eyes downcast, hands folded in front of her, palm-to-palm, right over left. Arta and I pushed our way through women's legs, straining to get a good look at my sister as the wedding party beamed at their new Nuse. But they couldn't sing just yet, for you didn't celebrate an acquisition in the house where others grieved a loss.

> Section XXV: "In the house from which the bride emerges, the Kanun does not permit singing or firing of rifles."

That would have to wait. In Albania, it was once they left our courtyard. In Brooklyn, it was the moment they hit the sidewalk.

Filanza draped a gold two-headed eagle around Jariyeh's neck. Then she scooped her hand into a small brown paper bag filled with candy, coins, and rice—symbols of sweetness, prosperity, and fertility. With a flick of her wrist, she tossed handfuls over my sister's head. We kids scrambled on the floor, grabbing for the money and sweets, while our women tried to catch the candies mid-flight—those had special powers. I had heard that giving one to a woman during a breech birth would flip the baby into position.

It was time for the temena, a custom from our Ottoman days meant to demonstrate humility and obedience. With eyes still downcast, Jariyeh slowly rotated her right palm up while softly cupping her fingers. She extended her elbow forward and lifted her hand in a half-circle toward her chin; a half-circle toward her forehead; then slightly up and out as she gently returned her right palm to rest over her left.

The groomsmen carried out the bride's dowry. In it were bedcovers, pillows, and doilies Jariyeh had embroidered meant to beautify her new home and confirm her ability to mend and sew. In America, it was easier to buy new clothes and socks, but the dowry tradition remained.

Baba escorted Jariyeh with Zogu, his middle son. Normally, it would have been his eldest, Bekim, but he had moved out after Jariyeh's engagement. We all followed my sister outside, the women teary-eyed over the hardships that awaited. Once they were officially off our property, a gunshot rang out, and the women in the wedding party began to sing. They sang about my sister's beauty, though she looked miserable. In truth, they were celebrating a successful "abduction."

♪ *Sa bukur na ka dal Nusja* ♪ How beautiful our bride turned out
Mashallah. Mashallah ♪ God has willed it. God has willed it ♪

God had chosen Mehmet for my sister, I thought. A heavenly match. If only she wasn't so sad.

Baba and Zogu guided Jariyeh into the back seat. Then Zogu banged on the car trunk three times, and called out, "Jariyeh! Jariyeh! Jariyeh!"

A ritual meant to help the Nuse release her sorrow. Holding it in was never good. If anyone could help Jariyeh get it all out, it was Zogu. Each sister, except for Roza, had a brother sidekick—I had Luan, Kamile had Bekim, and Jariyeh had Zogu.

We watched Jariyeh's car vanish down Church Avenue, then went back upstairs to feed our guests and mourn our loss.

Chapter 4

The Modern Brother

* * *

Unlike the girl's side, weddings on the boy's side were fun. Luckily, I had three brothers, and nineteen-year-old Bekim already had a fiancé. But we hadn't seen him since he had moved out. Why my big brother left, I did not know. I was too busy experiencing our new country of Brooklyn to think much about it. But my parents were upset, especially Baba. He hadn't come all this way to America to lose his firstborn son. Boys were never supposed to leave their parents' home, but Bekim never did what was expected.

Bekim was the third born, but as the first son he got special treatment. Rather than help with the crops or tend sheep, he played soccer—day and night and during all seasons. When Baba and his hard-working children posed for a picture in the cornfield, Bekim dropped his ball to join them. He looked out of place in his soccer shorts and striped shirt, wielding a hoe, but he couldn't pass up the opportunity to grace a photo with his presence. Bekim didn't think himself a farmer. He was a soccer star.

But in Kosova, his chances of making a team were slim.

My family escaped Albania in 1949 and went to neighboring Kosova, a Yugoslav province that was once part of Albania. They expected to be embraced by their fellow Albanians, but were met with suspicion instead. The Albanian Kosovars were oblivious to the suffering people had endured in Albania under Enver Hoxha's Communist regime. To them, Albanian immigrants were traitors. Who else would leave the motherland to live in a country ruled by Yugoslavs?

Bekim thought he and his high-school friends were above all that.

They were all soccer players, and promised to tell Bekim when the city-team tryouts were so they could go together. When he asked classmates why they weren't in last period and learned that they'd gone to the tryouts, he was pissed. Bekim rushed over and asked the gypsy groundskeeper to find him cleats. He tried out with one cleat too big and the other too small, but his skill was so undeniable the coach had no choice but to pick him.

In 1969, eighteen-year-old Bekim also made the statewide team. On the day of the big soccer tournament, he showed up early.

"They left without you," the groundskeeper said. "They gave you the wrong time because you're an immigrant."

Furious, Bekim told his father, "I don't want to be here anymore. Let's move somewhere else in Europe."

"No," Baba replied. "If we're leaving, we're going to the strongest country in the world—America."

———

Forty-six years later, when I asked Bekim why we came to America, he told me that story. "You guys have me to thank for getting us out of there before the war began," he said.[iv]

In 1998, Yugoslavia's president, Slobodan Milošević, used Serbian nationalism as a weapon to launch a genocidal campaign against Albanians in Kosova, but called it a religious war. For two years, my Aunt Fatime and cousins locked themselves up in their home praying not to get shot, hacked, or raped. We were safely in America, scared every day for them.

It was strange to think that a single soccer match may have saved our lives and cost Jariyeh hers.

I hesitated to ask my brothers about Jariyeh, sure that I'd be met with disapproval. But I knew that, of the three, Bekim would be the most open.

"I'm writing a book about Jariyeh," I said, hoping he'd share some stories.

"Nana was to blame for Jariyeh," Bekim replied without hesitation.

A passage on crime and punishment from *The Prophet* by Kahlil Gibran came to mind:

> "A single leaf turns not yellow but with the silent knowledge of the whole tree, so the wrong-doer cannot do wrong without the hidden will of you all."

At the time, the thought that my family may have been co-conspirators in Jariyeh's murder was disturbing. Was it possible?

"What do you mean, Nana?" I asked.

"She was angry at me for getting engaged without her permission, so she engaged Jariyeh to Mehmet out of spite."

Bekim took things personally, like most Albanians. We believed everything was about us—always—but I understood what he meant. My mother was spiteful, but even for her, this seemed extreme.

He was a man of few words and wouldn't say more, so I turned to his wife Saranda for details on their engagement. She went back to the beginning.

"Bekim and I met the first day you guys got to Italy."

———

It was October 1969—ten years before Jariyeh's murder.

A Catholic Albanian church in Kosova arranged for my family to take a freight train to Rome, then a bus to Cardito. Italy was where we'd get our visas to America.

On the bus, Bekim was surrounded by a group of boys, one of whom accidentally elbowed him in the eye. The shiner gave him an excuse to wear his sunglasses, a luxury not had by many. They made him look cool. Bekim liked cool.

He was looking out the bus window when he saw a striking girl with big chestnut eyes, full lips, and a regal nose that could have belonged to a queen in a previous life.

"She's mine!" he called dibs.

"What if she's Italian?" sixteen-year-old Jariyeh asked.

"I don't care if she's gypsy," he said. "I'm going to marry her."

Bekim believed he was above tradition. Above rules made for common folk. He was his own man. Nobody was going to tell him who to marry.

The bus dropped us off at a park. We would wait there until the church found us a place to rent. Sitting on the grass, Bekim saw his future-wife handing out bread and cheese to the immigrants from a headscarf. He leaned on one arm and smiled as she approached.

"Faleminderit,"--Thank you, Baba said to the young lady. "What's your name?"

"Saranda," the fifteen-year-old said, confirming she was a southern Albanian. "My mother sent me," she added. Having arrived from Macedonia nine months earlier, her mother knew what it was to sleep in the park for days, cold and hungry. "I'll be back with some blankets."

As Bekim reached for a piece of bread, Saranda noticed his well-groomed hands. The same hands she had seen in a recurring dream. She'd wake from it, knowing they belonged to her future husband, but wouldn't make the connection just then.

"She's beautiful, *and* she's good," Bekim said, knowing good was most important.

How dare he speak about me? Saranda thought, looking at this boy with the black eye and impeccably white sneakers. How did he keep them so white, she wondered.

The perfection demanded by our parents wasn't wasted on just the girls.

Baba rented a house in San Piaggio for the seven of us: Baba, Nana, Bekim, Jariyeh, Zogu, Luan, and me. I loved Italy. I loved hearing the church bells ring on the hour. I loved the pasta and mandarins the Red Cross gave us—I'd never had them before. I loved when Baba bought me ice cream from a truck and took me to watch him play bocce with the old Italian men who called me "Bella." And

I loved playing outside with my brother Luan.

Roza's family arrived soon after, and rented a home nearby. When Kamile came to bid us a final farewell, her husband decided to apply for a visa, convinced that working in America was the only way to support his large family in Kosova.

Now we were all headed *në Amerik*.

For Bekim, the best part of living in Cardito was that it was a twenty-minute walk to Saranda's. As he approached her house, he heard Italian music coming from her second-floor balcony.

"Tell your sister I want to borrow some records," he said to her little brothers, Ali and Ilmi, who were outside playing soccer.

Ali ran upstairs, eager to please the sharply dressed older boy with the sunglasses.

"Tell him to go away." Bekim overheard Saranda say. "What does the hillbilly know about Italian music?"

Bekim liked that she thought she was better than him—everyone should be allowed fantasies, he thought. This made him even more determined to set her straight and make her his.

After fourteen-year-old Zogu befriended Ali, Bekim offered to pay his brother to let him know if Saranda mentioned him.

"I don't care what you give me. I don't snitch on my friends," the righteous Zogu replied.

When Jariyeh visited Cardito, she stopped by Saranda's. The teenagers immediately connected. Unlike other immigrant girls, they both wore pants and left their hair loose. The friends gathered on Saranda's huge terrace to listen to Italian records and watch the boys play below.

"Who would you marry?" they whispered to each other. One by one, each pointed, giggled, and claimed a husband of their own.

Not Saranda.

"Why are you keeping quiet? Don't you like anyone?" Jariyeh asked, eager to know if she liked Bekim.

Saranda did like him, but another girl had already picked him.

"I'm promised to someone in America," she replied arrogantly.

Days later, she confessed to Jariyeh, "I lied about being promised. I don't want anyone here to ask for me. I have a big brother in America, and I want him to choose my husband."

Jariyeh couldn't *wait* to tell Bekim. It wasn't snitching. It was matchmaking. It was romantic. She wanted her brother to marry who he loved.

"Saranda isn't promised to anyone," she blurted out the moment she saw him.

When Bekim's handsome friend said he was going to ask for Saranda, Bekim said, "I hear she's engaged in America." Normally he didn't lie, but this was different. Bekim wasn't the best-looking of his friends, but he believed he was—and that was good enough.

His playboy days flourished after Baba bought him a used Volkswagen. Bekim dated only the most beautiful Italian girls. Girls he used for fun—like the Serbian ones before. Saranda was for marriage, but for now, he would keep her as a friend.

"I want to go out with her," he told Saranda, pointing to a sexy Italian girl buying gelato. Making her jealous was part of the plan. "Can you translate?"

Saranda agreed, but regretted it when the girls began sharing embarrassing intimate details. When one of Bekim's girlfriends moved to Rome, he'd bring Saranda her letters to translate, then dictate his response to her. Saranda added things she would have wanted to hear, like "I miss looking into your eyes"—still too innocent to know it wasn't their eyes he was interested in.

Before leaving with Baba for a cousin's burial in Belgium, Bekim went to Saranda with a final letter.

"This one is for you," he said, as if he were bestowing upon her a gift.

Feeling as though the entire world was watching, Saranda grabbed the letter, ran inside, locked herself in the bathroom, and read it—twice.

> *I fell in love with you the moment I saw you. But my parents are going to send a matchmaker to ask for Flutra. I told my mother that if they say yes, I'm not coming back from Belgium. I do not want her. I want you. But if they say no, I will return and ask for you myself.*

Flutra's family was from the northern mountains, where men often traveled for work and stayed away for years. This forced their women to become hard workers, making them excellent Nuses, and therefore coveted by other northerners—like Nana.

The Shkumbin River split Albania in two. North and south. Northerners spoke a nasally Gheg dialect; southerners spoke a more flowery Tosk. Same blood. Different worlds. The Tosk from the lowlands prized intellect, while the Gheg from the harsh mountains prized strength. Each was convinced of their superiority. Nana would never choose a spoiled southern city girl for a daughter-in-law over a northern female warrior like herself.

Bekim's love letter came as a complete surprise. Saranda wasn't sure how she felt about him. Mostly, he annoyed her. He was arrogant. He thought he was good-looking, honorable, smart—and he dated *all* the girls. But she did like his clean sneakers and blue eyes. Saranda dreamed of having blue-eyed children. But how could she marry a boy who made her so nervous? Whenever he spoke, her stomach felt funny, and she didn't know what to do with herself.

"Questo è amore"--That's love, Maria, the thirty-year-old neighbor explained.

"Love? How could I love him when I don't even like him?" Saranda asked.

"What makes you think the two have to go together?"

In the morning, Saranda gave Bekim a letter and ran away:

I also like you, but I'm too young to make my own decisions. Ask my mother.

Nana knew Bekim didn't want to marry Flutra, but she didn't care. Children didn't get to choose. Bekim was still in Belgium when she told Flutra's mother to expect a matchmaker.

"Bekim is going to ask for you," the mother said, giving Flutra the exciting news.

"He is not asking for me," Flutra replied. "His mother is. He has eyes for Saranda, and I have a boy I want to marry. If you make me marry Bekim, I will run away."

As much as her parents wanted to say yes to Lutfi Feza's son, they couldn't risk the disgrace of an elopement.

"Please don't send a matchmaker," she told Nana. "My daughter has someone, and says your son has eyes for Saranda."

Nana was *not* happy. Southern girls were much too modern for her taste. There was no way she would send a matchmaker to ask for Saranda.

Fate had other plans.

Chapter 5

The Love Plan

* * *

Gjile, Saranda's mother, heard the rumors and said, "I think Bekim is going to ask for you. So, what do you think? Should we try to fix Jariyeh with Ceni?" Gjile *loved* the spirited girl and thought she'd make the most wonderful Nuse for her eldest son.

"Yes!" Saranda exclaimed. She couldn't imagine a better Nuse for her big brother, and surely Jariyeh would like him.

Ceni was so handsome that photographers in Macedonia gave him a free portrait if he let them display his picture in their shop windows. Neighbors called him "as pretty as a girl," though he resembled a Greek god, and was very much a man. There wasn't a woman who didn't fall for Ceni—and now it was Jariyeh's turn.

The next time Jariyeh visited, Saranda handed her his picture.

"This is my big brother Ceni. In America, they call him Sam," she added, as though having an American name made him more special. "Do you want to marry him?"

Jariyeh looked at the tall man with shoulder-length curly brown hair, standing beside his '68 light blue Mustang.

"I'd marry him tomorrow if he'd have me."

"Great! Give me a picture and I'll send it to him and see what he says."

Jariyeh returned with a passport photo. Saranda immediately mailed it to her brother with a note:

This is my best friend Jariyeh. Would you like to marry her?

She prayed he'd reply before Bekim returned from Belgium.

When the blue-and-red trimmed airmail envelope arrived, Saranda anxiously waited for Jariyeh's visit, and practically yelled at the first sight of her.

"My brother said yes!"

The teenage girls hugged, then jumped up and down. They had many admirers, but they were good girls, waiting for their princes—or at least the Albanian version of one.

"Let's make a deal," fifteen-year-old Saranda said, feeling all grown up and in control. "You will marry my brother, and I will marry your brother. This way we can always be friends."

If they married elsewhere, they'd hardly see each other. Nuses didn't have friends outside their husband's family.

"It's a *deal,*" Jariyeh said, shaking Saranda's hand.

In the mountains, villagers mostly didn't read or write, so agreements were made by word of mouth and sealed by the power of their impeccable *besa*--word of honor. The spoken word was powerful enough, and shaking hands was like signing in blood. Though they had no power to make such agreements, the carefree girls believed anything was possible.

When Bekim returned from Belgium, he showed up at Saranda's first thing the following morning.

"Where is your mother? I came to ask for you," he said, as if doing her a favor.

Barbaric romance was a specialty of Albanian men.

"Wait here," Saranda replied nervously. She sent a boy next door to fetch her mother, who was using a neighbor's oven to bake bread.

"I want to marry your daughter," Bekim told Gjile, not wasting time.

Gjile remembered the words of her dying husband: "Promise me you'll let our children choose who they marry." She looked over at Saranda, who stood half in, half out of the doorway, embarrassed and trying to summon the courage to walk through the room and leave.

"Ask her," Gjile said.

Bekim turned to Saranda, who looked at him like a deer in headlights.

"Say yes," he directed. "So I can go home and tell everyone I'm engaged."

"Yes," she said, and ran out.

"How about you marry Saranda, and Jariyeh marries my son in America?" Gjile suggested.

"Ta jap besën"--I give you my word, Bekim said with confidence. Any man who went back on his word was not a man, and a man who wasn't a man was nothing. Bekim prided himself on his manliness—and then some.

"But they have to meet first," he added, wanting to make sure they liked each other. He wouldn't be part of the arranged-marriage bullshit.

Bekim came home with the news:

No matchmakers.

No permission.

Just engaged.

When I saw Saranda's picture, I was *thrilled.* We were going to have the most beautiful Nuse ever! I was six and too small to know my brother had broken the engagement rules—or that there were rules.

My parents took the news in their own way.

"Për hajr"--May it be blessed, Baba said, shaking his son's hand. He couldn't be a hypocrite when he had married who he wanted.

"She will *never* make a good Nuse," was Nana's response.

"I'm not marrying her to be a Nuse," Bekim said. He never liked the idea of women being slaves to the husband's family—but a slave to him was another matter. "And I'm not marrying her for you. I'm marrying her for me."

Me—a word Albanians never used because everything was about family. It was hard for Nana to have a child as *krye fort*--hardheaded—as herself. No one ever disrespected our mother, but he didn't see it that way. Bekim was just being Bekim. He always thought about himself. Not the family. Not the honor codes. Not the right way to marry. Although he knew the rules:

> Law §30: "The young man whose parents are alive does not have the right: a) To concern himself with his own marriage; b) To select the matchmaker; c) To interfere in his own engagement; d) To interfere in the token of engagement, in arrangements for the clothes or shoes, or in the setting of the marriage date."

Bekim didn't like rules. At that moment he had done away with a, b, and c. In Brooklyn, he'd cancel out d.

"Saranda has a brother in America for Jariyeh. I will arrange for them to meet," Bekim told his parents, proud to have found his sister a husband in America, where good suitors would be hard to find.

The next day, Baba went to Gjile's house with a *pesë-lirsh*--gold coin.

"May their engagement be blessed," he said, shaking Gjile's hand.

"May you be blessed," she replied. "But I must warn you. She's young. She's not ready to be a Nuse."

Years earlier, back in Macedonia, Gjile began Saranda's training to be a Nuse when she was ten, by showing her how to scrape the corners of the bread pan with a knife. When her pan failed inspection, Gjile sent it flying out of the kitchen window. The Macedonian neighbors shook their heads—crazy Albanians.

"She doesn't cook and isn't used to being around a lot of people," Gjile added. "You will have to teach her."

"Don't worry," Baba said. "If she takes after even your little finger, we couldn't ask for anything more." Gjile had sent food and blankets to all the immigrants in the park that first day, and Baba knew kindness ranked above all else.

After the token of engagement made it official, the news spread quickly among the immigrants: "Lutfi Feza's son is engaged to the girl with the pants."

Nana was passing by when she saw Gjile and Saranda in their courtyard. She reluctantly walked in and shook Gjile's hand.

"Congratulations," Nana said. But what she really meant was: You're welcome. They should have been thanking her for letting Saranda marry her well-bred son.

Before leaving, Nana pulled aside the girl Bekim had chosen over his own family.

No hello.

No congratulations.

Just: "Look at you. You're not good enough for my son. You're too skinny. You don't even have enough hair. And you're spoiled."

Nana didn't know if she was spoiled, but she couldn't imagine otherwise. She especially hated "spoiled." She never spoiled herself or her children—though she had allowed it of her eldest son. And look where that got her.

"I'm not sixteen yet," Saranda replied—not thinking Nana rude, only tough, like her own mother.

Despite Nana's reaction, the two best friends continued to dream. Jariyeh made up excuses to go to Cardito and snuck off to Saranda's. On the balcony, they listened to records and spoke of their glorious future.

"Tell me more about your brother," Jariyeh smiled.

"He escaped Macedonia at fourteen with two older men. But they had to leave him behind in Italy because America wouldn't accept minors without their family. He lived in a refugee camp for two years until my big sisters rescued him. They're all in America now, in a place called Staten Island."

"What kind of work does Sam do?" Jariyeh asked.

"He's a professional boxer. And he chops vegetables in a restaurant owned by Chinese people."

"What are Chinese people like?"

"I don't know."

Jariyeh pulled out Laura Pausini's LP and placed the needle on "E Ritorno Da Te"--I Come Back to You. After six months in Italy, Jariyeh could sing fluently in Italian. Love songs were always her favorite, and even more so now that she had Sam.

"I carved 'Sam' on an apple and ate it," Jariyeh smiled mischievously as she rubbed her belly.

"What is that supposed to mean?" Saranda asked.

"It means he will always be a part of me," Jariyeh replied, explaining her little witchcraft move.

Saranda never thought of carving 'Bekim' on an apple and wondered if it meant she loved him less.

"We're going to make such beautiful couples. But Sam and I will be more beautiful," Jariyeh teased.

"You can be more beautiful," Saranda smiled. She didn't mind Jariyeh having the best.

"Aww," Jariyeh melted at the sweetness of her friend and kissed her face all over.

Saranda wiped her face and smiled.

Our visas arrived after nine months in Italy.

Jariyeh couldn't *wait* to go to America.

———

Years later, when Saranda told me the love story, I was left with questions.

Why did Jariyeh, who was loved by everyone, say, "I'd marry him tomorrow if he'd have me?" Then I remembered that she was only sixteen, and didn't yet have the self-confidence.

And why did she believe she could marry who she wanted? I would never make such a plan. Did she think like Bekim, that the rules didn't apply to her? Or did she always have that fire inside her?

But more importantly: was Bekim right? Had Nana made Jariyeh marry Mehmet because he had dared to choose for himself?

Chapter 6

Bite Off His Face

* * *

"Were you there when Hamit came to ask for Jariyeh?" I asked my big brother.

"They did it when I wasn't around," Bekim said, annoyed. "I found out from Hava."

Hava was the matchmaker's wife.

"I was so pissed! She said it like it was a *mizhde*."

Mizhde meant good news.

"I told her, Mehmet Bici will never marry my sister."

———

During the day, Bekim worked as a janitor in a residential high-rise in Manhattan, and on the weekends, he visited Saranda in Staten Island. They sometimes took the bus to the movies. Neither spoke English, but the movies were his excuse to hold hands and kiss. One day, he took her into Manhattan and bought her a coat at Saks Fifth Avenue, worth two weeks' salary. At Rockefeller Center, he picked up a flier for computer classes. Thinking this was the future, Bekim signed up and Baba happily agreed to pay the $4,000 tuition.

"Mehmet Bici is asking for your sister," Hava broke the news to Bekim one Saturday.

"Mehmet Bici will *never* marry my sister!" he said, furious.

Bekim was nine when he saw eleven-year-old Mehmet playing dice at their elementary schoolyard in Kosova. He wanted to like the boy because their fathers were in jail, and because immigrants had to stick together, but the dirty, disheveled kid repulsed him. They weren't friends then, and they surely wouldn't be friends now. Mehmet was the last man Bekim wanted for his sister, and it absolutely was *not* going to happen.

Hava called Filanza.

"I don't know if they're going to give Jariyeh to you," Hava said, and held out the receiver for Bekim to hear.

"If they don't give her to us!" Filanza wailed. "We are going to steal her!"

In the old country, dishonorable families who couldn't get a Nuse the proper way resorted to stealing. These abductions were followed by rape to be effective. The girl's family had two choices: allow her to marry the rapist, since he'd taken her biggest asset, or kill him. But who would marry a girl who was no longer a virgin? Girls were especially vulnerable to abductions if the men of their family were weak, and although Filanza knew Lutfi Feza was not weak, she couldn't help herself.

The stupidity of the two women was aggravating, but not surprising. Bekim couldn't decide who to be angrier with: Hava, the instigator, or Filanza, the big mouth. Back in Kosova he remembered seeing Filanza pull up her skirt, slap the inside of her thigh, and yell, *"Une jam burrneshë!"*--I am a manly woman. A *burrneshë* was tougher than the average Albanian female, who was already pretty fierce. Bekim thought: You're not a burrneshë or a woman. You are an embarrassment to your family.

After Hava left, Bekim called Sam.

Sam had agreed to marry Jariyeh in a letter, but it wasn't until Saranda started sharing stories of how her friend sang all the time, made their mother laugh, and beat the unbeatable neighbor in arm wrestling that he began looking forward to the union.

"When are you coming to ask for Jariyeh?" Bekim asked. He had wanted Sam and Jariyeh to meet first, but time was of the essence.

"I was waiting for your family to settle in," Sam replied.

"We're as settled as we need to be."

Sam didn't have a matchmaker to send, so he went with his eldest sister and her husband. Luckily, Bekim would be there. Who better than the eldest son to vouch for him?

"We have come to ask for your daughter Jariyeh," Sam's brother-in-law said.

"We promised her to someone else," Nana replied.

I wondered if Jariyeh had been home. I imagined her in the kitchen about to serve the Turkish coffee when she heard.

Bekim was furious. If his parents had told him they had promised Jariyeh to Mehmet, he never would have invited Sam. He never would have sat there with them like an idiot. Bekim walked Sam and his family outside, then returned with a vengeance.

"I told you about Sam," he said to Nana, the one he figured was the culprit.

"You and your sister can't marry into the same family," Nana said.

It was true. The Kanun imposed many obstacles on whom one could marry:

> Law §39: a) There must be no blood relation; b) They must not be from
> the same clan; c) She must not be a niece of the clan; d) She must not

be a woman who has been rejected; e) There must be no spiritual relationship due to: 1) baptism; 2) marriage; 3) cutting of hair [God-parent]; 4) blood-brotherhood.

Blood connected us, but so did spirit, and marriage was spiritual. One didn't just marry a spouse; they married the entire clan. Intermarrying was avoided, for if one marriage failed, the disgrace to the family would be so great that the other couple had to split in order to save face.

But Bekim didn't believe Nana's excuse, not for a minute. Though his father had the final word, Bekim knew his mother was a master manipulator. She could get anyone to do what she wanted—except him. He figured she was mad at him for getting engaged without her permission.

"I gave my word to Gjile," he said, fuming.

How could his parents not honor his besa?

He was only making $80 a week—barely enough for rent, utilities, food, and a wedding—and now tuition too, which he was determined to pay himself. But he also couldn't live in a house where he wasn't respected. Bekim moved out and got a second job. He had no time to attend computer classes, but he'd still pay the $4,000 tuition because he had given his word and his word was worth something.

My big brother had left home once before, around age ten. Nana blamed him for something he hadn't done and went to get the iron tongs. Little Bekim was too proud to plead his innocence, hide, or run, but he wasn't dumb and snuck a pillow under his jacket to cushion the blows. After the beating, Bekim left home for three days and didn't talk to his mother for three months. That was then. This was now. Bekim found a basement apartment in Brooklyn and left for good.

Spite was a trait he had learned from his mother, and he learned it well. Biting off your nose to spite your face was child's play. Bekim would bite off his face to spite his nose if he thought he was teaching someone a lesson. He left to punish his parents for disrespecting him—especially his mother.

Not that she'd care.

I knew the power of Nana's spitefulness. But wondered—did she engage Jariyeh to Mehmet out of spite, or was she simply following the Kanun?

Chapter 7

The Rebel Mother

* * *

My mother, Kadire Kola, never spoke of her past. She never told me she was an infant when her father died falling down the mountain. She never said her five-year-old brother, Hamdi, inherited their one-room house with a dirt floor. She never spoke of the bitter winters, the rocks she hauled, or the rattlesnakes she killed to protect Fatime—her meek older sister. She never told me she was twelve when she threw away the neighbor's cucumber seed out of spite and shamed the family. Her sixteen-year-old brother nearly cut off her head with a scythe to save face. Luckily, a visitor stopped him. She never said her mother was a clean freak because dirty kids got lice, lice carried typhus, and typhus brought death. Nana was never to lend out the family comb or play with sick children—but she felt sorry for them. That was when she got typhus, lost her hair, and nearly died.

It was Aunt Fatime who told me all this.

"When Kadire got sick, our mom put her on a sheepskin in the corner of the room and pushed food to her in a bowl—like a dog."

Hearing this broke my heart. I thought Nana was tough on me growing up, but my struggles paled in comparison. If I had known, I wouldn't have felt so sorry for myself.

She never felt sorry for herself. The past was the past. Planning for the future was a luxury my mother didn't have. Survival happened in the here and now—which is where Nana resided.

"Did you know your mother married for love?" Aunt Fatime asked.

I stared at her, stunned, trying to process the words. Nana had drilled into us that we had no choice in who we married—while, all along, she had married for love herself.

This was my mother's most calculated omission.

———

In the mountains of Albania, my teenage mother Kadire and her girlfriends were singing outside when a wedding party passed through their village, delivering a Nuse to her husband on horseback.

"Who would you marry?" the girls excitedly asked each other.

Each one claimed a husband from the wedding party, then turned to their leader, Kadire. "Who would you marry?" they asked.

"I'd marry him—the one with the horse and saddle," she answered. If she could choose, she'd choose the best.

Because she had chosen Lutfi Feza, the most coveted bachelor in those mountains, rumors quickly spread across the river to where my father lived. He knew no one would marry the rebellious girl who dared choose him, and sent a matchmaker against his mother's wishes.

"Tell him he can marry my older daughter Fatime," Kadire's mother offered instead.

Baba wasn't interested and considered the matter settled.

Nana's brother Hamdi banned her from fetching water at the spring near the neighbor's house, knowing Lutfi Feza visited. Nana went anyway. When neighbors told Hamdi, he beat her. She went again. Her mother beat her. She went again.

News of her defiance reached her uncle Maliq. He went to the village elders and got permission to throw her off the mountain. How else to preserve his family honor?

When Kadire came home from a day of working the land, her friend warned: "Don't go tie the calf. I heard your uncle is waiting there for you."

Nana didn't want to give her mean uncle the satisfaction, so she decided to kill herself. But at the cliff, she couldn't bring herself to jump. Instead, she crossed the river and visited a married girlfriend.

An old man saw her enter the house and alerted Lutfi Feza.

Baba had tried to marry the rebel girl the proper way, with a matchmaker. But marrying a runaway hunted by her family would incite a blood feud. Still, he rode his stallion to the house and asked:

"Will you marry me?" he asked, figuring he was better equipped to survive the hunt.

"Yes," she said.

Baba's mother reluctantly accepted the union. But in private she told the rebel girl, "Look at you. You're not good enough for my son. You don't even have enough hair."

The same words Nana would later say to Saranda.

After the wedding, brother Hamdi and Uncle Maliq began hunting the man who had taken their blood without permission. Twice they set an ambush. Twice Baba's swift stallion saved his life.

———

"Your father left Albania because of the blood feud," Aunt Fatime explained. "He borrowed the neighbor's mule during the escape. When it returned home, there was a letter in its sack: I have not run away from Enver Hoxha. I have run away from Maliq Kola."

That surprised me. I had heard he escaped Hoxha's Communist regime.

Maybe it was both.

Once in Kosova, Nana's disgraceful past and Baba's blood feud were sealed behind Albania's Communist walls. Nana did all she could to preserve her husband's honorable name. She was the perfect Nuse, kept an immaculate house, and made sure her children did things by the book, especially when it came to marriage. The goal was to keep the family together. It was easier with boys because their wives would live with them. Girls, who had to live with their husbands' family, were more of a challenge. Marrying them to immigrant husbands who would return to Albania was a must, and northerners ideal.

Baba was the lenient one. After engaging Roza to a northern immigrant who he later learned drank too much, he told his daughter, "You don't have to marry him," knowing it could incite a blood feud. Roza married him anyway, saying he was her fate.

Next in line was Kamile. Our next-door neighbor, Elez, kept sending his matchmaker to ask for her hand. My parents kept saying no—not because he was poor, but because he was a Kosovar who would stay in Kosova. When Nana learned Kamile was in love with Elez, she rushed next door and told his mother, "If your son elopes with my daughter, I will burn your house down."

When Baba learned of their love, he found Elez and said, "If you include two plots of land in my daughter's dowry, she is yours." He knew such an act was unprecedented and embarrassing, but all he cared about was his child's happiness.

I understood why Nana didn't tell us she was a rebel. I understood why she didn't tell us she married for love. But why weren't we told of the kind things Baba did for his daughters? If Jariyeh had known, she would have gone to Baba, and he would have ended the engagement. Instead, she went to her mother.

"I want to marry Sam," Jariyeh told her.

"Selman Bici's son is better. He's from the north, and his family has money. You won't have to suffer."

"I don't care about money," Jariyeh replied. "I want love."

Nana was not an American mother. She didn't owe her an explanation. She simply walked away.

Jariyeh knew there was nothing she could do to stop the marriage.

> Law §43: "If the girl does not submit and marry her fiancé, she should be handed over to him by force, 'together with a cartridge'; and if the girl tries to flee, her husband may kill her...."

But Mehmet had options:

> Law §42: "If the young man so desires, he is free to reject the young
> woman to whom he is engaged, but he loses the token...."

Jariyeh called him.

"I don't want to marry you," she said the words girls didn't dare say.

"But I want to marry you," Mehmet replied.

"But I don't love you. I love someone else. You have to call it off," the seventeen-year-old begged for her freedom.

What she wanted didn't matter. She was a woman. He was a man. And it was a man's world.

Mehmet would not budge.

I didn't understand. What kind of man wants to marry someone who doesn't want him? Mehmet wasn't one to take a stand. Was he just being a good boy doing as his parents said?

Jariyeh called Saranda. They hadn't seen each other since Italy, but had been speaking on the phone every day about their exciting future. Now, they spoke of their ruined plan.

The Bicis refused to call off the engagement. Within weeks, an expensive groom's dowry arrived at our house. What was the urgency? Were they desperate for a Nuse to serve and clean? Or had Mehmet told his parents about Jariyeh's call? Were they hoping their lavish dowry would change her mind?

"I don't care for their jewelry," Jariyeh told Saranda. "All I want is love."

Chapter 8

Like Lions

* * *

Learning that Jariyeh tried to stop the wedding and was forced to marry Mehmet was heart-wrenching. Bekim's absence made it worse.

"Too bad Bekim didn't come to see Jariyeh off on her wedding day," I said to Saranda. "It would have made her happy."

"We did go," Saranda replied. "I begged Bekim for days, but was careful not to overdo it."

"You came? I don't remember seeing you guys."

―

From his basement apartment in Brooklyn, Bekim took one train and two buses to pick up Saranda in Staten Island. As they headed back to Brooklyn, Saranda said nothing, afraid he'd change his mind.

Standing in front of our four-story brownstone, Bekim said, "I'll wait here. Make it fast."

"You're not coming in?" Saranda asked, not yet grasping the depth of her fiancé's spitefulness.

"I never said I was coming in."

He brought Saranda because she and Jariyeh were good friends.

Saranda ran upstairs.

The friends burst into tears. "I just came to say good luck," she said, brushing Jariyeh's tear-soaked hair off her face, wishing she could make things better.

"I don't want to go. I don't want to marry him," her voice cracked.

"Maybe he's a nice guy. Maybe you'll love him." Saranda didn't know what else to say. She was only sixteen, and wisdom was not yet at hand.

"I could never love Mehmet. He will never touch me. I'll tell him I don't love him, and he'll let me go," the seventeen-year-old reasoned.

Saranda didn't know if that would work but thought it was worth a try. "Okay, but I have to go now. Bekim is waiting," she said.

He'd been nice enough to bring her. She didn't want to push her luck.

Saranda gave Jariyeh one last hug. "Call me." Then ran downstairs.

On the journey back to Staten Island, Bekim didn't ask a thing. Not "How was

Jariyeh?" Not "Who was there?" Not "Did my parents see you?" And Saranda knew better than to say.

Jariyeh went to the kitchen and called Mehmet, just to ruin his day.

"I'm going to wear the wedding dress for you," she said. "But my heart belongs to someone else."

The wedding party came. Sugar water, coffee, and cigarettes were served. Then they took Jariyeh to her new home in the South Bronx. The place where the Bicis would celebrate the taking of their new Nuse. Unlike in the northern mountains, where gypsies beat drums and filled courtyards with song, the celebration in their cinderblock apartment in the projects would be much more subdued.

What was it like?

I imagine an Albanian Imam performed the ceremony. That the women beat tambourines and sang. That Jariyeh stood in the corner of the living room. Her eyes downcast. Looking miserable. Holding a bouquet, an American invention Filanza adopted. I imagine Mehmet stood beside her—but he got to eat. Sit. Use the bathroom whenever he pleased. Not Jariyeh. Tradition demanded that she keep her position until the last guest exited.

The day my sister had dreamed of ever since she saw her first Nuse was a day of dread. No handsome husband to swoon over. No in-laws worth impressing. She didn't even care if her new owners thought her beautiful.

The newlyweds were escorted to their bedroom. Jariyeh stood in the corner.

Mehmet took off his clothes, eager to take possession and make sure she hadn't been with another. Once he took her virginity, she'd have nowhere else to go.

Mehmet lifted Jariyeh's veil, and her eyes pierced his.

"Don't touch me," she snapped. "I don't love you."

"You will learn to love me."

"I told you; I love someone else."

Mehmet pushed her onto the bed and pinned her down.

Jariyeh pulled her knees to her chest and kicked, sending her husband flying onto the floor.

The next morning, Jariyeh reported to Saranda on the phone:

"We fought like lions. I didn't let him touch me."

Jariyeh hoped Mehmet would send her home. That way, she could still be a virgin. That way, she could still marry Sam.

But he kept her.

What happened after? Did Filanza come looking for the bloody sheet that confirmed virginity? Did Mehmet tell her his Nuse had fought him off? Did he say she confessed her love for another? Was the eventual consummation a rape?

Chapter 9

Pale Pink Dress

* * *

Bekim's marriage would be different from Jariyeh's. She became a slave. He would become the master. Her marriage was a sentencing. His, a coronation. A celebration of manhood.

Baba would buy Saranda a most impressive dowry. Instead of crying, our house would sing and dance for weeks.

If it happened as it should have.

Moving out was bad, but moving to Staten Island, where his fiancé lived, was worse. It meant he had "followed his Nuse." People implied she was in charge, making Bekim worthless. But he couldn't care less what others thought or how it reflected on the family. Bekim did what he wanted. Nana may have modeled spitefulness, but Bekim mastered selfishness all on his own.

Things moved fast. We had arrived in Brooklyn on the last day of June. Jariyeh got married in September. Bekim married right after.

Saranda told me Bekim showed up at their house on a Sunday.

"I'm marrying your daughter on Friday," he told Saranda's mother.

"We're not ready," Gjile said, referring to the Nuse's dowry of embroideries and gifts for the groom.

"I'm not having a wedding. I'm just coming to pick her up," Bekim replied, not apologizing. He didn't have money to buy Saranda jewelry or fancy clothes. Dowries didn't matter. They had love.

Wedding arrangements were up to the groom's family. In this case, it was Bekim. His parents were cut out. They would not get to experience the joy of marrying off their eldest son. A son driven to live tradition-free—and no one was better equipped to do it. Bekim was used to getting his way. He'd done it all his life because Baba allowed it. If he wanted to get married on Friday, he would get married on Friday.

When Gjile broke the news to her daughter, Saranda was sad that she wouldn't get to be a Nuse. She had planned to wear a pale pink dress with puffy chiffon sleeves, and on her head a ring of flowers like the hippies wore on TV, but with a tiny veil. Nothing too fancy, she thought. After all, it would be a small celebration at her in-laws' apartment. But she wouldn't even have that.

On Friday, instead of sending a wedding party, Bekim went alone by bus. After lunch with Saranda's family, her brother Sam loaded his Mustang with gifts: bedsheets, a blanket, a vacuum, pots and pans. Then Sam drove the couple to their new apartment, which was bare except for the one thing Bekim imagined newlyweds needed—a mattress.

At the news of Bekim's marriage, my parents reacted in their own style. Nana cut her son off completely. Baba did his best to love him unconditionally. But inside, our father felt betrayed. Still, Baba trekked all the way to Staten Island to congratulate the newlyweds. He handed Bekim an envelope with $500 and whispered, "There's no need to mention this to anyone." By "anyone," it was understood he meant Nana. If she learned her husband had supported their selfish son, she would become unbearable to live with—and why stoke that spiteful flame?

The newlyweds had love but no money. On weekdays, Bekim worked two jobs at Plaza 100, a luxury residential high-rise in Manhattan: porter in the morning and manager at night. Saranda went to Wilfred Beauty Academy. When Sam had asked her, "What can you do?" she recalled trimming her friend's bangs with sheep shears and said, "I can cut hair." So he paid for her classes. Bekim's contribution was—he let her go.

To get by, the newlyweds lived on hot dogs and beans for an entire year and took turns riding the bus. One day Bekim took the bus to the ferry on his way to work; the next day, Saranda took the bus to beauty school. It was generous of my brother not to make his wife walk all the time. After all… he was the man.

Bekim considered himself a forward thinker. He called married women by their names, not "Nuse," like everyone else. Other Albanian men controlled their wives out of fear of seeming weak or being cuckolded, and only let them take office cleaning jobs after hours—when men weren't around. Bekim let his wife become a beautician—and even drive a car.

"You can do anything you want," he told her. "But if you ever cheat on me, I will skin you alive."

He wasn't the violet type and would never do it, but his point was made. Simple and direct, the way he wished others would make theirs and not waste his time. Bekim was focused, efficient, and always right. He was known to point at a white wall and say, "If I say it's black, you say it's black, and we will have no problems."

There was only so much Albanian one could take out of a man.

It was October 14th, the day Kamile and her family flew in from Italy, when Bekim and Saranda showed up, but only because she begged him to.

Baba was happy to see the couple. Nana was indifferent.

"You have to cook for everybody," she told our new Nuse.

"I don't know how to cook for everybody," sixteen-year-old Saranda said.

"If you're not too young to marry, then you're not too young to cook."

After everyone left for the airport, Saranda called her sister, crying.

"Don't worry," her sister said. "Just stay on the phone and I'll walk you through it."

When we returned from the airport, Nana called to Saranda from the living room, "We're not hungry yet. You don't have to rush." Like the Bible, Nana spoke in code. One had to decipher what she was really saying, which in this case was: If you were a northern Nuse, we would have been fed already.

"Oh good," naïve Saranda replied. "I'm not done yet."

Baba laughed at Nana's missed sarcasm and told his wife, "She's innocent. Don't ruin her."

He went into the kitchen to check on Saranda. She had made steak, rice, vegetables, and even *ravani*, a single-layer cake drenched in sugary syrup. Seeing dirty pots and pans everywhere and predicting Nana's wrath, Baba opened a cabinet and whispered, "Put those in here and wash them later."

After dinner, Bekim proudly gave us an update.

"Saranda is going to beauty school."

"That's very good," Baba smiled.

When Nana was alone with Saranda, she said, "Don't tell people you go to school. You're embarrassing me."

I was so happy my modern brother was going to let our Nuse become a bigshot beautician. I couldn't think of a fancier job. She'd then get to be a Telake and do Nuse makeovers. How fun was that? When my mother, Roza, and Kamile got cleaning lady jobs at 1 New York Plaza, I was proud of them too.

One weekend Saranda brought over a professional photo of her in a white dress and Bekim in a tux. My eyes filled with tears.

"What's the matter?" Saranda asked.

"We missed the wedding."

"We didn't have a wedding. We just rented these clothes for the picture."

That made me feel better.

———

I never knew Nana didn't like Saranda. Only now did I learn about the Sunday wedding, the bus rides, Baba's $500.

"I loved Baba," Saranda said. "He was so kind."

I loved him too, and hearing these stories made me love him more. It just broke my heart to learn he gave Bekim money in secret to avoid Nana's wrath. America may have been the strongest country in the world, but for us—especially Baba—it came with much heartache.

We hadn't come to America to become Americans. We came to live our old life in a new place—to honor our customs and follow their rules. And following those rules wouldn't have been a problem… if everyone played their part.

The Bicis did not.

And that was where the trouble began.

Chapter 10

The Missing Years

* * *

The Thursday after Jariyeh's wedding, she was due to come for a traditional three-day sleepover. On Saturday, her husband, his family, and their friends would come pick her up—but would first stay for the "groom's dinner." Mehmet would sit with the men for the first time as a son-in-law and be served the coveted sheep's head. He'd share some brain, eye, or tongue with those he respected—hopefully including Baba. Afterward, Jariyeh would eat with the women for the first time as our guest. The following Thursday, she'd come for another sleepover. On Saturday, my family and our friends would deliver Jariyeh to the Bicis and stay for the "bride's dinner." Our sister would serve us for the first time as a Nuse.

This was how Jariyeh and Mehmet were supposed to step into their new roles. How we'd all get to know one another—how we'd become *miq*--friends through marriage.

But none of this happened.

The Bicis didn't bring Jariyeh for the sleepovers. Mehmet wasn't the type to keep her captive, but he was the type to obey. His mother was likely telling him what to do, because like my mother, Filanza loved to be in charge.

The Bicis didn't even call us the next morning—now that we had phones—to say things were "fine," meaning Jariyeh had listened and was a virgin. If she wasn't, they would've sent her home, taken their dowry, and our family would be disgraced. But there were no calls. No Thursday visits. No Saturday dinners. And there was nothing we could do. My sister now belonged to the Bicis.

My parents were heartbroken. I missed my sister. Why didn't Mehmet bring her over, I wondered. Was the Bronx that far away?

Within weeks of Jariyeh's wedding, we moved from Boro Park to Flatbush. 50 East 18th Street was a seventy-one-family mini United Nations filled with people of every color. Baba, Nana, Zogu, Luan, and I slept on two queen mattresses on the floor of our one-bedroom while the rest of the world slept around us.

In America, kids had to go to school. I was seven and didn't know the alphabet—not in Albanian, not in English—and I couldn't count past twenty. My family was busy surviving and had no time to waste on matters of little importance, especially for a girl. It wasn't like I'd need to read or write to be a good Nuse. Nana was teaching me how to clear the table, wash the dishes, and vacuum in parallel lines. But Baba wanted more for his daughters.

In Kosova, he was the first immigrant to send his girls to school. Kamile and Jariyeh attended for a few years, but Roza was too old at thirteen. That was the age girls began preparing for marriage.

My father took me to PS 249 and insisted they put me in 2-1, the smartest second-grade class. He had faith in me, even though I couldn't understand my teacher. I tried to learn English on Sesame Street but wasn't allowed to speak it at home. Fifteen-year-old Zogu made himself the "enforcer of everything Albanian" and forbid it. He liked forbidding things. So I studied harder. I loved learning. What I didn't love was having to wear pants underneath my dresses. Children made fun, but Nana didn't want boys to see my underwear—that would have been embarrassing, and "embarrassing" was to be avoided at all costs.

"Can we go visit Jariyeh?" I asked Nana.

"No. They have to come to us first."

I didn't understand, but as the youngest I wasn't supposed to ask questions.

I wouldn't understand until much later that there were rules to visitations. The boy's family had to take the lead. Our going there first would be out of line. Intrusive. We were only the girl's family. We had to know our place.

America had a holiday called Christmas, with a Santa Claus who magically delivered presents. I liked that holiday and looked forward to our holidays. They came twice a year, and we'd get new clothes and visit our family and friends. They'd serve us sweets and give us money.

First came *Bajram i Vogël*--Small Bajram—which celebrated the end of Ramadan. Then came *Bajram i Madh*--Big Bajram—marking the day *Nuh*--Noah left the Ark and *Musa*--Moses crossed the Red Sea. In tribute, we sacrificed a lamb. In Kosova, Baba would slice the throat of one of our sheep with a single stroke, then drain its blood—per the halal ritual. In America, lamb came pre-cut in the supermarket freezer section. Everything here was easier. Even corn came pre-cooked in a can.

Days before our first Big Bajram, I came home from school to a familiar sound: "Baaaa." I followed it and found a sheep standing in our bathtub. Baba got his knife. Nana and Luan walked behind him. I sat on the couch and covered my ears. Later, I helped Nana stack the steaks in the freezer, then we cleaned out the stomach. I swore I'd never eat tripe pie again.

Nana made a huge lamb meal, complete with baklava from scratch, then waited for my married siblings to come for lunch.

Jariyeh didn't show.

It had been five months since my sister vanished into oblivion, and I couldn't understand why we couldn't do anything about it. I was almost eight and knew it wasn't normal. When Roza and Kamile lived with their in-laws back in Kosova, they visited us every *Bajram*.

Not Jariyeh.

I first learned about divorce from Maureen, a brunette Shirley Temple look-alike who lived on the sixth floor.

"My parents are divorced," she said.

Divorced? Luan and I shared a look.

The Sesame Street Muppets spoke of "understanding our emotions" and "talking about hard stuff"—concepts that didn't apply to Albanian children. Our grown-ups told us what we could talk about. The Muppets never spoke about divorce. Seeing our confusion, Maureen explained:

"My mother and father are no longer married."

What a horrible fate. We felt sorry for the Americans and were happy to be part of a culture that married forever. That's what honorable people did.

"I visit my dad on the weekends," she added.

She lived with her mother? That was crazy. Children belonged to their father, which could only mean one thing—he was weak. Another horrible fate. But we respected Maureen's dad after he warned her to stay away from Luan. She was the first girl he kissed. I was proud of him because she was so pretty. But it also confirmed what I'd been told: American girls were easy. I would never kiss a boy until I married.

Divorce existed—but not for us. It never occurred to me as a possibility for Jariyeh. I only wished God had chosen a better husband for my sister. But He must have known what He was doing. After all, He was God.

Over a year had passed when Nana told me Jariyeh had a baby boy.

Boys were good. Mehmet's family must have been happy, I thought. Not being able to see the baby added to our sadness.

I liked America but missed the simple life of Kosova. I missed petting baby lambs, chasing baby chicks, riding on huge turtles, and trapping rabbits with a box and a string. I missed pulling potatoes out of the ground. There, good came from the ground. Here, food came from supermarkets, but you needed money. American jobs took adults far from home. Nana worked till midnight in Manhattan. Zogu worked all day at a pizzeria in Queens. Luckily, Baba stayed home.

I looked forward to the weekends. Nana was home, and Roza and Kamile visited with the kids. Our nephews and nieces were closer in age to Luan and me than our siblings. We'd play outside with the American kids who taught us American games: hopscotch, bottle caps, freeze tag, and Chinese handball. We introduced them to games with rocks. Mostly we threw them at targets, but when we chose teams and threw them at each other, they opted out. Of course, we thought, they weren't as tough as Albanians.

We had moved from a one-bedroom to a two-bedroom on the fifth floor, still in the same building. This apartment faced the street. From the kitchen window, Nana could keep an eye on us—not that she did—but she used it to call us in for meals.

"Come eat," she called, making sure not to yell, because yelling showed no class.

This sparked competition among us kids. Everything with Albanians was a contest. We'd sprint up the five flights to see who'd come second, because Luan always came first.

We were in America two whole years. I was nine.

Weekends were the best.

They were about fun.

They were about family.

The only thing missing was Jariyeh.

Chapter 11

The Animals

* * *

I couldn't get over how the Bicis had kept Jariyeh captive. "It's crazy that they kept her from us for two whole years and there was nothing we could do," I said to everyone, hoping someone had information.

"Baba called me," Bekim said. "He asked me to go with him to the Bicis."

"Really?" I was shocked.

"Yeah. I went with him and Hasan."

Hasan was Baba's friend.

"Why Hasan? Why didn't the matchmaker go?" I asked, assuming the person who vouched for the Bicis would be the one to keep them in check.

"I don't know why," he said.

"How long after the wedding was this?" I asked, obsessed with timelines.

"I don't remember. But I remember the Bicis lived in a terrible place."

———

A rat scurried past Bekim as they approached the projects on Alexander Avenue. What a terrible place to live, he thought. The South Bronx was like a war zone—demolished buildings, broken windows, graffiti everywhere. Bekim figured maybe the wealthy Bicis had chosen this neighborhood because they were still in a blood feud that put Selman in a wheelchair. The place reminded him of a soccer safety zone where the home players had the advantage. No man in his right mind would seek vengeance here. You could die just by showing up.

The Kanun did not allow for Baba's visit. We had given Jariyeh to the Bicis. They could do as they pleased—except kill her without good reason.

> Kanun Section XXIX: "A woman is a sack made to endure as long as she lives in her husband's house. Her parents do not interfere in her affairs, but they bear responsibility for her and must answer for anything dishonorable that she does."

A man could even beat his wife without repercussion—unless her father was my father. Baba was not the kind of father who looked the other way.

It was time to set the record straight with the animals who held Jariyeh captive.

Not letting a Nuse visit her family was unheard of, disrespectful, and inhumane.

Baba knocked on the Bicis' door. After a few minutes, a waterfall of locks began to come undone. Filanza's lack of enthusiasm at the sight of guests, especially ones considered family, was discouraging. But Bekim took solace in the fact that his father knew what he was doing. Even if the Bicis didn't want them there, as guests they had to be welcomed and protected, or the Bici name would be disgraced.

Two-thirds of the Kanun's Honor section was dedicated to hospitality, starting with Law 602: "The house of the Albanian belongs to God and the guest." Guests were sacred. That was why all the Jews who escaped to Albania during WWII were protected.[v]

Baba, Hasan, and Bekim did not bring guns. This would be a peaceful meeting where men came to understandings—even if the understanding was that blood was owed at a later date.

Mehmet was at work, but his seventeen-year-old brother Agim and his father were home. Selman waited in his wheelchair in the living room, where the walls were covered with pictures of Albanian generals, Albanian artifacts, and the Albanian flag—just in case anyone forgot where they were from. The guests took their seats on the plastic-covered couch. Hasan, the eldest, took the honored spot farthest from the door. Bekim, the youngest, sat closest to the exit.

"We've come to find out why Jariyeh wasn't allowed to visit," Baba said, his voice calm but his tone firm.

Selman didn't respond.

"I will take responsibility for her actions. What did she do wrong?" Baba asked, needing the Bicis to know his daughter couldn't be treated any which way for no good reason.

Filanza—an obnoxious woman who never followed rules—came in and out of the room like the busybody she was. Baba ignored her antics and repeated his question to Selman. Agim, the short-tempered son who was anxious to defend his family name, the good name he thought they had, hovered in the doorway just out of sight.

Bekim sensed something brewing between mother and son, but stayed focused on the tension mounting between Baba and Selman.

Finally, Selman said, "She did nothing wrong."

Filanza left and returned. She placed a gun wrapped in a headscarf near Selman's leg—breaking every rule of hospitality. Instigation was Filanza's specialty.

Selman made no move for the weapon. He may have been embarrassed by what she had done.

Baba kept his focus on Selman as if nothing had happened.

Bekim, however, went on high alert. He had grown up among men and understood the rules early on: intelligence was strength, fear was an insult, and panic was weakness. He never panicked. At age five, he was walking home with his books strapped in a belt when a pack of feral dogs came charging. Bekim casually spun the books like a propeller and kept them at bay until he reached home.

Now, at twenty, he crossed his legs, slipped a hand into the pocket of his tan suede jacket, and formed a gun with his fingers, resting it on his knee and aiming it at Selman—as if to say: *Try something, and the patriarch will be the first to go.*

"Jariyeh must have done something," Baba said. "Why wasn't she allowed to visit?"

"We were busy," Selman mumbled.

Ah, shit, Bekim thought. We've got trouble. Selman has no real answers and he's getting defensive. Bekim kept his eyes on Selman's gun as he continued his charade.

Then he felt something cold and hard press against his temple.

"Drop it," Agim said.

Bekim realized he was holding a gun to his head.

Baba remained tranquil. He wasn't interested in games with idiotic women or impulsive boys. He knew fear led to more fear, which was when untried men did foolish things. Baba kept his gaze fixed on Selman.

"Take… your… hand… off your gun," Agim punctuated every word.

"First of all," Bekim said, "the man who scares me hasn't been born yet." Demonstrating a common Albanian trait—stupid brave. "And second, that man is definitely not you."

"I said, take your hand off your gun."

"I don't have a gun," Bekim said, pulling out his empty hand. His pocket fell flat. At least he was smart enough to do that. "You can shoot me if you want. But you can't scare me."

Bekim's pride didn't allow for fear. In fact, if he ever showed it, the first person he'd embarrass was himself.

Agim lowered the Colt .45—the biggest revolver Bekim had ever seen—not that it mattered. Dead was dead, no matter the size of the weapon.

The room exhaled and settled into the calmness that was Baba. During WWII, he once fell asleep against a tree and woke to a snake coiled around him. He stayed perfectly still until it slithered away. Compared to that, the Bici snakes were easier to handle.

"I'd like to talk to my daughter alone," Baba said.

"Of course," Selman replied, almost apologetic.

"Hajde moj bi,"--Come my daughter, he said with all the sweetness that was Baba. *"Se kto s'qenkan njerz"*--because these aren't humans.

"I'm not coming home," Jariyeh said, eyes downcast.

Why had she said no?

Was she angry at our parents for marrying her to Mehmet? Or had Agim and Filanza's antics made her fear that they'd kill Baba and Bekim if she tried to leave? Leaving had consequences? The bride-price was paid. Dowries exchanged. A marriage performed. Virginity taken. Her transaction was complete. Her blood was now Bici blood. Leaving could spark a feud. Clearly, there was no talking to a family who could pull a gun on a guest. They had no honor. They could kill all three of them right there and then, knowing American law would call it self-defense. Thank God Zogu and Luan weren't there. Three brothers were enough—but for revenge, more were better. No wonder boys were coveted.

"But you must come with me," Baba pleaded. He wasn't worried about shaming his name. He couldn't leave his daughter with these animals.

Jariyeh looked at the floor.

Heartbroken, Baba walked back to the living room.

He said, "We're done here."

Turned, and left without a goodbye.

That was all Bekim knew.

What happened after, I learned years later from Kamile.

"Tell your daughter to come home," Baba told Nana the moment he walked in. "She won't listen to me. Maybe she'll listen to you."

"Net vendos vet,"--let her decide for herself, Nana replied.

Was that because she didn't want to lose her husband or sons to a blood feud? Or was Nana worried that Jariyeh leaving would ruin her husband's honorable name?

The next day, Baba went to enlist Kamile's help.

"No one knows my worries, my daughter. That wasn't the Selman I remembered."

Had Filanza been his downfall? When a good man marries a bad woman, everyone suffers.

"Call your sister. Tell her to come home," Baba pleaded.

Kamile would have done anything for her father, but figured that if Jariyeh was scared to talk at the Bicis, she'd call from a payphone, and they'd go get her.

"Let her decide for herself," Kamile said.

Frustrated, Baba went to Roza.

"Let her decide for herself," Roza said, unknowingly repeating the exact words as Nana and Kamile.

Was this how destiny worked?

Baba stopped trying to rescue Jariyeh after that.

But his heart never stopped breaking.

Chapter 12

The Candles

* * *

"I wonder what Jariyeh's life was like during those two missing years," I said to Saranda in passing.

"Bekim and I went to visit her twice," she said, surprising me. "Once when Esat was born, and once on his first birthday. Of course I had to beg him."

"What was she like?" I asked, eager for a glimpse into my sister's mysterious life with the Bicis.

"I don't know. She was just different. We spoke two, three times a week."

———

Every time Jariyeh called Saranda, she'd say, "How's everybody? How's your mother?"

"She's good," Saranda said, always curious why her friend never asked about her own parents or anyone else by name.

"Who was at the house?" Jariyeh would ask after the weekend get-togethers.

"Everyone, just Roza wasn't there," Saranda replied, waiting for her to ask why. Nothing.

The calls were brief. Some only a few minutes long. Always surface-level. No details. No warmth. No emotion. The only time Jariyeh laughed was when she shared a story about her baby boy.

"I was changing Esat's diaper, and he peed on my hand," she cracked up.

Saranda loved hearing her friend laugh, but she wasn't the Jariyeh she remembered.

"What did you do last weekend?" Saranda asked.

"I ironed money."

Jariyeh lived with Mehmet, his parents, his brother, and two sisters. Like a good slave, she cooked. She cleaned. She ironed. Mostly, she ironed bills. Lots of bills, and stacked them into briefcases. While Filanza directed: "Make them look like new! Make them look like new!" Jariyeh obeyed. Like a robot, she stacked the bills neatly in a trunk. She wasn't impressed by the cash. She wasn't impressed by her mother-in-law's claims of grandeur. She wasn't impressed with anything at all. Not even the candles. Candles were a Catholic thing. Moslems didn't light candles. But in the Bici apartment, one was always lit in every room. The place constantly smelled of wax.

Jariyeh's life was uneventful until one afternoon in the summer of 1972, nearly two years after her marriage. She was sitting at the playground with her toddler when she heard someone shout: "Jariyeh!"

It was Avni. One of the immigrant boys she knew from Italy.

"How have you been?" he asked.

"Good, Avni," she said, happy to see him. "How have you been? How's your father and your mother?"

"They're good. How's your father? How's your mother?" he asked, not knowing she hadn't seen or spoken to them in years.

"Good," she replied, and started to feel uneasy.

When he asked about each of her siblings by name, the way Albanians did, something twisted in her stomach. After he left, she rushed up to the apartment, confused.

Filanza was sitting at the kitchen table. Jariyeh was preparing a bottle. In the background, the kitchen candle flickered. As she turned toward her mother-in-law, the flame shuddered once, then went out. They froze. Slowly, both turned toward the living-room candle and saw a thin ribbon of smoke curling into the air.

"Qish u ba moj Nuse?"--What's happening, my Nuse? Filanza shrieked, clawing at her cheeks with both hands.

For a moment, the room felt suspended in time.

Then a thought struck Jariyeh like lightning: *I have a family.*

She went to her bedroom where her husband was resting. Their candle had also gone out.

"We're going to my father's," she said.

"Okay," Mehmet replied, not moving.

"Now," she commanded him for the first time since their wedding night.

Then she marched to the kitchen and dialed Saranda.

"We're leaving this place," she said. "Tell Baba we're coming."

"Okay," was all Saranda could manage. She never imagined hearing those words from Jariyeh's mouth.

Bekim called Baba: "Jariyeh is coming over."

And just like that, the heaviness lifted.

Nana pulled steaks from the freezer, hoping they'd stay for dinner. Bekim and Kamile rushed over to await her arrival. When the buzzer rang, my parents and siblings lined up at the front door to greet the honored guests. I peered past them and saw an old woman in a headscarf, a short man, and behind them—my beautiful sister, holding her baby.

"*Bujrum*," Baba said, using the Turkish word for welcome, as he shook his son-in-law's hand, then Filanza's, then gently took Esat from Jariyeh and held him high.

"*Mashallah*," he said, the blessing that kept away the evil eye, and kissed Esat's forehead. "May he have a long life."

When Baba hugged his daughter, everyone got emotional. One by one, we embraced our long-lost sister, then settled onto the red-and-black plastic-covered couches. Saranda served soda and chocolates—our long-overdue gesture for a sweet marriage. I sat cross-legged on the carpet and stared at my sister, thinking how different she looked. How grown up. And how wonderful that she'd given her husband a son. He must have been so happy.

With hand-over-heart, Baba offered Mehmet a cigarette. Conversation flowed politely. No one brought up the missing years. Filanza spoke loudly and acted like it was a routine visit. But everyone knew: if it were routine, her husband would've come, and it wouldn't have taken two years.

"Come with me to the store," Filanza told Kamile. "I want to buy you something."

Kamile knew it was more about showing off her money than buying her a gift but didn't want to disrespect Jariyeh's mother-in-law. They went to Laytner's discount store around the corner.

"Pick something. Anything. Whatever you want," Filanza boasted, like she was buying her couture. "You're so beautiful. You're so smart," she repeated like a broken record.

How do you know I'm smart? Kamile wanted to ask. She quickly chose a blouse and hurried back—wanting every possible minute with her sister, not knowing when she'd see her again.

After dinner, Mehmet and Filanza went home, and Jariyeh and Esat went to sleep at Bekim's.

"Can you believe I thought I was happy?" Jariyeh told Saranda after they put their boys to bed.

"What changed?"

Jariyeh told her about Avni and how the candles in the kitchen blew out.

"Candles?" Saranda interrupted. "Why do you have candles?"

"I don't know. But there were always candles lit in every room. The crazy thing is, after the kitchen candle blew out, all the other candles went out too."

"How did they go out?"

"I don't know." Jariyeh shook her head. "First, I thought maybe it was the wind, but the windows were closed. But the moment they went out, I remembered that I had a family. It was as if the candles had cast a spell over me. Whenever I thought of the family, it was like they were strangers—like they were in a dream. When the candles went out, I woke up."

"Oh my God!" Saranda said, rubbing the chills from her arms. "Does Filanza do black magic?"

Our ancient Pagan beliefs in spirits and magic pulsed beneath everything. If somebody was depressed, couldn't have a baby, or life took a turn for the worse, witchcraft was the culprit. Surely someone had wished them harm and cast a spell. To break the curse, Moslem Albanians turned to a Sufi Dervish or a *Hoxhë*--who went to Mecca. They called on spirits and wrote scripts using passages from the Koran, giving the impression they were working with God, though Islam forbade such shenanigans. People weren't supposed to interfere in God's will, but that didn't stop us.

"I don't know if Filanza does witchcraft," Jariyeh said. "But every morning, she'd light candles in the nook by the bathroom, then place them in every room."

Had Filanza practiced black magic to make my sister forget her family? I wondered. Had someone called on good spirits to blow out the candles and awaken her from her slumber?

———

"I was just writing about when the candles blew out in the Bicis' apartment," I happened to mention to my big sister Roza.

"What do you mean?" she asked.

Surprised that she didn't know, I told her what Jariyeh had told Saranda.

"Really?" Roza said. "You know, one day Nana said to me, 'I feel so bad for your father. He won't stop worrying about Jariyeh.' Then she gave me five dollars and said, 'Give it to Bardhe. Tell her to give it to her woman. Tell her it's for Jariyeh.'"

Bardhe was a Catholic Albanian who cleaned offices on Roza's floor at 1 New York Plaza. She and Nana often helped each other out when they suspected black magic. Bardhe swore by the power of this woman who lit candles at her church and prayed to ward off spells.

"When was that?" I asked.

"I'm not sure, but Jariyeh came back after that. It must have worked."

Had it worked, or was it a coincidence? Part of me believed it and imagined how cool it would have been if Filanza's candles blew out the moment the church candle was lit. Another part of me was spooked by the idea of controlling people with magic. Whatever it was—it was over.

Jariyeh was back.

Chapter 13

Happy Days

* * *

Now that the "spell" was broken, Jariyeh was clear about three things: she didn't love Mehmet; she didn't trust Filanza; and she was never going back. She knew Baba would take her in—but she now had Esat, and leaving Mehmet meant leaving him. He belonged to the Bicis.

"We have to move," she told Mehmet.

She'd been trapped for two years. Now she wanted freedom. But wives weren't supposed to make such demands. And husbands weren't supposed to listen. Mehmet did. It was the first sign that he loved his wife. Why else would he listen? But to his parents it wasn't love. It was disgraceful. He had put Jariyeh before his manhood. Before his family name.

At first it wasn't too bad. Mehmet found an apartment in Queens—not too far from his parents in the Bronx, but not close enough to us in Brooklyn for people to say his wife was in charge.

Mehmet was working at his friend's gas station in Harlem. Jariyeh didn't trust his money and applied for welfare.

The weekend gatherings in our two-bedroom apartment finally felt complete.

We were nineteen in all—ten adults, nine children. In the living room, the men drank beer and smoked, except for Baba. He had quit years earlier. Cigarettes made him cough. In the kitchen, the women cooked and served. The men ate first. The women second. The children and our Nuse, Saranda, got the leftovers.

In Kosova, Baba sang after dinner, but in America he had stopped. Jariyeh's return inspired him to take down the çifteli that hung on the wall, sit cross-legged on the carpet, and begin to strum. Everyone was relieved to see him back to his old self.

"Eh heeee..." Baba began to sing *Halil Gashi*, his all-time favorite—a true story of brotherly love.[vi]

The song tells of Halil, a villager from the north who goes to town and meets Beqir, a city man. Out of the goodness of his heart, Halil offers to find Beqir a Nuse from one of the twelve houses in his village.

"Bring me your sister," the city man says.

"May you have a long life," Halil responds, thinking it was an offer of marriage.

♪ *Po nuk ta du o për miqsij*	♪ I don't want her for marriage,
O' nja tri net o me to poj rrij	For three nights I will stay with her
E masanej o ta kthej në shpij	Afterwards I'll return her home

When Halil leaves without a word, Beqir assumes the villager was too dumb to take offense. But then Halil returns with a gun, eager to educate the city man on the ways of northerners. He finds Beqir at a café and tells the owner:

"Roast me a coffee, o' coffee man. For Beqir Aga, roast two."

The only man allowed to spend the night with his sister was her husband. Beqir knew that if he accepted the coffee, it meant marriage. If not—it meant death.

♪ *Mos u ngut hej moro djal i ri*	♪ Don't be hasty young man
un kam lujt hej fare me tye	I was only playing with you

Beqir's admission that he wasn't looking to marry left Halil only one option:

O' i bjen o manxerre	With his gun he shot him
po brio o ne brije	from rib to rib
O' t'kjoft o per hajr more	Congratulations to you
motra o Hajrije	on my sister Hajrie
Hej s'ta ka shoqen	None can top her
ner dymdhejt shpije	from the twelve houses
Hej, nuk ka loj'o	There are no games
me robt e mij ♪	with my family ♪

There were no games with any Albanian's family. "An offense to honor is never forgiven," says Law §597. Disrespect was a crime worthy of murder, and songs were written of those who committed such "honorable" acts.

At nine, I didn't understand the entire song, but I understood the part where brothers protected sisters. And in that, I took comfort.

The following year, in spring of '73, Jariyeh gave birth to a second son and named him *Përparim,* which meant progress. Mothers weren't supposed to name their children, but she was no longer asking. Nana made a pan of baklava to symbolize a sweet life for the little boy, and we took the subway to their home in Queens. Perparim was the cutest little thing. So small. So helpless. Seeing the joy on everyone's face as we sat in the backyard on a blanket, I realized how hard those missing years had been.

A few months later, Jariyeh moved again—this time to Flatbush, one block from Prospect Park and five blocks from us. Living so close to us made it seem like Jariyeh was telling Mehmet what to do and that wasn't allowed. Maybe they moved closer because Baba wasn't feeling well. But to Filanza, reasons didn't matter. She was furious. Husbands were never supposed to listen to their wives.

Like in the Bible, the first book of the Torah.

Eve bites the "apple" from the "tree of knowledge" and is blamed for the suffering of mankind. When Adam follows suit, God punishes him in Genesis 3:17—"because he listened to his wife." But the harshest punishment came in 3:16, when God tells Eve, "...your desire will be for your husband, and he will rule over you."

Were these the words of God—or of lowly men desperate to suppress women who dared crave knowledge?

The moment Jariyeh left the Bici home, she became the villain who dared to want more. Filanza blamed us and made sure everyone heard: *Her parents should've put Jariyeh in her place—taught her to keep her mouth shut. To obey. To stay. To be the submissive Nuse she was born to be. Lutfi Feza isn't a man. He's ruled by his wife. She runs the show, tells her daughter what to do, where to live. They're the dishonorable ones—not the Bicis.*

Albanians avoided gossip like the plague. But what to do when you were related to Filanza?

"All she does is gossip," I heard my mother say to my sisters, but said nothing more.

———

On weekends, we gathered at Prospect Park. Tree trunks and piles of clothes served as goalposts. Young and old played soccer together, the women barefoot in their dresses. On really hot days, we kids ran through the open fire hydrants, clothes and all—having not yet discovered bathing suits. Mehmet was rarely there. One weekend, Luan and I took our nephews and nieces fishing with rods made from tree branches and caught black fish with wiry mustaches.

"They're called catfish," an old man explained. Wow, I thought. Fish that are like cats? America had everything. Did they also have dogfish?

Jariyeh and Zogu were excited to find *thânë*--cornelian cherries, from their sheepherding days and bit into the ripest ones. Their sour faces held such joy that Luan and I didn't want to be left out. We took a bite and instantly spit it out.

"American children," they cracked up.

At the end of a long, joyous day, we gathered on our blankets. We drank *qumësht*--watered-down yogurt, and ate *petë*--thin layers of dough filled with scallions. Watermelon was dessert.

As Jariyeh rocked little Perparim to sleep on her legs, she began to sing:

<table>
<tr><td>♪ Ka dyzet vjet</td><td>♪ It's been forty years</td></tr>
<tr><td>Ka dyzet vjet</td><td>It's been forty years</td></tr>
</table>

Që jam ne burg   Since I'm in jail

The rest of my siblings joined in on the repeating verse, typical of old Albanian songs. My parents smiled. They had been great singers, and now their children were carrying on that legacy.

♪ as njeri nuk vjen mem pa mu   ♪ Not a soul has come to see me
As njeri prej prindve t'mi   Not a soul from my family

I lay on the blanket and listened. The melody was soothing, like a lullaby.

As nanë, as babë   Not mom, nor dad
As nanë, as babë   Not mom, nor dad
As motër, vëlla   Nor sister, nor brother
Përveç se dashnja ime   Except for my lover
Që më vjen nga nji her m'pa ♪   who sometimes visits me ♪

Surely family would visit you in jail, I thought. I didn't know that Baba had been incarcerated in Kosova, and no one had been allowed to visit. Did Jariyeh feel abandoned when we didn't visit her those two years?

1973 was our summer of joy, the closest we ever came to living our American dream.

We were free.

We were happy.

We were together.

Life was perfect.

We didn't have to worry about what the Albanian Communists or the Yugoslav Secret Police would do to Baba.

Chapter 14

Firewood into Song

* * *

All I knew of my father was love and kindness. I knew nothing of his past. So I turned to my sister Kamile, who had a photographic memory.

"What was Baba like?" I asked.

"Baba was a saint," she said, her eyes filling with tears.

"Do you know the story of how we left Albania?"

"During World War II, Baba was a war hero," she smiled.

———

My father, Lutfi Feza Alija, joined the Partisans not because he believed in Communism but because he didn't want the Nazis to rule his land.[vii] He was a fearless soldier with expert knowledge of the mountains and saved the lives of many comrades. After the Partisans' victory in 1944, some rose to high positions in the Albanian and Yugoslav governments. One of them was Kadri Hazbiu. When he became Albania's Colonel Chief of Counterintelligence, he promised Baba a government position.

"How will people know to vote for me?" Baba asked.

"We will tell them who to vote for," Kadri explained.

Baba didn't like that, but continued to attend meetings in the northern villages. When a man who spoke against President Hoxha was shot dead and paraded through the village on a horse, for all to see, Baba said for all to hear:

"We said death to the Fascists and freedom to the people. Not death to the Fascists and death to the people."

Knowing he had signed his own death warrant, he galloped to the mountainside where his wife and baby girls, Roza and Kamile, were stationed. Nine other families had brought their sheep there to graze for the winter months. Baba's clan had over five hundred sheep—the equivalent of millionaires. While most men walked, Baba owned a stallion and a saddle.

"Gather your things," he said to his wife. "We are leaving tonight."

"We're coming too," said a spokesman for the families, knowing that if they were to get out of Albania alive, it would be with Lutfi Feza leading the way.

It was October 1949 when he led the moonlit escape across the border into

Kosova, Yugoslavia. The Yugoslav government feared that the Albanian Kosovars would befriend the Albanian immigrants and start a revolution, so they shipped Baba and the nine families to the abandoned concentration camps in Serbia.

Six months later they were crammed into a disease-ridden freight train along with other refugees. While the crew delivered livestock, they lived on bread and feta cheese. After a few months they were sent to live among Serbians. Every few weeks, officers arrived in the middle of the night on bull-drawn carriages and shipped them to some other room, in some other Serbian home, in some other Serbian town. Keeping immigrants confused and unsettled was the plan.

Refugee families received a monthly stipend from the Red Cross. Occasionally, Serbian officials kept it for themselves, leaving many without food. Not my family. They didn't rely on free money. After farmers harvested their wheat, my parents gathered the leftover grains, and Baba brought them to the mill for flour. When the millworker told officials about the hardworking immigrant, Lutfi Feza, they loaned him land.

"You can keep half of what you grow," they said.

After harvest, Baba gave the government exactly half. Not cheating them. Not cheating himself.

Impressed, they offered him work hauling lumber. Baba bought a mule and a horse and hired help. Between seasons, he built houses with mud and straw.

Nana worked just as hard while giving birth every two years. Not in a hospital. Not with a midwife. But by herself. Bekim was born in the concentration camp, Jariyeh at home, and Zogu in a barn—inspiring his siblings to tease that he was like Jesus.

After eight years, my family was better off than the other immigrants, and better off than their Kosovar and Serbian neighbors. They had a nanny and the finest tailored clothes on the holy days. People were envious, but Baba paid no mind and continued to work hard and live the abundant life he was used to, while he waited for the fall of Communism so he could return home.

In Albania, Kadri Hazbiu was promoted to Minister of Internal Affairs and sent word through his spies: "Tell Lutfi Feza nothing will happen to him if he comes back. His position is still available." Baba was not interested. Maybe because he didn't trust President Hoxha, or because going back meant returning to the blood feud with Nana's family.

Early one morning in 1958, a pregnant Nana was tossing layers of dough onto the wood-burning stove. She was sprinkling it with water, salt, and butter when two men in uniforms walked past her into the house.

"*Šta je?*"--What happened? she asked in Serbian.

The Secret Police didn't answer.

"*Šta je? Šta je?*" she repeated, following them in a panic.

The officers walked upstairs to the room my family lived in, and found Baba in his long johns. He hadn't been feeling well. The children looked up at the officers, confused. Roza was eleven, Kamile nine, Bekim seven, Jariyeh five, Zogu three. They were sitting on the floor waiting for breakfast.

"Shut up," the officer yelled at Baba, who had not said a thing. They grabbed him by the arms, not letting him dress or put on shoes.

"Why? Why?" Nana pleaded.

Baba quietly got up, knowing there was nothing to say to men who were obeying orders and enjoyed the feeling of power, and walked with them.

"Don't take my father!" Kamile screamed as she followed them down the stairs.

"Don't yell, Daddy's girl," Baba said gently. "Go back inside."

Kamile wouldn't listen. She followed them onto the tree-trunk bridge across the river, crying all the way to the police station. When they put her father into a room and shut the door, little Kamile sat on the floor screaming.

"Let my father come home! Let my father come home!"

The officers watched from behind their desks. After five minutes, one of them walked over to the little girl.

"Go, go. He's going to come home."

But Kamile wouldn't stop.

So he chased her out and locked the door.

Six months passed, and Nana didn't know whether her husband was dead or alive. Then she heard he was incarcerated in Banat, Serbia. Every night, Nana prayed he was alive, and every day she and the children worked. "Let's make your father proud when he returns," she said, to keep them from giving up, as well as herself.

Nana gave birth to her sixth child—a baby so beautiful she feared the evil eye. This "eye" was triggered by envy or overwhelming admiration and was believed to cause harm, illness, even death. To protect her daughter, Nana kept her hidden from the barren neighbor. But a year and a half later they crossed paths in town. "Can I see her?" the woman asked. Reluctantly, Nana removed the handkerchief meant to shield her from onlookers. "She is beautiful," the woman said, then quickly added, "*Mashallah*"--God has willed it. Words meant to ward away the evil eye. But it was too late. Nana felt the warmth of her baby's diarrhea and fear set in. She tried everything, but unlike her other children who recovered in days, the girl she named Hane died two weeks later.

My brother Zogu was four when she died. He'd see her on the terrace and they'd play tag—but he could never catch her.

Unable to live in a house filled with memories of her daughter, Nana sent Kamile to ask the authorities for a new location. Weeks later, they were shipped to a rundown barn in Ferizaj, Kosova. Nana and her children shoveled the foot-high dried manure and killed the rats that came swarming out. The barn was cleaned, whitewashed with chalk, and made pristine per Nana's standards. It was important for her husband to have a nice home to return to—*if he was still alive.*

Baba was never told why he was imprisoned. Although the Geneva Convention guaranteed prisoners the right to a fair trial, he was never given one. Still, he made the best of it.

He carved a *çifteli* out of firewood and sang to inspire the other inmates—like Selman Bici. Then carved himself a suitcase and agreed to make one for a guard in exchange for daisy seeds. When they bloomed around the prison, the warden asked if he'd plant flowers around his barracks. Baba requested roses, and made the prison a place of beauty—from the outside. On the inside, some were being tortured.

In a world of light and dark, Baba chose a different reality. What other men surrendered to, he transformed. He turned firewood into song and the prison into a garden. He spent the rest of his time memorizing the Koran and praying five times a day. Once back home, he'd chant verses like an Imam, but wasn't religious.

"God will forgive you for anything you do," he would later tell his children. "But people will not. Always be good to people, so you can die with a clean slate."

Two years after his incarceration, the warden had Lutfi Feza brought to him. "You are free to go," he said. "Your people did this to you."

Baba's suspicions were confirmed. Someone had told the Secret Police that Kadri Hazbiu had asked him to return to Albania—and claimed he was a spy. Was it an immigrant envious of his success, or a Kosovar jealous of his wealth? Baba never found out. But whoever it was would not change his ways.

It was a Sunday afternoon. Kamile was squatting in the courtyard, practicing the alphabet on the dry dirt with a stick. She saw a man and a woman walking toward her and raised her hand to block out the blaring sun. She recognized the female neighbor, but not the man with the big black mustache and gray hair, wearing a traditional Albanian costume. Those weren't allowed, she thought. He must be courageous.

The man smiled.

"Babë!"--Dad! she shouted from where she sat. Kamile was so happy, she

couldn't stand. She couldn't run. She couldn't laugh. All she could do was cry.

"Why are you crying, Daddy's girl?" he said, kneeling beside her. "If you want, I can go back."

Afraid he'd go back, she desperately tried to stop crying, but couldn't.

Baba picked up his platinum blond little girl and headed inside. Kamile couldn't wait for her mother to see Baba was here. To see *he was still alive!*

In the barn, Baba hugged his wife and rubbed his unshaven cheeks on her face, as he always did to make the children laugh. On those days, Nana would squirm and say, "Get away. Get away." But not on this day.

On the straw-covered dirt floor, Baba sat cross-legged on a handsewn mat.

One by one, the children returned from their chores to this wonderful surprise. One by one, they ran to him crying. Baba hugged them, kissed them, and wiped their tears. He even hugged and kissed the olive-skinned girl who ran into his arms.

"And whose child is this?" Baba asked his wife, smiling at the six-year-old with the thick brown hair.

"That's your daughter, Jariyeh," Nana said.

It was then that Baba cried.

It was then he realized how much he had missed.

A year later, after Luan was born, Baba told the authorities, "Either you give me a soldier's pension, or you let me buy land. Otherwise, I'm leaving."

They knew Baba had saved a high-ranking Serbian Partisan during the war, but immigrants weren't entitled to pensions or property.

"Fine, you can buy land," they said, assuming it would never happen. The Serbs wouldn't sell to an Albanian, and the Kosovars didn't want us around. But when Baba offered our Kosovar landlord one gold lira for a small plot of land, he accepted. It was a lot of money, and he liked Lutfi Feza.

Roza and Kamile helped him build a two-room house from bricks of straw and mud. In the center hallway, he installed a drain for washing dishes in winter—a luxury other wives didn't have.

At fifteen, Roza got married while thirty-eight-year-old Nana was two months pregnant—with her eighth child. Roza prayed no one noticed the bump her mother wore with such embarrassing pride.

When her labor pains began, Nana snuck out of bed and set herself up by the drain. It would make for an easy cleanup. She gave birth as quietly as she could, not wanting anyone to wake up and see the mess. Kamile heard the crying and picked me up.

I was born on May 1st under a waxing moon, which symbolized new beginnings. We only know the date because of the Workers' Day fireworks that evening. My family said I was born with luck—we finally owned our home, and Baba was out of jail.

My father walked in. "What do we have?" he asked his wife.

"*Cuc,*"--Girl, Nana replied in her northern Gheg dialect.

"May she be blessed," Baba said, smiling at his little girl. The daughter who would care for him in his final days.

Fathers preferred boys, but my father loved all his children.

"Are you good?" Baba asked his wife. A question other husbands didn't.

"I'm good," Nana replied.

Baba named me Hane, after the daughter he never got to meet.

——

Hearing these stories made me wish I'd had more time with Baba. I knew he was all kindness and love—but I had no idea he'd been a war hero, a millionaire, a hardworking, powerful man. Unlike the "tough" Albanian men, his strength came from a deep understanding of what truly mattered—gentleness, patience, and the courage to lead with his heart.

If Baba had been alive, I believe he would have found a way to save Jariyeh.

He had brought us to America to escape the blood feud with Nana's family, the Albanian Communists, and the Yugoslav Secret Police.

1973 was the closest we came to living our American dream.

In 1974, the danger would no longer come from politics or war, but from a far greater threat.

Chapter 15

Baba's Girl

* * *

I was ten and the family interpreter, but Baba spared me the translation when he took Bekim to his doctor's appointment. He was diagnosed with stage-four lung cancer and given a month to live. The doctors told him to stay in the hospital, but Baba came home instead. He made Nana and Bekim promise not to tell a soul—if the end was near, why spend his final days in sadness?

"You have to take care of your father after school," Nana told me. "He's not feeling well."

I thought he had a cold. I didn't know of any other illness. I wore my keys around my neck, in case Nana had already left for her cleaning job at 1 New York Plaza when I got home from school. Baba had worked there briefly as a janitor but had to stop because of his failing health. He had come to America with hope, only to be met with heartache. Not seeing Jariyeh for two years was hard, but watching his wife support the family was harder. In Kosova he had worked nonstop, and now he could hardly get off the couch. His dream of going home was gone. Baba was stranded on foreign soil, never to see his family again, with only his wife and little me to care for him.

While Luan played outside with our friends, I sat on the living room floor doing my homework at the coffee table. Baba lay on the couch in his long johns. It was my job to make sure he ate, then clean up after.

"Did you wash the dishes?" Baba asked one night, looking at the full dish rack.

"Yes," I said proudly, then noticed a line of grease on the back of a plate. Embarrassed, I looked at Baba.

He smiled. "Daddy's girl. You did such a great job."

His kindness made me want to cry. Was it really okay that I missed a spot? Was it okay that the dishes weren't perfect? The minute he walked out, I rewashed the plate, because Nana wouldn't be as nice. And because it was her love I craved. Perhaps because it wasn't forthcoming.

I'd look out the fifth-floor kitchen window at Luan playing below.

"What are you doing?" I'd yell out, careful not to be too loud. Luan shared his escapades so I wouldn't feel like I was missing out.

Whenever Baba heard me talking out the window he'd say, "Go. Go, daddy's girl and play outside."

"I don't want to go," I lied. How could I leave my sick Baba all alone? I'll go out once he gets better, I told myself.

"Çika Babës"--Daddy's girl, he'd call me often and kiss my face.

Something Nana never did.

After dinner, Baba and I watched television. I always wondered how they got the moving pictures inside the small wooden box. I translated *Abbott and Costello*. My father laughed his hearty laugh, which often turned into heaving coughs. What a horrible cold, I'd think, and couldn't wait for him to get better.

Baba's favorite show was *Star Trek*. He loved the Vulcan, Mr. Spock, who he called *"Vesh madhi,"*--Big ears.

"He's like an Albanian because he doesn't lie," Baba said. "One should always tell the truth."

I hated lies and decided to be extra vigilant. One day I came home from school eager to share what happened but couldn't recall exactly what was said or done— so I said nothing. If I didn't speak, I couldn't lie. I was already quiet, and became quieter still.

Luan, however, told the story and exaggerated for effect.

"That's not what happened," I said, as if I were the keeper of the truth.

"You calling me a *liar?"* Luan glared.

You never called anyone a liar. Especially not someone older, and a male. It meant you questioned their integrity, questioned their manhood. Coming from a younger girl, the insult was even worse.

"I didn't call you a liar. You made it bigger," I tried to explain, afraid he'd beat me up when Baba wasn't around.

On our way to school the next morning, Luan punched me anyway. I tried not to cry and show weakness, but a few tears escaped. What hurt most was the feeling of helplessness. The next time Luan exaggerated, I didn't want to get hit.

"That's not what happened," I said anyway. It was that Albanian *krye fort*-- hardheadedness that wouldn't let me drop it. It didn't matter that I risked another beating. Better a beating than a lie.

On weekends, I got to go outside and play with my nephews and nieces, but inevitably, Nana's call came from the kitchen window.

"Hane. Your father is asking for you."

I didn't understand. Bekim, Roza, Kamile, and Jariyeh were all there—why did he need me? I wanted to play, but I knew Baba preferred my *hizmet*--care. I'll play later, I told myself, and bolted up the five flights of stairs.

My Baba needed me.

He told Zogu, the new man of the house, *"Po ta la Hanën amanet,"*--My final wish is that you take care of Hane.

Was it because Baba knew my heart was kind like his? Or because he knew I was too sensitive for this world?

When he went to the hospital, I thought nothing of it. They'd make him better, and he'd be back soon.

During his final weeks, Baba started losing his ability to speak. Frustrated, he mumbled, "Hane." My siblings quickly came to get me.

I have no memory of this. It must have been hard to see Baba so close to death—something I didn't yet understand.

Kamile told me I stood at Baba's bedside and listened carefully, then turned to them and translated. My siblings looked at him to see if I'd gotten it right. He smiled and nodded yes.

I believe those months in my father's peaceful presence taught me how to listen with every part of myself—and hear even what wasn't being said.

The doctors gave Baba a month to live. He stayed nine.

"Wake up," Nana said gently the morning of August 24, 1974. "Your father has changed lives. Put on your best dress. He's no longer suffering."

I wanted to cry, but if I had to wear my best dress, did that mean we were celebrating? Was this how death worked? Was it normal to cry?

Nana was following Baba's directions.

"Don't mourn me," he had told her. "All my life I've been preparing for death." Baba lived his faith quietly—not through ritual, but through kindness. To him, the afterlife was what truly mattered, and goodness was the only way in.

This would also be my religion.

I put on my plaid dress from picture day. Luan put on his best button-down and slacks.

"Go to Jariyeh's," Nana said, "and watch her boys so she can come here to be with everyone."

I didn't want to go. I wanted to be with everyone too—but we had no choice.

Luan and I walked the longest five blocks to Jariyeh's apartment. Everything seemed different. The streets were quieter. The leaves more defined. The air more lonely. Jariyeh opened the door with a look of grief, not her usual smile. Did she wonder why we were dressed up to watch her kids? Or did she understand?

She gave us each a long hug.

"The bottles are in the fridge," she said.

I felt Jariyeh's thank you. Nana didn't hug us.

Esat was watching cartoons in the living room. Perparim was asleep in his crib. I sat on the couch, numb, staring at the screen. When Perparim started crying, I got his bottle. He wouldn't take it. He kept crying and crying—so I cried with him.

"What's wrong?" Luan asked.

"He won't take his bottle," I sobbed, not realizing that crying with Perparim was how I got some of my sadness out.

My father's death was the most heartbreaking thing I experienced. But what would come five years later would make it feel like a breeze.

Baba left me with a strict mother and a short-tempered brother.

He left Jariyeh in that marriage.

Now she'd have to fend for herself.

Just as I would.

Chapter 16

Please Hit Me

* * *

It was lonely without Baba. Luan was thirteen. I was eleven. All we had was each other. Nana left for work at 3:30 p.m. and got home after midnight. We waited up, afraid she'd never return, like Baba. If Nana died, we'd be completely stranded. She took a second cleaning shift and wouldn't get home until seven in the morning. She would've taken a third shift if they'd let her. I thought it was because we were poor. She later told me she couldn't bear to be home without Baba. I slept in his old spot on the trundle and prayed Nana would be asleep beside me when I woke up.

The new man of the house, nineteen-year-old Zogu, was never home. He'd rather work all day and play pool with his friends all night than care for us. I was lucky to have Luan. He taught me games. He was strong. He made me feel safe. We played outside all day. When mothers called their children in for dinner, they scattered, leaving us alone. No one called us home. Luan and I dragged ourselves up to our empty apartment and ate whatever we could find.

We never thought to go to Jariyeh's house. Though she lived close, somehow everyone felt distant. Even when we were together. Baba had been our glue. Now everything was falling apart.

"There's nothing to eat," I told Nana, feeling neglected—or maybe I just needed her attention. There was no other way to get it. Whining or feeling sorry for yourself wasn't allowed. And crying wasn't an option.

"What do you mean there's nothing to eat?" Nana snapped, opening the fridge. "Bread and grapes. Bread and feta cheese. Bread and watermelon."

Why didn't I think of that? I wondered, and felt stupid for complaining.

Luan cut the watermelon, and we ate it with bread in front of the television. It was delicious—or maybe we were just hungry. For dessert, I sprinkled fine Turkish coffee grinds and sugar on a slice of bread like Nana used to in Kosova, and surprised my brother. I hoped she wouldn't be upset that I used the sugar and coffee. She didn't say we couldn't use it—but she also didn't say we could. The bread was no problem. There was plenty of that.

Bread was sacred when you were poor. "Eat more bread than eggs," Nana would direct. More bread than meat. More bread than cheese. Just more bread. You never threw it out, and you never stepped on it—or else you'd get a headache, or something like that. When bread went stale, we made *pershesh*—torn bread with boiled milk and sugar, or homemade yogurt with a dash of salt, Baba's favorite.

Nana always made bread. It was easy here. In Kosova, we'd harvest the wheat, cut it, tie it, haul it to the farm on a horse-drawn cart, spread the stalks, and have the horses walk over them until the kernels broke off. The grains were sifted, then sent to the mill to be ground into flour. In America, we simply went to A&P and bought a bag of Hecker's All Purpose with the little boy on the label.

"Bake the bread," Nana would say when she left for work.

It was a small thing she asked of me. I didn't have to feed a wood-fired stove— just turn the oven to 375, light the burner with a match, and try not to singe my arm hair or lashes (which sometimes happened). Then wait for the five mounds of dough to turn golden brown.

Often I got lost in other things: playing, television, chores, homework, and I'd burn it. Luan and I did our best to salvage the bread. He'd cut off the scorched edges, and I'd push them to the bottom of the garbage so Nana wouldn't see.

One day I was playing and totally forgot the bread. When Nana uncovered three days' worth of bread with the bottoms cut off, my heart sank.

"You burned the bread again?" Nana said with utter disappointment.

I was mortified. I never felt she loved me, and now I had given her all the more reason to love me less.

Unlike Baba's overflowing affection, my mother's love came with conditions. I had to do as she said—and she said: *Watch the bread.* And I couldn't even do that. How could I be such a disappointment when all I wanted was to please her?

Nana had been upset before, but this time was different. She headed to the bedroom, knelt on the floor, sat on the back of her heels, and began one of her lessons, which were as sacred as our bread.

"How could you do this to me?" she said, looking up at God, The One who had damned her with this child.

Heartbroken, I sat in front of her.

"I'm sorry," I said, knowing "Sorry" wasn't a thing in our house. "Don't be sorry, just don't do it," rang in my head. But I *was* sorry. I didn't know why I got distracted. Had my forgetfulness been an unconscious rebellion?

Nana rocked back and forth and paid me no attention. She raised her hands in the air, then rested her forehead and arms on the floor, as if in prayer. Her heavy hands showed centuries of hard work. The bumpy right thumbnail, surrounded by tender red skin, was her only deformity. The doctor said it was due to harsh cleaning chemicals, but "real women" didn't wear gloves. Nana applied the prescribed cream religiously because defects showed weakness. She couldn't have that.

With her thick fingers, she fake-scratched her cheeks to show "her face had been shamed," then dropped her hands onto her lap—again and again. This horrible act of mine reflected on her failure to train me to be a proper Nuse. If people knew, they'd never send matchmakers.

"I will never burn the bread again," I pleaded, as tears ran down my face.

"You are not my daughter."

I couldn't believe it. I had burned the bread and ruined everything. I had no father—and now I had no mother.

"Hit me," I begged. "Please. Hit me."

She got up and walked away. She was done with me.

I followed her around like a puppy, trying to stop crying. Nana hated weakness. I prayed she'd ask me to do something. Anything. She ignored me as she ironed her light blue cleaning uniform—perfectly. The way she did everything else.

Her silent treatments were deadly. It was better when she spoke. At least then you knew what you were in for. Silence was the ultimate punishment. She knew that. She liked it.

I missed my Baba. If he were alive, she never could have done this. He wouldn't have let her.

I needed her to speak to me. To call me her daughter again. When will she look at me again? I wondered—day after day. What can I do? What will impress her? An immaculate house was a surefire way to win Nana's favor. Luan and I cleaned every day, but Fridays were special. That was when we washed the walls, and Luan scrubbed the carpets with a brush. I dried them with a rag, making sure no one could tell water had touched the surface—as Nana taught us.

Weeks later, she finally spoke: "Watch the bread."

Grateful for the attention, I barely left the kitchen and opened the oven door again and again. I would be Nana's perfect girl. Maybe then she'd love me.

Cracks were forming in my flawless world. The fear of Nana's spitefulness and Luan's beatings loomed over me, with no sign of rescue.

The reminders of Baba in our apartment had become too much for Nana. We moved to Avenue P and MacDonald Avenue, three miles from Jariyeh, one and a half from Kamile, and a short walk to Roza's. I got to see more of my niece Arta. It was our fourth move in four years. I didn't know it was no big deal for Nana, who'd moved every few weeks in Yugoslavia. But for me, it meant a new school and new children who'd pick on us all over again—because they didn't *yet know* how strong Luan was.

Things were changing. The good news was Nana's day job hours were extended, so she had to leave her graveyard shift. The bad news was Luan hit puberty, and Nana started treating him like a man—which meant more chores for me. It felt unfair, but I begrudgingly accepted my female fate.

I was at the laundromat when Luan came with his three Italian wannabe tough-guy friends. They had formed a gang called "The Aces," and Luan was their unopposed leader. Like Bruce Banner from Marvel Comics, when my little brother got angry enough, he could snap and demolish a person or group without knowing what he'd done. I never had the "privilege" of experiencing his Hulk-like wrath because I was the sister he swore to protect.

"Nana wants you home," Luan commanded.

"No, she doesn't. She knows I'm doing the laundry," I said, figuring he wanted to pass off a chore. Surely if I showed up, Nana would give it to me—*the girl.*

"I said Nana wants you home!" he yelled, angry that I dared speak back. Like all Albanian men, Luan took pride in the submissiveness of their women. How dare I not obey? How dare I challenge his "manhood" especially in front of his friends? They were all scared of Luan. I should have been too, but on this day, I felt safe. We weren't home alone. And there were witnesses.

In a huff, I grabbed a dime from my laundry change. "I'm gonna call Nana," I said, and walked outside to the payphone.

Luan and his entourage followed.

I put the dime in the slot.

Everything went black, except for a flash of white stars.

In the darkness, sounds came to me in echoes.

"Haneeee… Haneee… Arrre you okay?"

Luan's voice was muffled and distant.

I struggled to open my eyes. Everything was blurry.

"Are you okay?" Luan asked again. He was slapping my face.

He was panicking: *If I died, what would he tell Nana?*

Behind him, his friends stood frozen, staring down at me. I was confused. Why was I on the sidewalk?

Luan had punched me full throttle in the back of the head. My face smashed into the payphone, my brain slammed against my skull, and immediately shut down to save itself—and I dropped.

How dare he!

I tried to get up. But couldn't.

"Are you okay?" he repeated. "I'm so sorry."

I knew he was sorry. Real sorry. He always was after throwing me a beating. But his guilt no longer meant a thing. I was always careful not to push Luan to his breaking point, but I was getting older and growing less tolerant of his bullying with every punch. And now that I had challenged him once, who's to say I wouldn't again? Who's to say the next time he hit me, I'd come to?

Luan helped me up. I felt a dull, throbbing pain in the back of my head. He followed me into the laundromat. Being knocked out was no excuse not to finish the laundry.

"Do you need help?" Luan asked sweetly.

"I can do it *myself*," I snapped. Then pulled a "Nana" on him and pretended he didn't exist.

So he left.

Watching the clothes tumble, I started to feel sorry for myself. I knew Zogu would hit Luan when he found out, and Nana would yell at him. But that wouldn't change how I felt. I could no longer count on Luan—the brother who included me in everything and made life fun. The trust was broken. And with Baba gone, who would care if I died? Nana didn't seem to. It felt like she was just waiting for me to grow up so she could marry me off and be done with it.

But first, she'd have to marry off my brothers.

Chapter 17

Nusja Shpisë

* * *

My middle brother Zogu was Warren Beatty good-looking and dated the most beautiful American girls. But he knew better than to bring them around. When they called the house, Nana would shout, "Eat shit!" and hang up. That was the first time I heard my mother speak English. She had made sure to learn those words, thinking they would discourage "the whores" from stealing her favorite son. An Albanian girl would've been highly offended. The Americans were confused. When they told Zogu what she'd said, he laughed.

When my brother turned twenty-one, Nana decided it was time he stopped playing around and got married. She picked Vera, a northern Albanian girl, and took Zogu to her house for a viewing. Vera was a good server, but not as pretty as the girls he was used to.

"I don't want to marry her," he told Nana on the way home.

"You're not marrying her for you. You're marrying her for me," she enlightened the boy. Bekim had disrespected her by choosing his own wife. She wouldn't let *that* happen again.

Zogu obeyed, like most Albanian boys. It was easier to listen to his mother. To follow the rules. To put himself last. That way he could feel superior in his sacrifice, judge those who broke tradition, and be praised by the chorus of blind followers who called him "good" and "honorable."

I couldn't wait for Zogu to marry. Not just so we could celebrate a boy's wedding, but because his wife would become *Nusja Shpisë*--the Nuse of the house, which meant she'd do all the cleaning and serving and I could finally take a break.

Zogu would need his own room, so Kamile and Jariyeh found us a three-bedroom at 8747 Bay Parkway. It had a patched-up hole in the living room floor— left by tenants who had robbed Kay's Pharmacy below. The Polish superintendent was wary of renters, but my sisters convinced him we weren't thieves.

Three years later, this decision would cost him his life. 8747 would be where both he and Jariyeh would take their final breaths.

The first time I saw our new building, I loved it. It was fancier than the others we'd lived in. A low brick wall wrapped around the front. Behind it a garden of trees, roses, and bushes. What I loved most was the castle-like archway with small towers at each end—their slate roofs a patchwork of blues, grays, and purples. A great first impression. To reach our new home, visitors would pass under the gothic arch into a private courtyard before entering our vestibule. And with Zogu's wedding coming up, we'd have plenty of visitors to impress.

Our four-bedroom apartment was one flight up. I got to share a room and a half-bath with only Nana. Our room was so big we split the trundle and put a twin bed on each end. Best of all, Kamile was a fifteen-minute walk, and Jariyeh just a block away.

I was twelve on Zogu's wedding day and wore a long red dress with tiny roses on the rounded white collar. A glowing and very pregnant Jariyeh wore a flowing yellow gown. When the wedding party returned with our Nuse, everyone gathered around her. Vera stood quietly, eyes downcast. Jariyeh understood the stress of being in a house full of strangers. She played the tambourine and sang with all her heart to show our Nuse just how welcome she was.

♪ *Oh filiz filizi bardhë*	♪ Oh lily white lily
A e din se ku ke ardhë	Do you know where you have come
Zogu agën e ke marr	Master Zogu you have married
Shyqyr Nana	Happy mother
Ç'ka ka dhanë	for what she's given
Shyqyr vjerra	Happy mother-in-law
Ç'ka ka marrë ♪	for what she's taken ♪

Pleasing her new husband was important, but pleasing her mother-in-law ranked higher still.

"Don't love me. Love my family. I married you for them," Zogu told his wife, as if he'd done us a favor—when really, it was Nana he aimed to please.

Like a good Nuse, Vera woke up before everyone, put on a nice dress from her dowry, fixed her hair, did her makeup, and served her mother-in-law Turkish coffee.

"Good morning, Mom. Did you sleep?" she asked, placing the cup on the kitchen table.

At first, Nana answered. Later, she just sipped in silence while Vera stood by the doorway waiting for her to finish. As time passed, Vera left the coffee in Nana's room and went about her chores. Some days the cup was empty. Other days untouched. But the worst was when Nana walked into the kitchen and poured it down the sink right in front of her.

Vera cleaned the carpets and washed the walls every Friday, like Luan and I used to. At first, she failed our mother's inspections and had to clean until three in the morning.

Jariyeh stopped by often to check on our new Nuse. Vera enjoyed her visits but was shy and never looked her sister-in-law in the eye when speaking.

"Look me in the eye. Don't look at the floor," Jariyeh told her, wanting her to be more confident.

"Okay," Vera said, lifting her gaze.

The next day, Vera looked Nana in the eye. "Good morning, Mom," she said, thinking maybe that was what she was doing wrong.

"Why are you looking at me like that?" Nana snapped. "Are you telling me to eat shit?" Like in the animal kingdom, eye contact was an act of dominance. And no one dared dominate my mother.

Vera looked away.

She got used to Nana's moods, but could never get used to Zogu's constant yelling.

Jariyeh couldn't stand the abuse.

"Please, please, my brother. If you don't love Vera, leave her."

He said nothing.

Sometimes Zogu let his heart open to this woman who adored him so, and let her lie on the couch beside him while they watched TV. But when Nana walked in and saw this *outlandish display of affection*, she shot him a look of disapproval and walked out. As if to say this wasn't how a real husband behaved—even though Baba had shown Nana plenty of affection. He'd hold her hand when they went into town, something no other Albanian husband did. It embarrassed her, but deep down, she loved it. Just like she loved it when he rubbed his stubble on her cheek to make her wince and the children laugh.

To make his mother happy, Zogu went back to yelling.

He was rarely home. He worked all day, stayed out at bars all night, and played soccer on the weekends. Vera cooked, cleaned, ironed, did the laundry, and waited patiently for his return. But nothing stopped his yelling.

Jariyeh couldn't take it anymore.

"Leave him," she said—the very words she wished someone would say to her. "And don't worry about Zogu or Nana. I'll talk to them."

Talking a family into letting a Nuse go was the hardest part. But she was confident she could do it.

"I can't leave," Vera said.

Jariyeh figured it was either because Vera's family wouldn't take her back—or she couldn't afford to go. So one day, she showed up with $3,000.

"Take this and leave."

"The money isn't stopping me," Vera said. "It's my heart."

For Vera, it had been love at first sight. From the moment she served him coffee that day, she could think of no one else.

Realizing the tragedy of her situation, Jariyeh tried to give Vera what her brother wouldn't. She hugged Vera constantly, kissed her, brought her presents, and told her she was loved.

"I love you," she told her often.

"I love you too," Vera replied.

She could say it to Jariyeh. But not to the man she prayed would one day say them to her.

By some cruel fate, both my siblings found themselves in the same trap: loved by someone they couldn't love back. Which was harder—loving someone who didn't love you, or being forced to stay with someone you didn't love?

Chapter 18

The Gift & the Spies

* * *

May 13, 1976 News:

International: The United States and the Soviet Union initiated a treaty limiting the size of nuclear explosions.

National: Nebraska Republicans gave Ronald Reagan his fifth victory in 10 days over President Ford.

Metropolitan: James Sullivan bet $3 at the OTB and won $128,844.

Local: Jariyeh Bici gave birth at Coney Island Hospital.

"May you have a boy," everyone said at the news of her pregnancy. You never wished a girl on someone you loved.

"No. I want a girl. For me," Jariyeh replied each time. She wanted a daughter to cherish and spoil. A daughter to treat the way she would have wanted to be treated. She couldn't change her mother, but she would break the pattern with her daughter. She'd let her marry whomever she wanted, and kiss her all the time.

I wished with all my might that she'd have a girl. We all did. There were no ultrasounds, so we awaited the birth, eager to be the bearer of the *mizhde*--good news.

The mizhde tradition began before telephones and telegraphs, at a time when people delivered news on foot. The long journeys were motivated by the payment received for giving the scoop, such as a prisoner's release, a boy's engagement, the birth of a son. Never a daughter. But this was different. As many things were with Jariyeh.

On May 13, 1976, our phone rang.

"Ani mizhde," Nana said to Kamile, verifying she would pay for the good news.

My ears perked up. Hoping the mizhde was about Jariyeh, I eagerly waited for Nana to hang up.

"It's a girl," she said, smiling.

I wished I could tell Saranda and collect her mizhde. She said she'd pay a whole $20, not that she had the money. But she knew miracles happened around Jariyeh, and wasn't surprised when, days later, she found a crumpled $20 in her stairwell.

Telephones made it easy for one person to collect all the mizhdes, and I was sure Kamile had already called her. So I ran to Luan, who was napping between shifts at the gas station.

"Mizhde!"

"This better be good."

"Jariyeh had a baby girl!"

"Okay," he said and went back to sleep. Later, he gave five dollars.

When my sister came home from the hospital, I went to visit. Getting permission from Nana was easy now that Zogu's Nuse did all the chores. Jariyeh had dressed her daughter all in pink. Pink dress. Pink hat. Pink shoes. She couldn't get enough of anything girly.

"*Mashallah*. She's so beautiful. What's her name?" I asked, expecting something like *Lule*--Flower, or *Drandafile*--Rose, after her favorite bloom.

"Her name is *Dhurata*."

"Dhurata? I never heard that name before," I said, instead of what I was thinking—what a strange name.

"Dhurata means gift," Jariyeh explained, gently stroking her daughter's cheek. "And she is my gift from God."

I felt foolish for not knowing the word for gift, but was happy God had given my sister this gift. What a good God He was. We all loved Dhurata for bringing joy into Jariyeh's life. Even Esat and Perparim were crazy about their little sister, who we called Lata for short.

Jariyeh lived a block away at 8650 Bay Parkway, so I visited after school. One day, she showed me a picture of little Lata fresh out of the bath with a towel over her head.

"I entered her in a beauty contest," she said.

I felt so American.

When the newsletter came, with Lata in second place, I thought, not bad for our first attempt. Next time it'll be first, because Albanians excelled at everything.

I watched my sister cook while her boys ran around the apartment and tiny Lata lay in her carrier on the kitchen table. We loved our little girl *so* much that kisses—even hard ones—weren't enough. We bit Lata softly on her chunky arms and legs. When we got carried away, she made the most adorable "I'm about to cry" face. This made us want to bite her even more. To get it out of our system, I bit Jariyeh's arm. She bit mine. We laughed at the teeth marks, which we proudly wore as emblems of our love.

Between bites, Jariyeh sang and taught me how to embroider. I had just turned thirteen, and it was about time I began my dowry. Dowries took years to make, and I planned to have a most impressive one.

"You see," Jariyeh said, turning the cross-stitch doily over. "The back has to look just as good as the front. Never leave loose threads. Always find the shortest and neatest path to the next stitch."

Nana made us all perfectionists. I was following Jariyeh's directions when someone knocked on the door. She opened it and I saw two little boys run away.

"Who was that?" I asked.

"Tefik's boys," she said. Tefik was my friend Seba's father, and the building super.

"The little spies," Jariyeh added.

I laughed at the idea of little spies, but it made sense. Every time I visited, Seba's brothers knocked and ran. Were they checking if she was home? One day, they came inside. Jariyeh served them sodas—you never sent a guest away, no matter their age, or there'd be talk. The sneaky little brats drank their sodas in silence, then wandered into the other rooms.

Jariyeh and I looked at each other—did they think someone was hiding?

After they left, I asked, "Are they really spies?"

"Yes, Bici spies."

Jariyeh grew suspicious the day Tefik stopped by knowing Mehmet was at work.

"Is Mehmet home?" he asked, with a glint in his eye.

"He's at work," she replied. Normally, Jariyeh would have invited her male guest in, as her father had taught her—but she sensed something devious. "I'll tell Mehmet you came looking for him."

"That's okay," he replied, and never returned.

Tefik was a northerner who knew the Bicis. During World War II, Baba fought alongside his older brother. When Tefik arrived in America, Baba went out day after day, with his limited English, and found him an apartment. But Tefik disappeared without a word. His brother later told us he'd always been jealous and disrespectful. He hadn't given Mehmet the apartment out of kindness—for kindness did not live in Tefik's heart. He was a cruel man, even to his children, whom the state eventually took away. Did they know he once chained Seba to the boiler for not listening?

After Tefik's visit, Jariyeh wondered if the Bicis had arranged the apartment? Had he come hoping to report that she'd let a man inside while her husband was away? Or worse—had he hoped they'd fool around? There were rumors that he was sleeping with women in the building, meanwhile his wife was pregnant with their sixth child.

His Olive-Oyl-looking wife, tall, bony, with hair pulled tight, seemed to be in on the spying. She was always "running into" Jariyeh in the hallway or "stopping by for coffee." She constantly asked: *Who came over? Where did you go? Who did you go with? When did you get home?* It wasn't like they were friends. When I visited Seba, her mother even asked me questions.

Soon after, details no one else could've known came up in Filanza's gossip—confirming what Nana and Jariyeh already suspected: Tefik and his wife were Bici spies. Were they being paid? Or was Tefik simply happy to report on Lutfi Feza's "too good" family pro bono?

Just because we didn't think about the Bicis didn't mean they weren't thinking about us.

Jariyeh moved out of the Bici home seven years earlier but never broke free of them. Filanza was always there, lurking in the background, dying for something juicy about Jariyeh, her mother, her brothers, her sisters—anyone. Then she could do what she did best: whine, complain, and spread rumors, hoping to shame us into sending Jariyeh back. Gossip was Filanza's oxygen. And the building where she cleaned offices was a breeding ground for bored women hungry for morsels—especially about women who refused to sit and suffer like them.

Feeling invaded and unsafe in her own home, Jariyeh convinced Mehmet to move again. They found a three-bedroom apartment at 8735 Bay Parkway, right next door to ours.

———

Decades later, I sat in Central Park with thirty-something Lata. Her gap-toothed smile and fiery spirit reminded me of her mother.

"I heard there was a lot of gossip," I said.

"Yeah. My Aunt Drita told me women used to come to her house and gossip about my mom. And she'd tell them, 'That's enough.'"

Drita was Mehmet's sister. The only Bici Jariyeh liked, besides Selman. The only one she visited. I was happy to hear at least one Bici was on Jariyeh's side.

Chapter 19

American Summer

* * *

The summer of '76 was off to an exciting start. Jariyeh was next door. I graduated from junior high school. And America was turning two hundred years old. Patriotism was sweeping the nation, and I was excited, but wasn't sure how much I, as an Albanian, was allowed to join in the "Spirit of '76." Everywhere I turned there were flags with the original 13 stars, bicentennial T-shirt iron-ons, and fire hydrants painted red, white, and blue. Luan took me to Shore Parkway to witness "Operation Sail." We watched frigates, destroyers, tall ships from around the world pass under the Verrazano Bridge and into Lower Manhattan. They came to commemorate America's birthday.

The night before the big event, I watched a televised special with Bob Hope, Annette Funicello, and Princess Pale Moon. President Ford said: "Two centuries ago, the United States of America was conceived in liberty and dedicated to the proposition that all men are created equal." I liked the sound of that, but wasn't sure if "all men are created equal" included women.

On July 4th, millions of people went to watch the fireworks. I *so* badly wanted to go, but Luan was working. He had dropped out of school due to a learning disability no one tested for and now pumped gas at the Exxon station across the street. I was sitting at home feeling sorry for myself when Jariyeh burst into our apartment with her kids dressed in red, white, and blue, and tiny American flags attached to Lata's stroller.

"Let's go!" she shouted. "It's America's birthday! We're going to watch the fireworks by the water!"

Nana and Vera simply smiled. But I was ecstatic.

"You're coming too," she told Vera, who knew better than to invite herself.

As we crossed the street, Luan yelled, "Where are you going?"

"We're going to see the fireworks!" I yelled back, feeling bad that he couldn't join us. But he was happy to work because customers were giving big tips.

As we walked the two long blocks, cars passed with tiny American flags fluttering from their antennas. Some honked their horns, adding to my excitement. Shore Parkway was packed with people, but Jariyeh found us a spot on the grass.

We laid out blankets and unpacked the food. Once the sky darkened, we sat in silence, eyes fixed past the Verrazano on the Manhattan skyline.

BOOM! The fireworks began.

I watched in awe as colors exploded across the sky, then turned to Nana and saw the fireworks flickering in her smiling eyes. It had been two years since Baba passed, and we all wanted to see our mother happy, but it was Jariyeh who made it happen. After the grand finale, we clapped as a whiff of sulfur blew past us. But it wasn't over. Jariyeh handed out sparklers, making sure Nana took one, and lit them for us. Esat and Perparim ran around waving their glittering torches. I stood still, watching the bright white sparks in my hand that felt like hope. I was grateful to have a sister like Jariyeh, who made hope possible.

"In America, women can be free," she once told me.

It was true. Here, women could be free. Here, women could do more. I already had more of an education than my sisters, who never finished elementary school. And my mother, like the women before her, never stepped into a classroom. Zogu and Nana had given me permission to continue to the next grade. It was always a grade-by-grade, wait-and-see arrangement. But if I kept getting good marks and being a good girl, they just might let me finish high school.

We walked home with the crowd all abuzz. Another spectacular evening, thanks to my sister. Even if we didn't think of ourselves as Americans, that night we were proud to be in America. We were grateful that Baba had brought us to "the strongest country in the world." No one would mess with America—and for me, who was scared of everything—safety was imperative.

Things changed three weeks later. On July 29, 1976, the news reported that eighteen-year-old Donna Lauria was sitting in a car with her friend when two shots blasted through the window. The friend was wounded. Donna died instantly. People thought it was a one-off Bronx tragedy, but the killer struck six more times over the next nine months. The city spiraled into panic and assembled its largest police task force ever.

I was terrified.

Albanians only killed their enemies. Only those who disgraced their family. Only those who took their blood. Never strangers—and never for no good reason.

What was wrong with this man? With these Americans?

Was he targeting women who went out dancing? I had always envied American girls who got to go to discos, but not anymore. Now, I was grateful that the only disco dancing I was allowed to do was in front of my bedroom mirror. Even that, I did on the sneak.

He was killing girls with long brown hair. Beauty parlors were inundated with women dyeing their hair red or blonde. I wasn't allowed to color mine until I married. Jariyeh could, but she didn't. Was it because the attacks had only been in the Bronx and Queens?

A letter was left at the crime scene:

> *Sam is a thirsty lad, and he won't let me stop killing till he's had his fill of blood.*
>
> *—Son of Sam.*

Who was Sam? Was he possessed? Could this man ever be stopped?

The following July, Son of Sam changed tactics. He shot his first blonde, and he did it in Brooklyn—not just anywhere in this fourth-largest borough in the United States, but a short walk from where we watched the fireworks. My stomach turned.

New York was getting more dangerous by the day. Roza and Kamile's husbands took turns picking up the ladies from work because of all the subway crime. They'd get home after midnight. What if the Son of Sam killed them next? He wouldn't know they were just cleaning ladies.

I tried to calm myself: *God wouldn't let that happen.*

When police detectives parked at Luan's Exxon station for a meeting, he decided to do his own investigative work. Naturally, he included me.

"Let's follow the path the victims took," he said, pointing to the map in the newspaper.

Wanting to be brave, I went, but didn't have the nerve to go where they'd been shot.

After thirteen months, six dead, and seven wounded, Detective Edward Zigo of the 62nd Precinct followed a lead from a parking ticket and arrested twenty-four-year-old David Berkowitz. With his dark brown hair and round face, the unassuming postal worker looked a little like Mehmet—the man Zigo would be tasked with finding two years later.

With Son of Sam behind bars, my fears began to dissipate.

No one was home, so I turned on the radio and stood before the bedroom mirror, but couldn't bring myself to dance. America still didn't feel safe. Fear made me grateful for being locked up. Staying home kept me high on the matchmakers' list. It also kept me safe in a country where people killed for no reason.

I would soon discover that violence against women was everywhere and ever-present—even inside our very walls.

Chapter 20

The Future That Wasn't There

* * *

"When did Jariyeh first say she wanted to leave Mehmet?" I asked her best friend Saranda decades later.

"Right after Lata was born. It was like having a daughter made her feel like anything was possible."

"Since 1976?" I asked, surprised she had been thinking about it for four years.

———

Saranda and Jariyeh were best friends, but they couldn't have been more different. Jariyeh was bold. Saranda was meek. Jariyeh took chances. Saranda played it safe. Jariyeh married for Nana. Saranda married for love. Jariyeh questioned her husband. Saranda would wake up in a cold sweat if she dared dream of such a thing.

As they sipped Turkish coffee in Jariyeh's living room, All My Children played in the background. The headstrong Erica Kane had already dumped her first husband—nine more would follow. Though Jariyeh was also headstrong, her marriage didn't come with an exit strategy.

"I'm leaving Mehmet," Jariyeh said.

Mehmet had moved out of his family's home to please his wife, but she never learned to love him. Was it because he couldn't measure up to our father? In truth, Mehmet didn't even measure up to our brothers. Bekim and Zogu weren't Baba—but they would never marry a girl who didn't want to marry them. They would never sit among men and add nothing. They would never walk into a room behind their wives. Mehmet wasn't doing it out of respect; he simply couldn't lead—and that wasn't the nature of things Albanian.

Albanian girls were molded to be submissive, with the understanding that their husbands would be worthy. Husbands couldn't just flip the script midway and follow their wives around like puppy dogs. Wives expected their husbands to be alpha males—in charge and respected by their breed—not to fade into the furniture. When Jariyeh entered a room, it came to life. When Mehmet walked in, the oxygen headed for the exits.

She couldn't fall in love with the emptiness of his space. She just couldn't—

and eventually, that "couldn't" turned to hate. Hate that she'd married him. Hate that she couldn't leave. Hate that he even existed. It wasn't anyone's fault, really. Mehmet couldn't become strong. Jariyeh couldn't accept weakness. So, there they were, two vastly different people, a mismatch from the start.

"How will you leave Mehmet?" Saranda asked.

"I don't know. But I can't see myself getting old with him. I try to, but I just can't."

It was true. Jariyeh wasn't going to grow old with him—or anyone else. Had she somehow looked into the future and seen she wasn't there?

"It's going to be him or me. If I don't leave, I'm going to die," Jariyeh shared a gut feeling. Not that she thought Mehmet would kill her.

She had mentioned dying to Saranda once before:

"The other day I was on the bus and wished it would crash so I could just die. But I felt bad for the kids. When I gave my seat to an old woman, she said, 'God will bless you, my dear.' What do you think she meant?" Jariyeh asked, hoping Saranda would say, It means God will make things better. Instead, she said, "It means you shouldn't be thinking about dying."

That's when Jariyeh realized she'd said too much. Normally she kept it vague: I want to leave Mehmet. I can't stand him. Never serious complaints, because when she did, Saranda would cry and cry.

"If you really think you're going to die if you don't leave him, then we have to figure something out," Saranda said. She didn't know what that something was— but knew Jariyeh couldn't just walk away.

Seeing the panic in her friend's face, Jariyeh backtracked.

"Don't worry. I'm not going to die if I don't leave him. Nothing's going to happen to me. Forget it."

But Saranda couldn't forget it.

"Why don't you ask Mehmet to leave you? He'll do anything for you."

"Yeah, but he won't do that."

"Does Nana know how you feel?"

"She does. I told her, 'He's stupid. I want to leave him.' And she said, 'A smart woman can live with a stupid man.' Then she told me a story about how a smart woman had stayed and got to marry off her children and buy a house. Does Nana think all I care about is marrying off my kids and buying a house? Or was she trying to manipulate me into staying—just to prove I was smart?"

Saranda shrugged. She'd been raised by a different kind of mother. One who was direct. No sarcasm. No eye signals. No stories to decipher. "My mom says, 'If you have a stupid husband, run as far as you can.'"

Jariyeh laughed. She loved Saranda's mother.

"Did Gjile really say that?"

"She did. But on my wedding day, she also said, 'As long as your husband works, comes home at night, puts food on the table, and doesn't hit you, you've got nothing to complain about.'"

> Law §32: "The Duties of the Husband are: a) To provide clothing and shoes, and everything necessary for the conduct of life; b) To preserve the honor of his wife."

But "The Duties of the Wife" were more involved.

> Law §33: "a) To preserve the honor of her husband; b) To serve him in an unblemished manner; c) To submit to his domination; d) To fulfill her conjugal duties; e) To raise her children with honor; f) To keep clothes and shoes in good order by sewing."

These laws were made at a time when women lived in harsh environments and depended on men for survival. In America, with its supermarkets and indoor heating, where women could make a living—mothers still taught their daughters they were nothing without men.

The woman who gave you life was not your friend—she was the guardian of the family name. She didn't hug and kiss. She didn't ask about your feelings, desires, or opinions. They didn't matter. In our house, Nana was the boss. She made the rules. We obeyed. That was our job. You couldn't quit, though being disowned was an option.

Jariyeh knew all this. Still, she hoped that maybe—just maybe—Nana would one day take her side, as Baba would have.

If only her father were alive.

If only she'd left Mehmet the day Baba begged her to.

If only she'd been allowed to marry Sam.

But life didn't work with if onlys.

The following year, 1977, Jariyeh saw Sam in person.

He was engaged to Hasi, an Albanian girl from Paris. He'd flown there to meet her. Sam told his sister there were no sparks, but she had a nice smile and came from a good family. Besides, Sam was twenty-seven. It was time he had children and brought a Nuse home to help his mother.

We all went to congratulate Sam and his family. The men were seated in the fancy living room with the ornate Roma furniture. The women were led into the small family room. After sodas and chocolates, Gjile passed around a photo of his fiancé. I couldn't wait to see the girl who got to marry Sam—and was disappointed. She wasn't nearly as good-looking. When Gjile praised her honorable family, I thought, *of course, that was most important.* She's probably a good listener.

Kamile spotted a tambourine on top of the armoire, and my sisters began to sing. Jariyeh grabbed a handkerchief and pulled Saranda and her sisters up to dance. When the excitement died down, Jariyeh went to the living room and returned with Zogu and Sam.

The sight of the groom reignited the singing. Jariyeh spun her handkerchief wildly as she led the men in a line dance. The women rushed in, grabbing Sam's hand. My niece and I joined at the end of the line, where kids belonged. After two loops around the cramped room, Jariyeh shamelessly headed toward the men's living room, knowing Mehmet wouldn't mind. Roza stepped off the line, knowing her husband wouldn't approve.

The men looked up and broke into smiles—now this was an engagement party. As we approached Bekim, I wondered if he'd be mad at us, especially at Jariyeh, for being so bold. Instead he stood, got in between Zogu and Sam, and started singing along.

We circled the coffee table twice, then made a loop through the kitchen, around the dinette, and back into the living room. Knowing not to push her luck, Jariyeh steered us back to the women's alcove. Gjile smiled. Nana beamed. Once again, her children brought joy to a celebration—like their father used to.

After midnight, we got up to leave, and Sam's family walked us to the door.

"Thank you for coming," they said to us—but especially to Jariyeh.

"Till next week!" she said, letting them know she wasn't done with them yet.

They laughed with anticipation.

———

"Jariyeh was heartbroken at Sam's wedding," Vera told me years later. "She danced all night. She danced so much that her heel broke, but she wouldn't stop."

I imagined my sister flying around the dance floor in her peach gown, desperate to prove she was happy for Sam—while dying inside.

Had my sister fallen in love with him again during those home visits? He was the most handsome man I'd ever seen, and so charming. There was something warm and inviting about him, something that reminded me of Baba. Was that what Jariyeh fell for?

Chapter 21

Family Fun

* * *

It was 1978, four years since Baba passed, when our weekends were fun again. I especially loved it when my niece Arta came over. She and I were best friends. Unlike my American friends from school, with her—it was easy. I didn't have to explain our traditions or make excuses for our ways. We were in it together, living almost parallel lives. I was fifteen. She was fourteen. I was the youngest of seven. She was the oldest of four. Nana and Zogu were strict. Her parents were stricter. But compared to Arta, who did all the serving and cleaning after her mother left for work, I was spoiled—I had Vera.

Arta lived two miles away, too far for me to walk alone, so we talked on the phone every day and constantly interrupted each other with song lyrics. Every word reminded us of the latest hit. If one said, "Do you know"—the other sang, "…where you're going to…" If one mentioned "ladies," the other belted out, "It's ladies' night…" then we'd finish the verse together. We could hardly get through a sentence without a song interlude.

Every phone call ended with, "Are you coming over this weekend?"

Saturday nights were when my siblings came over, but ever since Arta's uncle, on her father's side, arrived from overseas, they started going to New Jersey instead. The father's side always came first. We were only the mother's side. On their way back, they often stopped by because we stayed up late and knew how to have fun.

Vera served the men beers, the women sodas, and prepared meze plates of fried beef cubes, baked chicken legs, and Nana's pickled cabbage, green tomatoes, and cucumbers.

"We are three brothers and have four sisters," Bekim said. "We should each choose a sister to call our own."

"Jariyeh is my sister," Zogu called dibs.

"Who said you get to choose first?" Bekim playfully pulled rank.

"Don't even think about it. You get Hane."

"That's fine. I'll take her. We've got the blue eyes—and we're the best looking."

Everyone laughed. Like all Albanians, we claimed to be the best at everything:

best looking, best dressed, most intelligent, funniest—it didn't matter that we weren't. We believed we were, and that was good enough.

"So that makes Jariyeh my sister," Luan said. "She and I look alike."

They did. They both had thick brown hair and olive complexions, which was why Zogu had nicknamed her *Maxhupe*--gypsy. Any other purebred Albanian would have been insulted, but Jariyeh took it as a compliment.

"Get outta here," Zogu said. "Jariyeh's mine. We grew up together. We're friends."

Family was important to Zogu, but friendships ranked higher still, and in Jariyeh he had both. They were inseparable back in Kosova and had *"eaten a sack of salt together,"* as the saying went.

Zogu and Luan went back and forth—neither one would give up. Roza and Kamile didn't get upset. They understood Jariyeh's magnetism.

As usual, the women migrated to the family room and began to sing. The men gathered around the dining table for a game of poker. While the adults did their thing, the children ran around unsupervised. Fathers paid no attention, and mothers only stepped in when there was crying or blood.

"Good for you. Who told you to fight?" was often the most sympathy they got. Sometimes it was followed by a slap. Jariyeh slapped her boys when they misbehaved—never her daughter. Once a child was done sulking in the corner, they'd run back to their crew and rejoin the fun.

"Who farted?" Luan asked, swatting his nose.

The kids laughed. Farting was taboo—they knew better than to do it in front of grown-ups and snuck one in amongst themselves.

"Not me." "Not me," all the kids said.

One brave soul volunteered to find the culprit and went sniffing from ass to ass. When the sniffer turned away disgusted, we laughed hysterically.

As aunt and uncle, Luan and I were supposed to keep the kids from crying—but his version of babysitting was inspired by the World Wrestling Federation. The center of the large bedroom Nana and I shared was our ring. Luan selected two "gladiators" from the seven nephews aged between six and twelve. The rest of us jumped on the twin beds at opposite ends of the room, ready for a show of strength. Luan served as ringmaster. At the end of each bout he lifted the winner's hand as if they'd won a championship belt.

After a few bruised rounds came the grand finale: seventeen-year-old Luan vs. fourteen-year-old Arta and fifteen-year-old me.

"In this corner, Luan the Liiiooooon!" he roared. But his name meant lion, so his title wasn't that impressive. Still, the boys cheered.

With fists in the air, Arta yelled, "And in this corner, THEE

DEESTROYERS!!!"

Then we jumped him as planned.

Luan tossed us off like paper.

We dove back in.

The kids went wild.

They had all tasted a beating from "the Lion" at some point, but still wanted him to win—to prove boys were tougher. We knew he could kick our ass, but we'd put up a good fight. Arta kneeled behind Luan. I pushed him over. She caught him in a headlock. Next thing we knew, we were trapped beneath him. Minutes later—red, bruised, and pinned to the floor—Arta and I surrendered. But we were proud of our performance.

Afterward, we snuck into my closet, where I kept a teen magazine hidden under my neatly folded shirts. I turned on the light, closed the door, and opened to the centerfold of the Hardy Boys. My secret crush was Shaun Cassidy, the TV detective. He was such a hunk. I imagined him coming to Brooklyn and somehow bumping into me. I didn't know how, since I wasn't allowed to go out—but it happened. He'd be so impressed by what a "good girl" I was that he'd ask me to marry him. I'd kiss him on the cheek, but only once—then break his heart by saying I couldn't marry an American.

As the evening progressed, one by one the children went to their mothers mumbling, "I'm tired." Their moms found them a spot on a bed, a couch, or a floor cushion. They'd fall asleep fully dressed.

I wanted Arta to sleep over so we could go to Jariyeh's the next morning to listen to her records and dance.

"Can Arta sleep over?" I asked Roza, so she could ask her husband—because I didn't dare speak to him myself.

We knew Roza couldn't bother him when he was doing "manly things": smoking, drinking, gambling, and conversing with the other men—so we waited for him to head to the bathroom, then ran to Roza.

"Ask him now!"

She'd walk over and ask as if it just occurred to her, "Oh, can Arta sleep over?"

"We'll see," he gave his typical response, which meant: I'm in control. Ask me again on the way out to see how I feel. A straight "yes" was on par with a miracle.

Nana stayed up as long as she could to watch the festivities. Not being with her family in Albania must have been hard, but these Saturday nights made American life worth it. If we were in Kosova, she wouldn't have seen her daughters this often, or gone to sleep surrounded by *all* her grandchildren.

Around 2 a.m., Vera, drunk from exhaustion, climbed onto the kitchen table and started to dance. Jariyeh grabbed the tambourine.

♪ *Xhixhile moj Xhixhile*   ♪ Gigileh, my Gigileh
Xhixhile moj e malit e'   Gigileh of the mountains

Roza and Kamile clapped in rhythm and sang along. In the dining room, Bekim and Zogu joined in. To urge Vera on, Jariyeh climbed on a chair and played the tambourine near her face:

♪ *Tunde moj belin o e bukur o*   ♪ Shake your waist oh beautiful

Seeing Vera on top of the table, Zogu laughed. "She's drunk! She's drunk!" he said, delighted that his wife was becoming like his family.

Vera laughed—happy for her husband's attention.

Jariyeh got off the chair, grabbed a bill from the men's betting pile, climbed back on, spit on the dollar, and smacked it onto Vera's forehead. The women cheered. Vera danced harder:

Veç një natë me ty të fle   Just one night to sleep with you
opopopo moj olelele   O' my goodness, ooh la la
le të vdes të bëhem dhe ♪   I can die and become earth ♪

The song ended, and Vera climbed down.

When the men finished gambling, they summoned their wives.

"Let's go!"

Arta and I helped the mothers wake the children. As we slipped their shoes on in the foyer, where the fathers waited, we glanced at Roza.

She turned to her husband.

"Can Arta sleep over?"

"Another time," he said.

Arta and I exchanged quiet looks of disappointment.

Everyone marched out. The husbands first, the wives behind them with their half-asleep kids in tow. There was no such thing as DUIs or seatbelts, so the kids lay on top of one another in the backseat while their drunk fathers drove them home.

Once in a while, Zogu asked the brothers-in-law if our sisters could spend the night. Mehmet was fine with it, but Kamile and Roza's husbands needed a little begging. Who would make them coffee, cook their meals, or get up to change the TV channel?

When all three sisters slept over, it was a treat. Arta and I curled up with the kids on the floor cushions. Roza took my bed. Jariyeh spooned Kamile on the couch so she wouldn't fall.

"Let's go jogging," Jariyeh said in the morning.

The Complete Book of Running had just come out, and the newly formed New

York City Marathon was becoming popular. Joggers were no longer seen as "mental," and Jariyeh wanted in.

"Jogging? But we don't have sneakers," Kamile said. "Or clothes to run in."

"Come on! Hane has sneakers and we can run in our dresses. Since when are you so fancy?"

Kamile and Roza wore my sneakers with extra tube socks, then we walked arm in arm to Shore Parkway.

"To the Verrazano and back," Jariyeh proposed—a six-mile run.

They agreed. None of them had jogged before, but they were Albanians who could do anything. Besides, how hard could running be?

Ten minutes in, Kamile said, "My legs itch like crazy."

"Mine too," Roza added. "We should stop."

"No! We can't stop!" Jariyeh shouted. "Hane, rub our legs while we run!"

I took turns running behind each sister, trying to rub the itch out of their thighs with my forearms as we laughed.

I was impressed by Jariyeh's willingness to try new things. To be more like the Americans. I wanted to be like her—carefree. Jariyeh believed life was supposed to be fun. So fun was what she made it.

Chapter 22

The Mother's Curse

* * *

"I remember when you and Jariyeh went to see Grease," I said to Vera.

"Yeah," Vera said with a childlike smile. "She didn't even ask Zogu. She just told him she was taking me. She was so much fun."

"She really was," I said. Then it hit me, as it often did. "I'm still trying to figure out what happened."

Vera looked at the floor, then back up at me. Her smile faded.

"It was my fault," she said quietly. "I killed her."

"What do you mean, you killed her? It wasn't your fault."

"Jariyeh died because of my mother's curse."

———

In the summer of '78, Grease was the word. It had groove, it had meaning, and it had the sexy John Travolta and Olivia Newton-John. Jariyeh loved them both and just had to see the film.

"I'm taking Vera to the movies," she told Zogu, knowing it was best to tell than ask. "And don't worry. *Kërkush s'ka me hanger,*"--No one is going to eat her. She joked, meaning Vera wasn't going to disappear.

"Okay, okay," Zogu replied. He couldn't say no to his favorite sister and appreciated that she did things with his wife, so he didn't have to.

The two friends headed to the movies arm in arm. A "smart" Albanian woman had warned Jariyeh, "Don't walk like that. In America there are women who sleep with other women called lesbians. People will think you're one of them." That explained the stares, but Jariyeh wouldn't change a thing. To her, all love was beautiful.

Grease was inspiring. Not only could good girls be bad girls—they could also get their man. On their way home, Jariyeh sang what she remembered of "You're the One That I Want," as she and Vera danced arm in arm down 86th Street as if they had no care in the world.

Vera would recall this memory often.

A year after *Grease*, life wouldn't be as simple.

Zogu was being nice to Vera, who was pregnant with their second child. He even laughed that laugh that always melted her heart. Naturally, Nana suspected foul play. She searched the apartment for signs of witchcraft. Finding none, she told Luan to look in Zogu's checkered cab. In the trunk, he found one of Zogu's undershirts tied in a knot—confirming Nana's suspicions. Undergarments symbolized intimacy, and a knot symbolized union. Vera had cast a love spell. Nana was sure of it—and she was *pissed.*

"You did black magic!" Nana snapped. "That's why Zogu's fighting with everyone and has been up your ass!"

Not knowing what to do, Vera called her mother—a short woman with a hunched back and a big nose who resembled a witch but was a kind soul. She fiercely loved her daughter and got on the very next train to come to her defense.

"My daughter didn't do anything," she told Nana. "But you have climbed on her neck." Meaning she was bullying a Nuse who wasn't allowed to defend herself.

"We'll see," Nana replied, and took her to the Albanian psychic on Church Avenue for an "objective opinion."

"The woman in question is pregnant," the psychic said, confirming her abilities. How else could she have known Vera was expecting? "Go home and say no more. You are becoming indebted to her soul," she warned my mother.

Back home, Nana said she wasn't convinced of Vera's innocence. But Vera's mother wasn't having it.

"Paç hak e hile, bija jeme mos koftë,"--If my daughter was deceitful and at fault, may she not exist, Vera's mother said, removing her scarf and throwing it onto the living room floor.

She bent down, picked it up, and continued.

"If my daughter has been dishonest, may she see, and may she pay."

She flung the scarf again.

To seal the curse, she picked it up one last time and looked Nana dead in the eye. "But if my daughter has done nothing, then *you* will see. And *you* will pay."

She threw the scarf for the third and final time.

"Don't you swear in my house!" Nana snapped, remembering Baba's warning. "Words have power. Never curse someone or wish them ill. For if something happens, you'll have no one to blame but yourself."

Nana hadn't cursed anyone. But the force of Vera's mother's words was chilling. If Vera was innocent, then Nana would see...and Nana would pay. What that payment would be, no one could know—until it happened.

———

Vera finished the story staring at the floor, heavy with guilt.

I didn't think to tell her that I had asked Nana why she had been so mean to her. Nana said, "I was jealous of Vera because after your father died, Zogu took his place."

"I know words have power," I said gently to Vera. "But your mother's curse didn't kill Jariyeh."

"It was my fault," Vera said. "Ever since Jariyeh died, I've never cursed anyone. And if someone curses me, even as a joke, I make them take it back."

"You didn't kill her," I said, reaching for her hand.

Vera was quiet for a moment. "I know Jariyeh wasn't happy. She once told me, 'I wish I could take my children and go far, far away and live in a house high up on a hill. Only then could I be happy.'"

Then she smiled softly, lost in memory. "Remember her last New Year's Eve? She was so happy. Remember the angel bell on her tree?"

"How could I forget?"

Angel Wings

* * *

Jariyeh used any reason to throw a party, and New Year's Eve was the perfect excuse. We would ring in 1979 at her house, just like the years before. Luan and I helped crisscross streamers across the ceiling. Jariyeh taped holiday cards on the wall around the New Year's tree. She and her children had decorated it together, and near the top she hung a white ceramic bell.

"When the bell rings, it means an angel got its wings," she explained.

I didn't grow up with Santa Claus, but I loved that American children had something magical to believe in. Jariyeh and I had watched "Miracle on 34th Street" glued to the TV. We cried when it was proven that Santa was real. Maybe Santa wasn't real—but angels had to be. Why else were they mentioned in the Koran? Why else would Christians adorn their churches with them? I believed angels were God's helpers. I just hoped I'd hear one get its wings before Jariyeh took down her tree.

Everyone came dressed in their finest. The women wore gowns. The men wore suits or button-downs. The children were freshly combed and pressed. The tables were filled with meze and drinks. The grown-ups gathered in the living room while the children played in the bedrooms.

Jariyeh decided to play a joke on Nana.

"Take Nana into the kitchen," she told Kamile.

The minute they walked out, Jariyeh planted a whoopee cushion in the couch.

Farting was a big no-no for Albanians. It was highly disrespectful and very not funny—especially for women. Even we kids made sure not to let one slip in front of the grownups. My mother explained just how serious an offense it was through a cautionary tale:

> One time, a new Nuse accidentally farted in front of a little boy. Later, when she was put on display before her in-laws and guests, the boy blurted out, "The Nuse farted." She was so embarrassed, she went to the back of the house and shot herself.

I couldn't believe it really happened, but knowing our obsession with shame, it was possible. Regardless, the point was made as only Nana could make it—*don't disgrace yourself unless you were ready to kill yourself.* I knew I wouldn't have the courage to do that, so I never farted in front of others. But neither did anyone else. Including the men.

When Nana returned from the kitchen, Jariyeh led her to her seat.

We held our breath. Nana sat, and the farting sound erupted—*brrrrrt.* She froze. Slowly she looked up, mortified, and scanned our faces. When we all burst out laughing, she realized she'd been tricked, and let out a laugh. I had never heard my mother laugh so hard. For months afterward, every time she recalled it, she would chuckle and shake her head. Of all her children, Jariyeh was the only one who could make her laugh like her husband used to.

"Let's make a wish on a shooting star for the New Year," Jariyeh said.

The women crowded around the window, looking up at the dark sky. Within minutes, a star streaked across the sky. We looked at each other—stunned.

At that very moment, we heard the ringing of the ceramic bell.

Ding ding ding.

We turned to see which kid had touched the tree and set it off—but no one was there.

"You see!" Jariyeh exclaimed. "An angel just got its wings. All our wishes are going to come true."

Of course angels got wings in her house, I thought. My sister was special. It reminded me of the time at Coney Island Amusement Park when she gave a homeless woman all the change in her purse—except one dime which she needed to make a call. At the phone booth, she slipped it into the slot, but no dial tone came. She kept flipping and flipping the return lever. Suddenly, change came flooding out, filled the coin return, and spilled onto the floor—giving her back far more than she'd given. I was shocked. "You see," she said, "If you give with all your heart, you will always get." I planned to listen to my sister. She seemed to know what she was talking about.

As midnight approached, Jariyeh turned on *New Year's Rockin' Eve with Dick Clark* and gave Zogu the champagne—an American tradition we'd happily adopted. He walked around like a waiter, filling martini-shaped plastic glasses for everyone, including the women. We laughed and took pictures of the hysterical sight. My brothers often joked about being "submissive," saying things like, "Let me ask my wife for permission," or "I made my wife coffee this morning," or "I washed the dishes." And we'd all laugh at the absurdity of it.

With the countdown near, Arta and I ran to get the children so we'd all be together to ring in the New Year. We grabbed festive hats and noisemakers and waited for the ball to drop.

"Ten…nine," Jariyeh began, and we joined in. The boys came screeching into the room, not wanting to miss it.

"Three…two…one! From shepherds to champagne drinkers!" Jariyeh toasted as she lifted her plastic glass.

Everyone smiled at her brilliant toast.

"From shepherds to champagne drinkers!" the grownups repeated, clicking their glasses.

We hadn't come to America to stay, but where would we go? Albania was still Communist (and would be for another twelve years). And Baba was gone. For now, we would enjoy America's easier life—but not its ways. Ours, we still believed, were better.

We all hugged and kissed on both cheeks, exchanging wishes for a better year. Jariyeh loved seeing her family happy—especially Nana, who had never quite recovered from Baba's death. She offered her a champagne glass, but Nana playfully pushed her hand away.

"Kamile," Jariyeh called to her sidekick. "Grab Nana."

Kamile held down Nana's arms and Jariyeh tipped the glass to her lips.

Smiling, Nana shook her head and finally gave in.

Triumphant, Jariyeh raised her glass and burst into song:

♪ *Si dukati vogel je*　　　　♪ You are like my little gold

Everyone joined in the drinking anthem as Mehmet and Roza's husband smiled from their seats.

♪ *Hajde shpirto ri me ne*　　♪ Come my soul, stay with us
Naj ka çel nji gonxhe re　　A new bud has sprouted
Era karajfil poj vjen　　　It smells of carnations
Hajde, cakrroma gotën　　Come on, click my glass

The drinkers raised their glasses on cue.

Hajde pim raki　　　　Come on, let's drink brandy
Mos pi shum se u pime　　Don't drink too much and get drunk
Hajde! ♪　　　　　Come on! ♪

Nana beamed.

"To a better year than the last!" Jariyeh wished.

"For many more to come," Nana added.

New Year's Eve was a time for wishful thinking.

How were we to know this would be Jariyeh's last?

How were we to know Mehmet would join a drug cartel?

II. HER FINAL YEAR

1979 New Jersey:
Jariyeh and I dancing at an American wedding.

BROOKLYN

1979

Chapter 24

The First Kilo

* * *

"A mechanic from Staten Island gave my dad his first kilo to sell," Perparim texted me out of nowhere.

Jariyeh's younger son was now a New York City firefighter in his forties. I had asked him and Lata many questions about their dad, but never thought to ask about his first kilo.

"A mechanic? Jerry, Saranda's brother-in-law?" I texted back, then immediately called her.

Saranda was just as shocked as I was.

"How did they know each other?" she asked. "Maybe they met at Sam's wedding?"

I called Perparim with our theory.

"No," he said. "Pop knew this guy from the Lower East Side. They used to be friends. Pop said he never would've taken the kilo if it wasn't for your mom. He was mad at her, because she told the mechanic that he was doing drugs, when he wasn't."

That didn't make sense. I called Saranda hoping she knew more.

"Can't be," she said. "Nana doesn't lie. And where would she have talked to Jerry? He never came to your house and Nana never went to their house. And why would she talk to a stranger about her son-in-law?"

She had a point. An Albanian parent would never badmouth a son-in-law, because if he heard, he could take it out on their daughter. I tried explaining this to Perparim. He was Americanized and didn't get it. I told him my mother doesn't lie. He wasn't buying it. Why would he? He didn't know us. He grew up with the Bicis.

I always thought of Mehmet as quiet, messy, and spineless—never a liar. So why had he lied to his son? Was he trying to excuse himself by making us villains? Or had Jerry lied to him? He probably knew that telling Mehmet that his mother-in-law said he was doing drugs would piss him off and he'd sell the kilo out of spite. But there was no use in trying to defend my family to Perparim, so I moved on.

"Do you know how the sale of the first kilo happened?" I asked, thinking it might make a good story.

"When the mechanic called my dad, he was very excited," he said.

Excited? I'd never seen Mehmet excited. Was he lonely? Was he eager to see his old friend? Did he even have friends besides Zogu? I never saw any.

———

Xhevdet Mustafa, aka Jerry, fled Albania at twenty-three. He was one of the two older men who agreed to take Sam to America, but since Sam wasn't family he left the teenage boy behind in Italy. In 1965, Jerry landed on the Lower East Side and befriended the streetwise seventeen-year-old Mehmet. They lost touch when Jerry moved to Staten Island, married Sam's older sister, and became a mechanic. After years of sixteen-hour days, he opened his own auto body shop.

Mehmet hadn't seen him for over a decade.

"Jerry called for you today," Jariyeh said, handing her husband the phone number.

Mehmet immediately dialed his old friend.

"Come to my shop," Jerry said.

Mehmet rushed over. Did he hope they'd reminisce?

Jerry wasn't the nostalgic type. He was a workaholic with a mission. He planned to assassinate Albania's dictator, Enver Hoxha, so King Zog's son could take his "rightful place." This was the reason he escaped Albania. Jerry was a businessman, and talking about old times wasn't going to bring him closer to his goal. The man with the boyish looks didn't seem the type to pull a trigger or even touch drugs. Yet he slid a kilo of cocaine toward his old friend and said:

"I thought we could make some money."

Mehmet had never sold drugs, but they were always around him, even at the deli where he worked. Every day he made sandwiches for the dealers of East New York. One regular who drove a Rolls-Royce came to mind.

He looked at the kilo.

"Okay," he said. "I'll do it."

When the guy in the Rolls-Royce stepped up to the deli counter, Mehmet pulled him aside and took out the brick of cocaine.

"I don't know how this works. But do you wanna buy this?"

The dealer laughed, grabbed the coke, and came back with $70,000—the same amount Pablo Escobar got paid.[viii] Mehmet was shocked. He expected $2,000 tops. He strutted back to the autobody shop with the life-changing cash. Jerry took 60,000 and handed Mehmet 10. Though he felt cheated, Mehmet happily took the score.

I thought it was just a good story. What I didn't understand was that after selling your first kilo—there was no turning back.

A switch flipped in that moment. Mehmet was hooked.

The quick 10,000 was intoxicating. Jerry's respect an added plus. The high-risk, high-reward rush had rewired Mehmet's self-image—from deli worker to player in a dangerous game. He liked that. Most dealers sold drugs out of desperation, ambition, or rebellion. Mehmet didn't have those traits. They'd come later. Impressing Jerry was the goal, and Jerry was impressed.

He introduced Mehmet to his "associates." Albanian men who would help Jerry fund his assassination plot. Men who would later end up dead or in jail. But these were the honeymoon days. The time for fantasizing about beating the system, getting rich, and feeling invincible.

I didn't know Mehmet had an entire circle of friends. Men he never brought to our family gatherings. Our worlds would overlap at Lulu's House.

Jerry introduced Mehmet to Lulu's, a Catskills resort where Albanian families gathered. Jariyeh loved the place and convinced us all to go. There was a volleyball court, two swings, an in-ground pool, and lots of grass. I'd never vacationed anywhere else, so to me, it was the Taj Mahal.

Lulu's wife cooked three meals a day. I didn't have to clean, but I helped clear the tables, in case someone there knew a family looking for a Nuse. This way they'd know I wasn't spoiled.

Though we all went to Lulu's House, Jariyeh was the one the owners and guests looked forward to. While the adults lounged poolside, Jariyeh stood fake microphone in hand, deciding what song to sing next. She chose the new Serbian one, "Zašto su ti Kose Pobelele, Druže"--Why Has Your Hair Turned White, My Friend.

Having learned Jariyeh's routine, the men came prepared. They thumbed dollar bills over her head like they did to singers at nightclubs and weddings. Their wives laughed and Mehmet smiled. He enjoyed the effect his wife had on his friends. Jariyeh basked in their attention, unaware these men were small-time drug dealers, on the brink of going big. Not that they needed the money. There was no reason for Jariyeh to suspect a thing.

Skender owned a travel agency in Staten Island.

Nazmi, aka Nicky, owned several gas stations.

Bari, who went by Benny, owned a pizzeria in New Jersey.

Mehmet, who was called Mike, was the poorest of them all.

During drug deals the men spoke only Albanian, making wiretaps useless, and their besa meant no one talked. Even their wives were oblivious.

Benny was the nice-guy "John Gotti" of the crew, their money man. Like Jerry, he wanted to "free Albania" and often sang a ballad about his homeland that he'd written himself:

♪ *O' Shkodra Ilirie*	♪ O' Illyrian Shkoder
O' vendi njerziz	O' land of the people
Sa shum m'ka marr malli	How much I miss you
Per ti du me këndu	For you I want to sing
Sa bukur natira	How beautifully nature
në ti ka qëndis ♪	Was embroidered in you ♪

"That's not how it goes," Jariyeh interrupted, making everyone laugh.

Then the two of them sang in perfect harmony. By the end, everyone had joined in. For the homesick, songs were a way back home.

The men bought their sons BB rifles to "practice being men." The boys practiced by shooting at birds and trees.

"Let's take a picture with the army in training to free Albania," Benny said.

The ten youngsters lined up at attention, rifles on their left shoulders, right hands raised in salute. Benny, with his thick black mustache, looked like Stalin as he saluted beside them.

The fathers hoped to instill in their boys a desire to fight for a homeland they'd never seen, while they themselves slipped deeper into the criminal world. Mehmet didn't care about revolutions, but felt the pull of their world. He was chasing status, power, cash—and figured Jariyeh wouldn't mind once she saw the money.

He was so wrapped up in the possibilities that he couldn't see the life he was chasing would be the beginning of her end.

Chapter 25

Jesus' Son

* * *

In February 1979, Skender used his travel agency to fly in the cartel's first drug shipment from Kosova.[ix] Xhevdet Lika, aka Joey Lika, distributed a kilo at a social club on the Lower East Side. Joey wasn't a household name like Al Capone, but in the underworld he was known for his violent streak, like Joe Pesci's character in *Goodfellas*.

The following month, Zogu told me Mehmet shot at a man at Benny's House of Pizza, then called him from the station. Zogu bailed him out and drove him home—no questions asked. Did my brother think Mehmet was defending his honor? Who did he shoot—a rival? I found no record of a trial. Did the man fear for his life and drop the charges?

Also that March, Mehmet's boss bought a Burger King franchise and asked him to manage the last six months of the deli lease. But Mehmet barely went in and did what dealers should never do—sample his own product.

"Mehmet's not working," Jariyeh told Nana. "He's bringing home friends and they're doing drugs."

———

For decades, I told myself Mehmet loved my sister and could never have killed her if he hadn't been high on coke. Growing up, the only drugs I knew of were marijuana and cocaine. On TV, pot made people loopy and coke made them crazy. Crazy was how I imagined Mehmet on the night he killed her.

I began my research online. I read that coke made users paranoid and aggressive. *I knew it!* Mehmet must have imagined my sister was having an affair and overreacted. For weeks, I researched cocaine addiction and mapped-out how his coke-fueled frenzy may have unfolded that night.

I figured Mehmet's addiction began after he sold his first kilo at the deli, which I believe was around 1977, and before March 1979, when he began doing drugs at home with his friends. He had to be a full-blown addict by then, because in his right mind he never would have upset Jariyeh like that.

"Do you know when your dad started doing coke?" I texted Perparim.

"No, I don't. But my dad wasn't a coke addict. He did heroin," he replied.

Heroin?

Didn't heroin make you sleepy? *Oh my God*—he was always dragging himself around. Heroin made more sense.

The realization shook me. I had spent decades clinging to a false memory of him crazed on coke when he killed her. It disturbed me to see how easily the mind could reshape the past.

I had to stop writing. I needed time to shake this off before I could begin again.

Knowing absolutely *nothing* about heroin, I started with blogs of firsthand accounts. Then, to better understand it, I watched heroin addicts portrayed in movies. But I still had questions. So I invited Xavier, a writer friend and ex-junkie, to my local Italian restaurant for dinner.

"The last thing heroin wants is to kill," he told me.

Great. Exactly what I didn't want to hear.

"Tell me more," I said. "I want to understand what it was like for Mehmet and for my sister."

———

On the streets, heroin was called H, dope, horse, smack, junk.[x]

So *that* was why they called users junkies.

Mehmet wasn't smart enough to stay away from the drugs he sold, but he knew better than to use a syringe. Instead, he did "one and one" in each nostril. As the drug entered his capillaries, a warmth radiated from his nose and slowly made its way into his brain. Then...

Ahhh—all was right with the world.

Someone could point a gun at his head, and he'd still feel fine. All was beautiful. All was perfection. Heroin wasn't named after "hero" for nothing.[xi] The Velvet Underground sang about how this wonder drug could make you feel—*like the son of God.*

He lay on the floor, invincible yet unable to move. When the nausea hit, it took everything in him to crawl to the bathroom and throw up. Afterward, he went "on the nod," drifting in and out of wakefulness.

Unlike alcohol or cocaine, he woke up with no headache, no hangover—just the afterglow of that amazing buzz. Nothing bothered him. Not the monotonous deli job. Not the extra thirty pounds his wife complained about.

All was chill.

Why not take another hit, Mehmet thought. I won't get addicted.

But by March 1979, he was a full-blown addict.

Saranda told me he was high all the time—she thought he'd been drinking.

"Why is he drunk again?" Saranda asked Jariyeh one morning.

Jariyeh opened the freezer and pulled out a foil-wrapped package. "He's drunk from this."

"He takes marijuana?" Saranda asked, naming the only drug she knew of.

"No. It's something else."

"Please Jariyeh, throw it away."

"I can't. Mehmet says it costs a lot of money. He keeps telling me to take it."

"No, don't take it," Saranda warned. "And don't smoke those funny cigarettes either. They will make you stupid."

Jariyeh assured her friend she'd never take it. She wished Mehmet would stop, but it wasn't her place to tell her husband what to do.

After a while, she'd had enough. "You have to stop with these drugs."

"But Jariyeh. That's how I'm losing weight. I'm doing it for you," he said, rubbing his thinning gut.

Mehmet always looked sloppy, and the extra thirty pounds made him look sloppier still. Jariyeh bought him nice shirts and kept them ironed, trying to make him more presentable. He'd put them on and tuck them in, but before long they'd stick out, followed by his belly. The drug that turned hourglass models into gaunt "heroin chic" bodies was helping him shed those extra pounds. But now Mehmet hardly bathed and began to smell of old perspiration.

"I don't want you to lose weight like this," she begged.

"Okay, I'll stop," he replied in all sincerity. Mehmet so believed what he was saying that he could have passed a lie detector test. But the biggest lie was the one he told himself: *I can stop at any time.*

Heroin—H—had sucked him in like quicksand. The harder he tried to pull out, the deeper he sank. The addiction was getting expensive, but thanks to the dowry his parents gave Jariyeh, he didn't need to rob others or prostitute himself.

"Did you take my jewelry?" Jariyeh asked.

"No. I swear it wasn't me."

Eventually, Mehmet lived to get high and got high to live. He grew distant, like he was being dragged through the earth while existing on another planet. Even when he was physically present, he wasn't really there. His eyes were dead, no longer accessible. Disturbing to be near.

"Mehmeti ma ka pru shpirtin te huna,"--Mehmet has brought my soul to my nose, Jariyeh told her mother, her sister, and sisters-in-law—meaning he was sucking the life out of her.

She thought it was hard being married to a man she didn't love, but being the wife of an addict was pure torture. No matter how tough she thought she was— she wasn't. She found herself growing angrier by the day.

"What the hell is wrong with you?" she burst out, as he shuffled past.

After a long pause, he'd look up with droopy eyes and slur, "Nothing." Denial helped him maintain the illusion that he wasn't destroying his life—or anyone else's.

"You have to stop with these drugs."

"Okay, okay," he'd say—again and again. Mehmet wasn't lying. He was surviving. He'd say what he must to get another hit—or he'd surely die.

Stopping would've taken real willpower, something he didn't have. As much as he wanted to do what his wife asked, he now had a new ruler. A new love.

Heroin.

And leaving *her* would be a motherfucker.

If he stopped, the first to go would be his confidence. Then would come the fever, twitching, itching, insomnia, vomiting. Six hours in, the heroin-induced constipation would release, and he'd lose control of his bowels. After twenty-four hours, the most excruciating pain of all would begin. The sensation of his bones being pulled out of his skin from the inside.

Why would Mehmet stop? Why should he have to? He was fine, really. Just ask him.

On heroin, he thought he was brilliant. Thought he knew everything. And that everything was *okay, all the time.*

Now, if only Jariyeh would stop harassing him.

One night, she came home to find a bowl of watermelon on the kitchen table.

"Did you eat the watermelon I left for you?" Mehmet slurred when she entered the living room.

"No, I threw it out. It was spoiled."

He stormed into the kitchen, muttering, "That shit's too expensive to waste."

As she watched him grab the watermelon from the trash and devour it like a wild animal, juice dripping down his forearms onto the linoleum—Jariyeh realized it wasn't spoiled. It was spiked. He had sprinkled it with drugs, hoping to get her high. Better yet, to get her addicted. Then she wouldn't tell him to stop. Then he wouldn't feel *so alone.* She'd be with him. No more secrets. No more lies.

Mehmet had no idea the demons he'd encounter when he started. As long as he was high, he wouldn't have to face them. But with each hit, the buzz grew weaker. What once lasted 24 hours now barely held for five. He'd forever be chasing that elusive, initial mind-blowing high.

Dealers knew of this obsession. They cut drugs with additives for greater profit and to keep regulars from overdosing. But every so often, they left a few bags of "the pure shit" in the batch, knowing that when one of their clients died, others would ask, "Where did he get it?" Not from fear, but from hope that it was the high they'd been seeking—because surely they'd survive the hit.

Xavier explained that addicts rarely give up this quest.

Sometimes they got high on uppers, then eased the crash with downers. Eventually they needed a hit just to feel "normal." Every hit carried risk. Breathing could slow and even stop.

For Jariyeh, that could've been an easy out of her godforsaken marriage. But she didn't want Mehmet to die. The children needed their father.

I remember him walking into the room—arms limp, shoulders slumped, sniffling, drooling. It frightened me.

But all I could think was—*Poor Jariyeh.*

Chapter 26

A Song is a Song

* * *

My sister filled the void Baba had left behind—a void Nana didn't know existed. I was fifteen and still not allowed to hang out with my American friends after school. Jariyeh's home became my refuge. After she moved next door, I stopped by almost every day. She was always happy to see me.

On weekends, I woke up early and walked into her apartment to the smell of pancakes—my favorite. Jariyeh flipped them at the stove while her children ate and got syrup everywhere. It was hard to see their mess without wanting to clean it up, but refreshing that Jariyeh didn't care. Around Nana, sloppiness wasn't allowed, no matter the age. This made us all clean freaks, but Jariyeh accepted imperfections. One time, she left her children with a bowl of watermelon while she cleaned. Esat watched as Perparim and Lata discovered the joy of putting the slices on their heads. When she found them soaked in watermelon juice, she didn't yell or slap. Instead, she called Kamile. "You have to see them," she said, cracking up. "They are so cute."

I grabbed a plate, and Jariyeh stacked it with steaming pancakes as she sang:

♪ *Gitarrja ime*	♪ My guitar
bashkë me zemrën time	together with my heart
Shkojnë e bëjnë pushime	Go on vacation
te dashnorja ime	to my lover's house

Songs were part of Albania's oral tradition. Through them, we told stories of war, heroes, marriage, and unrequited love. For some reason, my sister favored the latter. I sang in English but longed to sing in Albanian. But I wouldn't because I didn't know the words, and singing it wrong was unacceptable. Nana had instilled such a striving for perfection in me that if I couldn't do it right, I wouldn't do it at all.

"Hane. Sing with me," Jariyeh said.

"But I don't know the words."

"Okay. Listen, and repeat after me."

♪ *Ajo ma kujtonte*	♪ She remembered

kohën a kaluarë	the days of our past
Ajo ma shëronte	She healed
zemerën e helmuar ♪	my poisoned heart ♪

Seeing me struggle to get the words right, Jariyeh turned off the stove and sat beside me with pen and paper.

"Let's write it down."

"Okay! Can you also teach me wedding songs?" I asked eagerly. I always wanted to sing with my siblings at engagements and wedding parties. We all had beautiful voices—except tone-deaf Zogu. But he sang anyway. Why let them have all the fun? Nana had stopped singing after Baba died, but when her children sang, she held her head high. I wanted her to be proud of me too.

"I'll teach you *all* the songs," Jariyeh said, pinching my cheek.

"What about the one with the moon and the river?" I asked.

My sister sang that one often. She always looked at me when she mentioned the moon, because my name, Hanë, meant moon in Albanian. Jariyeh's name was Turkish. We imagined it meant "beautiful"—like her. It turned out to mean "enslaved woman"—like her—like all of us.

"Okay, let's do that song first."

She began singing as she wrote down the lyrics in her elegant European script.

♪ *N'atë anë detit*	♪ Beyond the ocean
n'atë anë bregut	beyond the shore
Kish fillu hana me dal	The moon began to rise

"Now, let's sing together," she said.

I anxiously looked at the page. No one had taught me how to read Albanian, but if you spoke the language, it was easy to decipher.

♪ *N'atë anë detit*	♪ Beyond the ocean
natë anë bregut	beyond the shore
Kish fillu hana me dal	The moon began to rise
Vjen nji djal	Approached a boy
por si bir mretit	like the son of a king
Me nji vajzë, po rrin tu kja ♪	With a girl he sits and cries ♪

I loved the image of a handsome prince, but knew our princes weren't like the ones in American fairy tales. I didn't grow up with fairy tales or happily-ever-afters. We didn't marry who we loved—we married who we were told to. For us, love was a dirty word, and its victims often cursed.

At the end of the song, the girl married someone else, and the prince was left a lonely bachelor. Why did my sister love that song so much, I wondered.

Jariyeh finished writing the lyrics and handed them to me with instructions to practice. I couldn't wait. As she wiped the pancake syrup from her children's hands and faces, I cleared the table and started the dishes.

"Hajde!"--Come on! "Leave the dishes," she said, kissing Lata before picking her up.

Many rules were broken at my sister's house. It was invigorating. The boys and I marched behind our leader to the record player. Unlike me, who had to wait for Zogu and Nana to leave before turning on the radio, no one told her she couldn't play American music or sing American songs. She knew all the latest tunes and had the coolest records: Queen, The Beatles, The Rolling Stones, Elton John, and of course, the King—Elvis Presley. Jariyeh wept when Elvis died.

Elvis's "Hard Headed Woman" reminded me of her and Mehmet. She was tough. He was soft—not sweet soft, more spineless. I believed he loved my sister, everyone did, but she didn't love him. And I didn't see how she could. She was stylish. He was messy. She was fun. He was dull.

Jariyeh pulled out the *Saturday Night Fever* soundtrack. The movie was filmed in our neighborhood. It showed the Italian Guidos with their slicked-back D.A.'s cruising under the 86th Street L in their "Daddylacs"—short for Daddy's Cadillacs—as the trains rumbled above. They'd lean back in the driver's seat, one hand on the wheel, disco music pumping from the windows, trying to impress the Guidettes in their Farrah Fawcett haircuts.

Eighteen-year-old Luan fit right in with his thick, neatly combed hair and impeccable white Cadillac, which he bought himself. He'd take me cruising on 86th Street and show me off to his friends: "This is Hane, my baby sister." At first they didn't believe it—we looked nothing alike. The boys were polite—afraid to disrespect "Al's sister." I liked that.

Jariyeh placed the needle on "Stayin' Alive." The children watched as she and I sang along with the Bee Gees and mimicked John Travolta's finger-pointing moves.

"Now, which song?" she asked, leafing through her records.

"Wone-wee boy," Perparim said in his adorable lisp, while winding his Evel Knievel motorcycle.

Jariyeh put on Paul Anka's "Lonely Boy." It was cute watching Esat and Perparim sing along, but I didn't like it when they sang about being "lonely and blue" and "left all alone."

Was it a premonition?

The lyrics didn't bother Jariyeh.

"A song is a song," she'd say. But in reality, for her, songs were everything. They were how she shared her joy, her pain, her longing for love—a longing I wasn't aware of.

Mehmet walked in, and my shoulders tensed. Jariyeh kept flipping through her records—as if nothing had changed—but I could tell his presence annoyed her. It was a different kind of annoyed, maybe because he was a different Mehmet. He was still his typical quiet, non-existent self, only heavier. I stayed a little longer, then left.

I was glad to be away from him, but felt guilty for abandoning Jariyeh.

I hated that this had to be her life.

Chapter 27

The Making of Mehmet

* * *

Who was Mehmet? Not the man who killed my sister—but the boy he used to be. Maybe if I could go back to the life that shaped him, I could understand why he killed her.

I asked Bekim and Kamile, "What do you remember of Mehmet in Kosova?" They recalled very little.

I turned to Perparim. "Do you know anything about your dad's childhood?"

"He was fourteen when they immigrated to the Lower East Side," Perparim said.

What was the Lower East Side like back then? I wondered. What was his home life like? Who were his friends?

———

Mehmet Selman Bici was born April 17, 1948, in the village of Bicaj, Albania— hence the surname Bici. It was fifty-four miles as the eagle flies from my father's village of Aliaj. Like us, they were Lumjan from the northern mountains.

During World War II, Mehmet's father, Selman, was a hero in his own right. The Nazis suspected him of hiding Jews, but he refused to give up his guests— even when they burned his hand with a heated gun barrel. He still had that scar.

Like Baba, he escaped to Yugoslavia with his family after the war, and in 1958 was a political prisoner in Banat, Serbia—the place they first met. While the Lumjan men served their time in Serbia, their wives and children lived in Kosova, not far from one another.

Kamile recalled how Filanza constantly bragged about her firstborn son, and sat in front of her house making up rhymes:

Oh Mehmet,	Oh Mehmet,
të past Nana	may your mother always have you
Babën ta ka marrë hapsania	Prison has taken your father
Në ta l'shofshin babën sivjet	If they release him this year
Do't bajmë nizafet	We'll have a celebration
Ta thirrim UDB-në	We'll invite the Secret Police
e shkupin krejt	and all of Shkup

Then Filanza would pull up her skirt, slap the inside of her thigh, and declare: *"Unë jam burrneshë!"*--I am a manly woman!

In 1962, the Bicis joined the new wave of European refugees and immigrated to America. They settled in Manhattan's Lower East Side, in a low-rent apartment on the corner of Rivington and Ludlow, two blocks from Katz's Deli and three from where The Velvet Underground rehearsed. The neighborhood was steeped in crime. Mobsters shot people in the streets, and kids joined gangs for protection.[xii] As an outcast in Kosova, fourteen-year-old Mehmet may have been prepared for violence, but not for the drug scene.

In the mid-sixties, flower-power hippies smoked marijuana, Timothy Leary urged Americans to try LSD, and thugs pushed heroin in the ghettos—the poor man's drug.[xiii] There was no Drug Enforcement Agency, so narcotics were sold "open air" in Tompkins Square Park, bodegas, liquor stores, and abandoned buildings. Guys in suits, strung-out junkies, and old ladies lined up at a door with two slots, one for receiving cash, one for dispensing drugs.

Mehmet told his son he tried all kinds of drugs but never got addicted. Where did he get them? At Tompkins Square Park, or one of those doors with the double slots?

The year before JFK was assassinated, Filanza gave birth to her sixth child. The next day she left the baby girl diaper-less on top of newspapers and went to her cleaning job. Meanwhile, her golden boy cut school, hung out with delinquents, and played dice on street corners—as Bekim had seen him do in Kosova.

Mehmet had just turned seventeen when his father Selman was shot and paralyzed. There were rumors as to how this happened.

Before leaving Kosova, Selman promised his eldest daughter, Drita, to a neighbor's cousin in the States. She was twelve. He was in his twenties. When the Bicis arrived in Manhattan, they accepted the token of engagement—but called it off two years later. This wasn't allowed.

> Law §41: "The token binds the young woman, and if faith is not kept a blood-feud results between the parents of the young woman and the family of the young man."

The story that followed was where fantasy and reality collided. Filanza told Kamile that *she* had broken off the engagement, and that the fiancé fired at *her* outside their building—but Selman jumped in front of her. This story made Filanza a fearless woman, and her husband a hero. But women didn't have the authority to call off engagements, and even if they did, they weren't shot at in blood feuds. Their men paid the price for not having controlled them.

Later, Filanza told Lata that it was Drita who didn't want to marry the man, and that Selman had called it off, despite her warnings. She claimed the jilted fiancé fired at them as she and Selman hailed a cab on their way to work. The taxi part didn't ring true. I couldn't picture the frugal Bicis taking a cab to their cleaning jobs.

Would Filanza ever fully tell the truth?

I knew breaking an engagement could result in a blood feud, but I still had trouble believing it would happen in 1960s America. Then Perparim sent me a front-page New York Times article, dated May 27, 1965:

"Rejected Albanian Suitor Seized in Shooting of Father of Girl, 14."[xiv]

> At around 2 a.m. Selman was stepping off a city bus on his way home from his porter job when he was greeted by gunfire. The fiancé and his brother shot Selman in the back. Two bystanders were also hit—one in the leg, another in the arm and chest. The brothers were arrested and charged with felonious assault.

Selman didn't press charges—that's not how blood feuds worked. The suitor must have considered the debt paid because he never shot at Selman again, and Drita was allowed to marry another.

The broken engagement had disgraced the Bici name, so age-appropriate suitors didn't want to be related. Drita married a man nearly three times her age. Selman's paralysis became a reminder to all of what happens when a father chooses love for his daughter over keeping his *besa*--promise.

I was surprised how similar Mehmet's family was to mine. Both our sisters didn't want to marry their fiancés. Both our mothers would rather their girls be forced to marry than bring them shame. Both our fathers put their daughters' happiness before the honor codes—and themselves.

I wonder if the goodhearted Selman would've allowed Baba to call off Jariyeh's engagement. And if he had, would Filanza have pushed him to shoot my father in defense of the family name? Selman may have ignored his wife, the way he did when she placed a gun on his wheelchair the day Baba went to ask why Jariyeh wasn't allowed to visit. But would her sons have listened to her? When Agim pressed the Colt .45 to Bekim's head, surely it was at Filanza's direction.

She was an unforgiving woman. Filanza never stopped berating her crippled husband for forcing her to become the breadwinner, while Selman quietly shuffled around on crutches, doing all he could to care for their children and comfort his bitter wife.

To help with the bills, Mehmet, who was already cutting school, dropped out and got a job at Benny's House of Pizza in Queens.

That same year, 1965, he befriended Jerry—one of the first Albanians who would influence the direction of his life.

Two years later, in 1967, the Bicis moved to the Mitchel House Development in the South Bronx, just blocks from what *Time Magazine* dubbed "The Most Dangerous Square Mile in America." The homicides, shootings, and drug use were so out of control that the Red Cross refused to send volunteers. [xv]

In the summer of 1970, the Bicis heard Lutfi Feza had arrived in Brooklyn with a daughter of marrying age. If sixteen-year-old Jariyeh hadn't fallen in love with Sam's picture in Italy, would the marriage have stood a chance? Or was it destined to be as it was?

Around this time Benny arrived in America, followed by Nicky. Benny helped him purchase his first gas station. A few years later, the friends opened an Albanian social club on Church and MacDonald Avenue, simply called "the café"—where Albanian men gambled, drank Turkish coffee, and were served by sexy girls, mostly Russians. Never Albanians. A place where men lived double lives and wives weren't allowed to ask questions. I knew men gambled and drank there. I learned years later, from Nicky's son, that they also snorted coke and heroin and slept with mistresses. "I saw Mehmet, Jerry, and Joey Lika there all the time," he said. I wondered if Mehmet's addiction went back further than I thought.

When Nicky needed someone to run his gas station in Harlem, he hired his friend Mehmet. Nicky did well until 1973, when the U.S. support for Israel caused gas shortages and soaring prices. Fined heavily for price gouging, he began losing his gas stations and turned to selling weed in industrial-size garbage bags and smuggling coke in from Miami.

Could this be where Jerry got the first kilo he gave Mehmet?

Was Mehmet gravitating toward what he knew, or was it written in the stars? From age fourteen, he lived on the drug-ridden Lower East Side, where violence was a daily threat. Even after leaving his parents' home in the South Bronx, he worked in Harlem, then at a deli in East New York—places soaked in drugs, danger, and desperation. His home life offered no refuge. No wonder prison, violence, even death didn't seem to faze him.

When Jerry asked him to sell that first kilo, did he make the only choice available to a man shaped by those streets, that home, and those friendships?

In that case—did Jariyeh stand a chance?

Chapter 28

Kuq e Zi

* * *

J ariyeh was late.

"Where is she?" an impatient Bekim asked his wife.

Saranda shrugged.

The door burst open.

Jariyeh strutted in wearing a new satin outfit the colors of our flag: *kuq e zi*--red and black. With hands on hips, eyes straight ahead, and a big smile that proudly displayed the gap in her front teeth, she took long strides in her strappy high heels that should have been left at the door. Like a runway model, she swayed her arms, swung her hips, and exaggerated her stride. Her hair flew as she spun to give the full effect of her flared satin skirt. Doing this in front of Kamile's husband was inappropriate, but such rules were for other women.

The men smiled and shook their heads.

Nana chuckled, completely taken by her daughter's essence. Jariyeh was *si nji shpatë*--like a sword. A warrior. She commanded attention everywhere she went. Nana loved that about her. Of all her children, Jariyeh's spirit reminded her most of her husband.

"Hajde!"--Come on! Jariyeh said, as if they had kept her waiting.

My siblings were heading to Il Galletto, an Albanian nightclub in New Jersey. On weekends, the Lulu's House couples went to private parties, Port Said, the belly-dancing club, or Il Galletto. But this night, Sam and his wife were going to be there, so Jariyeh had convinced her siblings to join them. I wished I could go, but everything good had to wait until I married—makeup, fancy dresses, sexy shoes, and dancing at nightclubs with my siblings. I couldn't wait.

At Il Galletto, Jerry waved them over. A round of *raki*--brandy was ordered for the men, and screwdrivers for the women. As the band played, their table filled with singing and laughter. A glassy-eyed Mehmet returned from the bathroom and grabbed Jariyeh by the arm.

"Let's go!" he snapped, pulling her toward the dance floor.

Embarrassed, Jariyeh yanked free. She was nobody's property.

He pulled again, this time harder.

Sam placed his palm over his drink, picked it up, and slammed it on the table—shattering the glass beneath his hand. No one said a word.

Another man's wife wasn't his business, but Sam couldn't stand injustice of any kind. The former professional boxer who cleaned up his gang-ridden neighborhood and defended the weak wasn't going to sit back and watch a woman be manhandled by her husband.

"Another round," Jerry called to the waiter, breaking the tension.

The five-foot-five Mehmet sat down, knowing he was no match for the six-foot Sam, who was nicknamed "Lightning."

Flustered, Saranda stood. "I'm going to the ladies' room."

"I'll come with you," Jariyeh said, grabbing her purse.

In the bathroom, Saranda warned, "You shouldn't have pulled away from Mehmet like that. It was a mistake."

"I'm unpredictable," Jariyeh replied. "I act how I want, when I want. Mehmet knows that. There's nothing to worry about."

She made it sound like a joke, but she had seen the shift. Mehmet had never been that forceful with her before, but she wouldn't say that to Saranda and make her worry. But Saranda had noticed. Everyone had.

Would Jariyeh have been more cautious if she knew he was in a drug cartel?

What had set Mehmet off that night? Was it a bump of cocaine? A hit of heroin? Did being a drug-dealer unleash his aggressive nature? Or did he suspect something between Jariyeh and Sam?

———

"Why did Sam and Hasi divorce?" I asked Saranda many years later, wondering if it had anything to do with Jariyeh.

"Sam hoped to fall in love with Hasi," she said. "But after a while, he didn't even like her. She was cold, jealous, and didn't like children. What woman doesn't like children? It came as no surprise to my family when he left her."

"Was her family upset?"

"Yes, but there was nothing they could do since she didn't want children."

"I should've known it would end like this," Sam had told Saranda. "We had a civil ceremony in Paris to start the visa process. Afterward, I went to the bathroom to wash my face. I looked down at my wedding ring and thought: *I guess this is it.* The ring cracked in two and fell down the drain."

Did Jariyeh know this story? Had she taken it as a sign that they were meant to be?

Jariyeh called Gjile. The two shared a special bond ever since Italy. Even during Jariyeh's two missing years, when she forgot she had a family, she never forgot to ask about Gjile. Saranda's mother was a tough old lady who adored Jariyeh. She hung photos of her grandchildren in the living room, but when my sister gave her a picture of herself in a fuchsia dress and said, "So you won't miss me," Gjile placed it on her nightstand.

Jariyeh often called just to chat.

"Hello, Gjile!" she said warmly.

"Sam!" Gjile called out to her divorced son.

Why did she do that? Had Gjile sensed the heartbreak behind Jariyeh's dancing at Sam's wedding? Did she think letting them speak would ease the pain?

Right after that call, Jariyeh rang Saranda and was already laughing when she picked up.

"I just called your mom. And the moment she heard my voice she called out to Sam—"

"I don't want to know," Saranda cut her off. "This way, if anything happens with you guys, I can swear I had no part in it."

Saranda knew that if they eloped, Jariyeh would be disowned and Bekim would be told to leave her. That was why families didn't intermarry. But maybe, Saranda thought, if she stayed out of it, he might keep her.

Jariyeh understood and changed the subject.

After they hung up, Saranda realized there was no guarantee Bekim would keep her even if she didn't know. Maybe if she left him before they eloped, Nana would be more likely to accept Jariyeh and Sam. Saranda had already spent nine years with the man she loved. It was Jariyeh's turn.

She called Sam.

"If something's going to happen with you and Jariyeh, you have to tell me first. That way, I will leave Bekim, and you guys can have a chance at happiness."

"Don't worry about it," Sam said. "Don't rush into anything."

Chapter 29

Live, Love, Laugh

* * *

Saturday came, and I waited.

May 1st was my sixteenth birthday—in America that was a big deal. I wasn't allowed to go to my friends' birthday parties, but I wished my mother had at least let me attend their sweet sixteens. Why did we have to be so different? It's not like I was going to fall in love with one of their brothers and run away—I knew better than that.

I was the first girl in our family to turn sixteen in America. My birthday fell on a Tuesday. All I got was a phone call from Arta. Then Saturday came—and nothing. What was I supposed to do—my homework? Watch television?

Nana got dressed. *"Shkova,"*--I'm leaving, she announced, and walked out.

Birthdays were an American thing my sisters picked up on—but not my mother. Kamile and Jariyeh took turns throwing parties for Luan and me. Because our birthdays were five days apart, we always celebrated together. But not this time—this was a sweet sixteen, and it would be just for me.

I was walking around the house, feeling lost, when the phone rang.

"It's Jariyeh," Vera said, handing me the phone.

"Get dressed and come over," she told me and hung up.

I was ecstatic. *Was this it?*

I put on my new outfit: a pair of brown slacks, a button-down shirt in shades of brown and beige with tiny flowers, and an earth-tone wool sweater. It was a little warm for the sweater, but I couldn't break up the set. My love of fashion came from my parents, who custom-tailored our clothes in Kosova.

"I'm going to Jariyeh's," I told Vera, in case Nana asked when she got back.

I walked as fast as I could in my wedges. Normally I wore sneakers—but this was a special occasion. I made my way down her block-long hallway, all the way to the back of the building, rang her doorbell, and anxiously waited.

"Erdha!"--Coming, Jariyeh yelled.

Would she take me out to eat for my sweet sixteen, I wondered. Would we go to Burger King or the diner on 86th Street with the fancy burgers?

Jariyeh opened the door.

"Surprise!" everyone yelled.

I jumped back, startled.

I looked at the crowd of women and children and was surprised to see Nana. So this was where she was going? She never attended our birthday celebrations. This was a big deal. Even Saranda's sisters were there with their children. Jerry's boys had brought their BB rifles. Normally, you didn't invite a Nuse's family, but as far as I was concerned, the more the merrier.

Feeling like a celebrity, I hugged everyone.

Jariyeh had gone all out. There were birthday plates and hats. Mine was shaped like a crown, and for the first time, I felt like a princess. The table overflowed with chips and dips, and Jariyeh made her Italian specialties: chicken parmesan and baked ziti. Mehmet had taught her. Eating at Jariyeh's was always a treat. Nana only made Albanian dishes: cabbage stew, potato stew, scallion pie, beans with beef strips she dried over the stove, and pasta smothered in butter—her version of Italian.

Saranda served our guests as Jariyeh put an LP on the record player so we could dance. All my siblings were good dancers, but Jariyeh was by far the best Albanian folk dancer at any gathering. And I was quickly becoming really good at American freestyle.

Months earlier, I got the chance to show off my skills at the wedding of a distant "cousin." He claimed he was marrying the rich American for his "papers," but that may have been an excuse for betraying us by falling in love with a non-Albanian. I wore a white dress with tiny roses. Jariyeh wore a tiered black-and-white chiffon cocktail gown. We were the only ones left on the dance floor. Jariyeh kicked off her sandals. Like a good girl, I kept mine on. Nana and the rich guests smiled at us as the fancy photographer snapped away.

Dancing was my first love, and where better than at my birthday party to show off my moves? Whenever Arta slept over, we'd go to Jariyeh's and choreograph new steps for our routine. Then we'd call her in for approval. She'd smile big and clap hard, yelling "Bravo! Bravo!" each time.

Now we'd show everyone.

Jariyeh grabbed her 8mm movie camera and set it on a tripod.

Arta and I stood in front of the wallpaper mural of a waterfall, our hearts racing. When Jariyeh first put it up, she proudly showed it to us. "It reminds me of Kosova," she said. "I wish I could jump right in." That would've been an easy escape, back to a time when life was simple—before husbands and children.

Jariyeh called all the kids in to watch. The room was all abuzz. The grownups lined the couches, while the kids sprawled across the floor or leaned against the waterfall. Smiling, Jariyeh put Rod Stewart's album on the record player, held the needle over our song, and looked to me for a signal.

Arta and I grabbed hands.

I nodded.

The needle scratched down onto "Do Ya Think I'm Sexy."

The beat kicked in and my nerves were gone. Arta and I launched into the Hustle—pulling each other close, then pushing apart, as our bare feet glided across the rug. I twirled her, she twirled me. We dipped, kicked, and pointed to the ceiling, *Saturday Night Fever* style, as Rod Stewart sang about our sexiness. Thank God Nana didn't speak English. These weren't the kinds of songs a virgin daughter should be dancing to.

Jariyeh couldn't sit still. She sang along as she ran her hands up and down her body, acting out how "sexy" she was. From the outside, no one could tell she wasn't happy.

The song finished.

Arta and I ended with a bow.

Everyone clapped—even Nana. I was thrilled to see my mother smiling up at me. I was her good girl. Marriage was coming, and she was preparing me to be obedient, quiet, and a good cleaner, so I'd attract many suitors.

Jariyeh brought out the Carvel ice cream cake, our birthday staple, and everyone sang "Happy Birthday" to me. I closed my eyes to make a wish. But what to wish for when I had everything? I had an honorable, respected, modern, fun family, and I was sure I'd have plenty of suitors. Then it came to me: *I wish I would love the man I married.*

I cut the cake neatly and filled the plates.

Everyone took their children and ice cream into the living room. Arta and I stayed behind with Jariyeh and Saranda, who fed their little girls.

Saranda got some chocolate ice cream on her lip and was about to wipe it off when Jariyeh yelled, "Don't move."

Saranda smiled, thinking her best friend wanted to wipe it for her. But Jariyeh had something else in mind. She'd noticed Saranda never ate leftovers, like a good Nuse should, but instead made herself peanut butter and jelly sandwiches. At first, she figured Saranda just loved peanut butter and jelly. But when she saw her pour a new glass of water every time someone took a sip from hers, Jariyeh understood: Saranda was "picky and spoiled"—the Albanian version of a germaphobe. And my sister had the perfect cure.

She grabbed Saranda's face with both hands and licked the chocolate off—knowing it would drive her crazy. Then she continued licking the rest of her face.

Saranda couldn't get mad at her friend and laughed hysterically.

"Wait," Jariyeh said. She took a sip from Saranda's cup and held it to Saranda's lips. Cracking up, Saranda drank from it. She wasn't cured, but afterward she even drank from her kids' cups and ate her husband's leftovers. Unlike therapists, Jariyeh cured with love.

I opened Nana's gift first—a watch. Exaggerating for the movie camera, I gave her a theatrical kiss, as Jariyeh would have. Nana laughed. I got clothes, my favorite kind of present, and charms to add to my charm holder.

Jariyeh saved her gift for last—a gold pendant with the words Live, Love, Laugh—her commandments. I planned to wear it always and make those words my own.

I still have it. Curiously, the "L" in Live broke off.

"Zemra jeme"--My heart, Jariyeh said to me in front of the camera, as if we were acting out *Romeo and Juliet*.

I played along, gazing at her in adoration, soaking in her love.

She kissed both my cheeks, grabbed my face, then kissed my forehead again and again. I laughed. Then she kissed my face in a circle. When she reached my laughing mouth—she faked a spit.

Everyone roared.

Mission accomplished. Jariyeh smiled and walked off.

I never felt as loved as I did that day.

Chapter 30

Houdini Nights

* * *

Mehmet hardly worked at the deli he was asked to manage. Why would he—when heroin paid better. Instead of making sandwiches, he went to Albanian social clubs to gamble and possibly sleep with mistresses. He went to American discos to deal and hang with VIPs. The underworld's sense of influence and belonging was addictive. Mehmet enjoyed the thug prestige. It made him feel powerful, cool, important—and everything else he wasn't. At Studio 54, he ran into his look-alike.

"I met John Belushi," he bragged, knowing how proud we'd been when we learned that the *Saturday Night Live* star was Albanian. We were impressed, not realizing that besides their looks, they had heroin in common.

It was springtime, months after the cartel's first heroin shipment arrived.

Jariyeh knew her husband used drugs. She didn't know he was selling them. Then one night, Mehmet came home with a briefcase and spilled stacks of bills onto their mattress.

"Look, Jariyeh!" He smiled. "That's four hundred thousand dollars."

Jariyeh stared at the money, then at Mehmet, stunned. Never in her life had she seen so much cash. But he wasn't working, stayed out all night, and was always high. There was no question where it came from.

"Get this dirty money out of my house!" she shouted.

"Never bring dirty money into your home" was a Baba rule we all obeyed.

"But Jariyeh, it's a lot of money," Mehmet said.

"All the curses that mothers put on you for selling drugs to their kids could one day hurt *our* kids. Get it out of my house!"

"Okay, okay," he replied meekly. As dangerous as he was, Mehmet cowered around his wife. Like a scolded child he gathered the bills and stuffed them into the briefcase.

So many "tough" Albanian men went silent when confronted by their wives. Even Baba avoided Nana's wrath. Albanian girls were suppressed from birth, but some turned that pressure into a fierce inner strength. The way coal turns into diamonds. No matter how tough a man was, it was hard to contend with that.

Mehmet grew up watching his father submit to his mother. This shaped his marriage. Like Filanza, Jariyeh was in charge, but she had no cruelty in her heart. Like his father, Mehmet was passive, but he had no integrity to fall back on.

"I won't raise my children on dirty money," she told Mehmet. Then she called Kamile, who was promoted to supervisor. "Sis, I need a job, right away."

Within twenty-four hours, Jariyeh was picking up trash, vacuuming, and emptying ashtrays at 1 New York Plaza. Leaving the children with Mehmet was hard, but knowing I was just next door gave her comfort. She didn't give her paychecks to her husband. She loved having money of her own. Clean money. Money she would spend wisely. A lesson we learned from Nana:

> Once, there was a wealthy man and a poor man. The wealthy man offered his riches to the poor man. "Why would you give it all away?" the poor man asked. "Because with great wealth comes great responsibility," he explained. "One must do the right things with it."
> After giving away his wealth, the man rode off relieved of his burden.

Jariyeh sang Albanian songs as she cleaned the empty offices. And every night, after 9:00 p.m., she'd sneak into a vacant conference room to call home. If no one picked up or Esat answered, she knew Mehmet had left the kids alone. Her next call was always to me—her emergency sitter.

"Hane, you have to go watch the kids."

"I can't," I protested, not wanting to be in her apartment without her there.

I didn't know why Mehmet stopped working or why Jariyeh started, but being around him made me uncomfortable. He had changed since the previous summer.

We were all at Coney Island beach. Mehmet arrived late carrying two Katz's Deli bags filled with heroes, pickled tomatoes, and sodas. I thought how generous. Just as we took a bite, he said, "By the way, they're pork." We froze. Not eating pork was the closest we came to being religious, aside from the women fasting during Ramadan. The mouth-watering meat suddenly became disgusting. We were about to spit it out and save ourselves, when Mehmet laughed. "I'm only kidding."

Mehmet was always just there, but now he was different.

One day, he stood too close to me in the foyer and said, "You're becoming a beautiful girl." It wasn't the words. It was the way he looked at me when he said them. I stiffened. If he touched me, I'd be ruined and my family disgraced. I told myself Mehmet respected Zogu too much to cross that line, but I still worried. I didn't tell anyone because if Zogu found out, it could cause tension in the family, and Mehmet could take Jariyeh away.

"Please, Hane. You have to go," Jariyeh begged. "The kids are alone."

As much as I didn't want to, I couldn't leave her seven-, six-, and three-year-old kids by themselves. I grabbed my books and headed over. Minutes later, the phone rang.

"Are the kids okay?" Jariyeh asked.

"Yes. They're sleeping."

They were almost always sleeping.

I'd hang up, then climb on a chair, unlatch the kitchen cupboard, and go junk-food hunting. Nana didn't understand the concept. Jariyeh had everything: Ring Dings, Devil Dogs, Twinkies, chips, and sometimes Cracker Jacks with the toy surprise inside—my favorite. Jariyeh never minded the raids. When the hard-core junk was gone, Ritz Crackers and orange juice would do—they went so well together. I sat in the living room with my treats while I did my homework, watched TV, and prayed Mehmet wouldn't show up.

The door opened and he walked in.

"Oh. You're here," he said, feeling caught.

"Yeah," I replied, as I quickly gathered my books and left.

Most of the time, Jariyeh got home first. It would be after midnight, and I'd be asleep on the floor near my books, or on the couch with the TV on. She'd wake me gently and hug me tight.

"Thank you, Hane. Thank you. Thank you," she whispered, kissing me again and again.

Seeing how worried she was, I felt guilty for giving her such a hard time but still dreaded those late-night calls.

I didn't understand her pain until Kamile told me decades later.

Whenever Mehmet left the kids alone, Jariyeh would call me then go into an empty conference room and cry in the dark. Sometimes her supervisor found her.

"Go home to your children," Billy would say. "Kamile will finish your floor."

"Thank you, Billy, but I can't."

"Don't worry. I won't dock your pay," he added gently.

But it wasn't that. Jariyeh couldn't risk losing her job—or worse, getting Billy fired. At times, Jariyeh accepted his kindness. She'd go to the locker room, change out of her uniform, run to the subway, and once in Brooklyn, sprint the two blocks home.

When Mehmet arrived, she'd yell at him. He'd swear he'd never do it again—every time.

One night, during a junk food raid, I found nothing. Refusing to give up, I reached further back in the cupboard and found a small, tightly wrapped brown paper bag. Hoping it held some hidden treat, I opened it. It was just flour. We always bought Hecker's, so this had to be something special. Or maybe it was fine sugar. I thought of tasting it, but spotted the Ritz crackers.

A few days later, I overheard Saranda and Jariyeh in the kitchen.

"Is Mehmet still putting drugs up his nose?" Saranda asked.

"Yes. And he keeps leaving it around the house."

I'd seen people in movies put drugs up their nose. It looked like flour. Had I found cocaine, I wondered. Thank God I didn't taste it.

"One day I found his drugs in the refrigerator," Jariyeh said. "I'm scared the children will find them."

I was scared too, sure it could kill them.

During one of Mehmet's Houdini acts, Jariyeh did what she never wanted to do—she called Bekim. The brother who never wanted her to marry Mehmet. The brother who thought so little of Mehmet that he refused to set foot in their house except on New Year's Eve.

"Mehmet left the children home alone again," she said.

"What do you want me to do?" he asked.

Jariyeh wasn't sure what she wanted him to do. She knew he wouldn't tell her to leave him, but she had hoped her big brother—the one who had taken her father's place—would have a suggestion.

"If you want me to call the police, I'll call the police," he offered. "And then they'll take your children away."

"No, I can't let the police take my children."

"Then why don't you quit your job and go home?"

"But Mehmet isn't working. And I don't want his kind of money."

Bekim knew exactly what she meant.

Mehmet once said to him, "Come work with me. You can make $300,000 just like that." He snapped his fingers, acting as if he were offering Bekim a way out of his concierge job—when in fact, he was hoping to bring him down to his level, then maybe he'd respect him.

Sa i mençum asht budalli?--How smart is stupid? Bekim thought. I'm going to risk my life for dirty money I could never spend in good conscience? But what he said was, "Thanks, but I'm fine."

Jariyeh never called her brother again.

Chapter 31

Kosova Connection

* * *

Just over a month before she died, Jariyeh came over with an unusual request: "Can you take the kids to Lulu's House for a week? Mehmet wants to take me to Mexico."

Mexico? That sounded exotic. Other than Lulu's House, Mehmet had only taken her to Kosova on vacation. I didn't want her to miss the opportunity, but there was much to consider. I wasn't sure I could handle all three kids by myself, and Nana and I were preparing to go to Kosova, so we had much to do.

"I don't think Nana will let me go," I said.

"I asked her, and she said yes."

"I can't ask her to pay for me."

"Mehmet will pay for you." Jariyeh smiled.

A free vacation—*how could I say no?*

Jariyeh and Mehmet dropped me and the kids off at Lulu's House. I'd been babysitting since I was nine, but this was the first time I realized that being a mother was exhausting. Between outfit changes, baths, meals, and watching them like a hawk so the other kids wouldn't make them cry, I barely had a moment to breathe. I couldn't wait for Jariyeh and Mehmet to return.

The week passed slowly.

Before picking us up at Lulu's, Jariyeh and Mehmet stopped by our house. He went to the living room with Zogu. She went straight to Nana's bedroom.

"Mexico wasn't a vacation," Jariyeh told her. "It was a drug deal."

"What are you saying?"

"We went in a limo with his friends, and they said, 'Why is she here?' I didn't understand what was happening till they started talking about drugs. I told Mehmet I wanted to leave."

"Did you say it in front of them?" Nana asked.

"Yes, I did."

"My daughter, you must be careful."

"I don't care," Jariyeh replied.

Nana wondered if this was what people meant by *M'bytëm se plasa*--kill me 'cause I'm dying. Did her stubborn daughter hate her life so much that she was trying to get herself killed?

"Did you know any of them?" Nana asked, hoping she didn't.

"They were Albanians," was all Jariyeh said.

Later, the DEA would call them the Balkan or Kosova Connection. While less known than the Sicilian or French Connections, they would move as much as 40 percent of the U.S. heroin supply. Heroin they sourced from Turkey.[xvi] Had Mehmet and his crew gone to Mexico looking for a faster, cheaper route?

Vera walked in with Turkish coffee, eager to hear about her friend's trip.

"So, how was Mexico?"

"Brooklyn is better," Jariyeh changed the subject. "We're picking up Hane and the kids from Lulu's and will stay the weekend. Why don't you take Samir and come with us?"

Vera was eight months pregnant, a little vacation with her baby boy sounded wonderful. She rushed to ask her husband.

"No!" Zogu yelled in typical Zogu fashion.

When Jariyeh offered to take twenty-month-old Samir, Vera didn't ask again. Her husband didn't change diapers, give bottles, or care where his son was. Vera packed a bag for her boy and walked with Jariyeh and Mehmet to the car.

When she returned alone, Zogu shouted, "I didn't want either of you going." Not bothering to explain that he had a bad feeling.

I was happy to see Jariyeh and Samir at Lulu's House. Not so much Mehmet.

After dinner, the kids begged to go into town for ice cream. Jariyeh was happy to take them. Mehmet insisted she drive, though she didn't yet have her license.

"I don't want to drive," Jariyeh said.

"Drive. Drive." Mehmet insisted.

At a time before car seats and seatbelts, her three kids piled into the back seat. Not trusting a drugged-up Mehmet to hold Samir, she put the toddler on her lap.

"There's something wrong with the brakes," she warned.

"It's fine. Just drive," Mehmet slurred.

She gripped the wheel tighter and drove with extra caution, but on a sharp turn, the brakes gave out—and they crashed.

Samir's face slammed into the steering wheel, cushioning Jariyeh's blow. Blood poured from his little chin onto her lap. At the hospital, ten stitches closed the gash, but his swollen and battered face looked far worse. Jariyeh's arms and knees were bruised. Her three children and Mehmet walked away without a scratch.

Later he said the mechanic found the problem. But she suspected foul play.

When Vera first told me this, I was sure Mehmet had tampered with the brakes.

But looking back now, it doesn't make sense. Why would he put himself and his children in danger? Was he too high to realize what he was doing? Or was Jariyeh being paranoid—unless she suspected someone else. Was one of the dealers from the limo at Lulu's House that day picking up his family?

Jariyeh wouldn't go anywhere with Mehmet afterward. She didn't understand why he had taken her to Mexico—none of the other men brought their wives.

"Ta jap besën,"--I give you my word, Mehmet said. "I won't take you to another drug deal."

No matter how she felt about her husband, she wanted to believe that his word meant something. So when Mehmet said, "Get dressed, we're going to a party in Manhattan," Jariyeh didn't hesitate.

The moment she walked in and saw who was there, Jariyeh went pale. Not only did his word mean nothing, he was still involved.

"How dare you take me to those people *again*?" she snapped at him on their way home.

"I'm sorry, Jariyeh. I was afraid to go alone."

Why did he say that? Was Mehmet becoming a liability to the cartel? Had he made some mistake, or was bringing Jariyeh to Mexico the thing that crossed the line? Did he take her thinking her charm would impress the dealers? Or was he also too scared to go to Mexico alone?

Had the dealers threatened to kill him? Her? The children?

One day Mehmet said to Jariyeh out of nowhere, "We're moving to Canada."

Jariyeh told her sister during their train ride to work, "Mehmet said we're going to Canada."

"Why don't you let him go by himself?" Kamile asked.

"Believe me, sis. I don't want to go. But he won't leave me here with the kids."

Weeks later, Jariyeh told Kamile, "Mehmet ripped up some papers and flushed them down the toilet and said, 'We're not going to Canada.'"

Kamile wondered what those papers were, but didn't ask.

"I'm happy you're not going."

"I'm not happy," Jariyeh said.

Kamile was surprised that her sister was willing to move so far away. Did she no longer feel safe in America? But Kamile didn't press. The more she knew, the more she'd worry.

Chapter 32

Suspicious Minds

* * *

Mehmet started following Jariyeh like a fumbling Inspector Clouseau—crouching behind bushes and ducking behind parked cars, thinking no one noticed. He wasn't the brightest bulb, and the drugs had dimmed his judgment further still.

One day, Jariyeh left the house in her latest Candie's heels, a flowing summer dress, and Jackie O sunglasses. She looked ready to board a private jet to Paris for a fashion show, but she was headed for the subway to her cleaning job.

"Yo! Sweetheart!" construction workers catcalled and whistled as she walked past.

Jariyeh turned to nod a thank you when she spotted Mehmet behind a tree. She marched over.

"What are you doing?" she asked.

Mehmet stood still, certain she hadn't seen him.

"I see you."

"Aw, okay," he said, laughing his weak laugh as he stepped out like a bashful boy caught in the act. "I was just playing."

One morning he called out from the foyer, "Bye, I'm leaving."

Jariyeh heard the front door close. Later, when she opened the hallway closet, she saw his feet sticking out beneath the coats. Had the drugs made him so delusional that he thought if he couldn't see her, she couldn't see him?

"What are you doing?" she asked.

"Aw, you found me," he said, as if they'd been playing hide-and-seek.

She shook her head, took her shoes, and shut the closet door.

Jariyeh told Vera, "I don't know why he's following me around. Maybe it's because he sees I'm happier now that Sam's divorced."

Before heading out, Mehmet started asking, "Are you going anywhere today?"

If she said she planned to go shopping, but didn't—he'd come home and say with a smirk, "So…you didn't go shopping, did you?"

"I think he tapped the phone," she told Vera.

Maybe it wasn't a tap. Maybe he waited outside all day. Or maybe the Bici spies were at it again. Filanza lost her daily surveillance when Jariyeh moved next door to us, but her gossiping never ended.

———

Years later, Lata helped me understand what was happening at the time.

"Pop said he was hearing rumors all the time," she said.

"What were people saying?" I asked.

"They were saying my mom was having an affair."

"What did they see?" I asked. It was more than forty years since Jariyeh's death. I was dying to know what proof they had.

"Someone saw my mom walking outside, and a man was walking a few feet behind her, acting like they weren't together."

"Who was this man?"

"I don't know."

He could've been a total stranger, but that somehow became evidence.

"After a while he couldn't take it" Lata continued. "Pop said, 'I'd stay outside. I'd stay with my friends. I didn't want to hear.'"

———

It was late August when Jariyeh came over with an envelope.

"Can you hold onto this for me?" she asked Nana.

"What is it?"

"Ten thousand dollars."

This had to be the money from the sale of Mehmet's first kilo. Whether he hid it and she found it, or asked her to hold onto it, I'll never know. What I do know is that she took it without his permission.

"I want you to hold it for me in case I have to take the children and run away. I'm afraid I'm going to die like that Italian lady."

She was referring to the Italian woman killed by her Albanian husband because she wanted a divorce. Then there was the Albanian woman who learned her fiancé was married with children. When he walked in to find her packing, he shot her several times, then pinned the murder on his "jealous" wife. She obediently took the rap and went to jail.

"Nothing will happen to you while I'm alive," Nana assured her daughter.

Jariyeh believed her. We all would have. Nana was the toughest woman we knew.

In Kosova, when Baba was in jail, an eighteen-year-old Serbian girl pulled a chunk of hair from eight-year-old Kamile's head. Kamile slapped her so hard the girl ran home crying. Her stepmother grabbed her spindle, marched past a pregnant Nana, went upstairs, and beat little Kamile bloody. Nana was chopping wood when she heard the noise, and with an axe in hand, she ran upstairs and told the woman to stop. When she didn't, Nana hit her so hard with the back of the axe that the woman died of internal bleeding a few weeks later.

Luckily, the judge didn't believe a woman could have done such damage.

Now, Jariyeh was in need of her mother's help. Nana reached into her bra for her key. From beneath her bed she pulled out her slim gray briefcase and unlocked it. Pushing aside our green cards and Baba's keepsakes, she grabbed a .38.

"Take this. Use it if you have to. Rather than I cry for my daughter, let his mother cry for him."

"May my children never be without a father," Jariyeh said. She didn't want Mehmet dead. She just didn't want to live with him.

She took the gun, just in case.

Chapter 33

The Final Rose

* * *

From the moment Nana told me I was going to Kosova with her, I began counting down the days—but kept my excitement from Luan.

"Nana's a double-crosser," he said.

I felt bad. Luan should've been the one to go. *I was just a girl.* He was older *and a boy.* But Zogu got him a job at George Bassolino Plumbing, and three weeks off wasn't an option. I loved Luan. He was the only one who hit me, but he was also the only one who went out of his way to make my insignificant Albanian-girl life more American. He took me to see *Star Wars* on opening week. He took me to see *Rocky.* Afterward we ran home punching the air, singing, "Ta-na-naa! Ta-na-naa!" Luan also gave me driving lessons in his Cadillac, in case my husband would let me drive, and taught me how to ride a dirt bike just for fun.

Nana and I were leaving at the end of August, which meant I'd miss the start of my sophomore year—but Nana didn't care about school, and I couldn't pass up the opportunity. It was our first time back to Kosova since we left ten years ago—when I was six. I looked forward to going back home. I had fond memories of sheepherding, shooting birds with slingshots, and playing rock games with our friends. One of them threw a huge rock onto my big toe—I lost that nail.

Nana and I went to Canal Street, where everything was cheap. She made sure to buy gifts for everyone. American clothes, especially Levi's jeans, were coveted in Kosova. Nana let me choose the styles. I couldn't wait to see my cousins' faces.

I dropped the shopping bags off and was headed to Jariyeh's when I spotted it—the most perfect pink rose. It stood alone in a fenced-in garden, as if it had been waiting for me.

Should I steal it?

Jariyeh gave so much and expected nothing in return. The joy of others was payment enough. Little things made my sister happy: singing, dancing, and roses— but not just any rose—a stolen rose. A store-bought one didn't carry the thrill of being pinched from a garden. I hated breaking rules but was always on the hunt for that perfect bloom—and there it was.

My heart pounding, I scanned for witnesses, reached over, and snapped it off like the rose-stealing pro I'd become. Then ran straight to Jariyeh's.

Music seeped through the door as I rang her bell.

"Erdha,"--Coming, she said.

I hid the rose behind me. Jariyeh opened the door. I looked into her eyes as I swung the rose out with a smile.

"For me?" she said, her eyes lighting up.

"For you," I replied.

She hugged me as if it were the first time I'd given her a rose. I didn't know if I stole roses to make her happy, or just to feel her love.

"What a beautiful rose," she said, breathing in its scent.

Billy Joel's "My Life" came on as I walked in. It had become my sister's anthem. She sang along. I imagined she was singing to Mehmet, wishing he'd *go ahead with his own life and leave her alone.* That made me sad. It must be hard to be married to an addict. I prayed I wouldn't get stuck with one, but there were no guarantees. If God could give Jariyeh an addict, why not me?

As my sister continued to sing about "her life," I thought about how I didn't have any control over mine. But surely she did. She was older and freer than most—but more troubled. Not that she complained to me, and I never asked. What good was knowing when there was nothing I could do but get sick to my stomach? I wanted the world to be a happy place, and if anyone deserved happiness, it was her. I hoped God would make things better—soon.

"I went to see Susan," Jariyeh said.

"Oh really?" I replied, honored that she'd confide in me.

Susan was the 86th Street gypsy. As a child in Kosova, I was told gypsies wandered around looking to steal children. But in Brooklyn, they didn't sneak. They lived in shops with neon lights, tempting Americans to look into their future—if they dared. Bleached-blonde Susan lived over a boutique and read tarot cards in her front room, just two blocks from Kamile. Kamile hated fortune tellers. She said they robbed people of their power. She didn't want Jariyeh going to psychics for answers, but it wasn't that simple. Jariyeh knew her situation was complicated and hoped the spirit world could change what she couldn't.

"What did Susan say?" I leaned in.

"She said she saw dark energy around me."

Energy was a word Americans seemed to use for anything unexplained.

"Did someone do witchcraft?" I asked, concerned.

"She didn't say. But she gave me candles and told me to light one every day and pray to get rid of the darkness."

Looking back, I wonder why Jariyeh told me about Susan. Maybe she sensed my worry and thought that hearing about the candles would give me hope.

I knew all magic—white or black—dealt with spirits, and not all spirits were good. I hoped Susan worked with the good ones, though I wondered if it was a scam. But there was no harm in lighting a few candles. Maybe it would work. For two weeks Jariyeh lit one every day and said her prayers. But nothing changed. If anything, Mehmet got worse.

Billy Joel's LP ended, and Jariyeh flipped through her records.

"I bought this one for us," she said, pulling out "We Are Family" by Sister Sledge.

I couldn't believe she bought it.

She placed it on the record player, and the two of us sang along and danced. During the chorus, we looked at each other as we sang about *having all our sisters with us*. I pictured Roza and Kamile dancing next to us. Sister Sledge had five sisters. We were four.

I was the luckiest girl in the world.

When the song ended, I turned to Jariyeh. "I should go pack."

"I'm so happy you're going to Kosova." She smiled. "Who knows. Maybe you'll meet a boy and fall in love?"

Wouldn't that be nice? I thought, as I hugged and kissed my sister goodbye.

I didn't know it would be for the last time.

Chapter 34

American Girl

* * *

When Nana and I arrived in Kosova, everything seemed smaller, poorer, and less colorful than I remembered. We stayed with her sister, *Teze* Fatime. Teze meant aunt on the mother's side, which wasn't as important as the *Hallas* on the father's side—but she was the closest family we had in Kosova. Everyone else was stuck behind Albania's Communist walls.

Teze lived in Prizren, a picturesque city nestled in the foothills of the Sharr Mountains. The Ottomans had favored it during their occupation, so much so, that they littered it with mosques. The lyrical morning prayers coming from the minarets made me want to be more Moslem.

My Teze had only one child, a son named Isa, which meant Jesus in Arabic. Isa was a blood technician, but they called him *doktor i gjakut*--doctor of blood. Exaggeration came with being Albanian. My mother and sisters weren't just cleaning ladies at 1 New York Plaza. "I clean the 41st floor, Salomon Brothers," Nana boasted, as though she ran the company. Jariyeh sang as she wiped desks at Oppenheimer Funds. Kamile cleaned the law offices of Fried Frank on the 28th floor—until she got promoted to supervisor and oversaw all the firms. Nothing Albanians did was insignificant. They worked hard and took immense pride in a job well done.

Isa took me to "his" hospital and gave me a blood test.

"You're A-negative," he diagnosed.

I was disappointed. I wanted to be A+ because it was a better grade in school.

It was exhilarating to be in a place where people spoke my language and understood my ways. No explaining necessary. The Kosovars didn't have much money, or jobs, but it didn't matter. They seemed to enjoy life more than us. We lived in apartments, worked all the time, ate too much, and had no social life except for family. They lived in homes with courtyards, ate just enough, and wore the same clothes over and over without a need to apologize. I tried not to change every day, but I had so many nice outfits—and Nana wanted to show off her beautiful, stylish daughter.

After dinner, everybody dressed up and went to *korza*--a stroll around the city center. It was a poor man's night on the town, yet more exciting than anything I'd ever done in America. Family and friends walked arm-in-arm, stopping at cafés and ice cream parlors, hunting for future wives and husbands, either for themselves or their relatives.

I was surprised to learn that some girls secretly dated.

Walking between Isa and his wife, I felt like a movie star in my American dress and sandals.

"Kjo asht Amerikane,"--She's an American girl, Isa introduced me to his friends.

I wasn't sure if he was being playful or testing me to see what I'd say. Albanians loved to test—but I didn't like it.

"I'm not American. I'm Albanian," I responded every time.

Isa would laugh; happy I hadn't forgotten where I was from.

Growing up in Kosova, he couldn't understand my plight. In America, no real Albanian wanted to be called "American." It meant you had no shame and put your needs before the family.

I may have had fancier clothes, and spoke with an American accent, but I was proud to be Albanian. To speak Albanian. To dress and act appropriately for an Albanian girl. In America, I felt like an outsider, and now that I was "home" in Kosova, my people saw me as American.

Who was I? Where did I fit in?

When Isa's eighteen-year-old brother-in-law, Fisnik, came to visit with his family, there was instant chemistry. It was then I was happy to be different. To be "American." To have beautiful clothes. I blushed as we shook hands. Then like a good girl, I sat quietly while the grownups exchanged greetings.

Everyone asked Nana about my siblings who vacationed in Kosova. However, the focus always turned to Jariyeh. She had the gift *mi ba njerëzit për veti*--to make people for herself. My sister had a way of bringing a person's guard down and sneaking into their hearts. Some never knew what hit them.

"That Jariyeh," Fisnik's mother said with a big smile. "She was something else. Whenever she was around, all we did was laugh and sing."

I was happy Fisnik was there to hear about my amazing sister and hoped he had also met her. That would give him all the more reason to like me.

"How could one person be so lovable?" added his older brother.

"Thuj mashallah"--Say God has willed it, Isa's wife interrupted.

"Mashallah. Mashallah," they said in unison, as the mother fake-spit on the floor.

I had heard Christian and Moslem Albanians alike say mashallah to Jariyeh to counteract the evil eye they may have unintentionally triggered. It wasn't just dislike or envy that activated this "eye." It often happened by loving someone too much—and too much was how everyone loved my sister. I understood why we loved Jariyeh—but how did she make strangers love her during such a brief time?

Then it hit me.

I'm going to be just like her—loved by all.

And just like that, life felt electric.

If I were like my sister, everything else would fall into place. Nana would love me the way she loved her. Families would be clamoring to send matchmakers—at least the modern families like mine. The old-fashioned ones might see me as a rebel, but I wouldn't want them anyway. As soon as I get home, I'll watch her every move. I'll learn to dance like her, sing like her, love like her. *I'll be her!* But for now, there was this beautiful boy sitting before me.

I caught Fisnik looking and immediately stared at the carpet. Could this be happening? Could life be this amazing? Had Jariyeh called it?

All I wanted was to stay at Teze's house and wait for Fisnik to show up, but there were people to visit.

I loved the farms. I loved the sheep. I loved the horses. Even the food was better—so fresh, so flavorful—except for their skinny chickens. I liked the fat American chickens; unaware they were crammed together and injected with hormones. Nana tried not to visit during mealtime because people were poor, but they still insisted on feeding us.

"We'll cut a chicken," they'd offer a costly dish, then call a child to cut its head and boil off its feathers.

"No. No. We don't want meat," Nana would say to show we weren't big shots from America. "We'd prefer some beans or fried peppers with *gjiz.*" I loved their drained yogurt.

Our hosts always put up a fight, then eventually gave in. To show I liked their food, I ate a lot, making them happier—and me fatter. Fat was good. It showed wealth. Skinny meant poor.

We went to Ferizaj, where I was born, to spend a few nights at Kamile's in-laws.

"Mehmet was just here," they told us.

That was strange. Why was he there without Jariyeh and the children, I wondered. And why didn't he visit us at Teze's?

I was in the backyard, sharing a bowl of beans with a girl my age, when two flies crashed into each other and fell inside the dish. A nightmare for me back in Brooklyn. I hated bugs. No matter how immaculate our apartment was, roaches made their way into everything. This made eating a chore. I inspected every bite before putting it into my mouth. But this was Kosova. It wasn't my house. And people here didn't have much food.

"I'll get another bowl," the girl said, standing up, her face bright red.

What would Jariyeh do? I wondered.

"It's not a big deal," I said, as I scooped out the flies and bravely put a spoonful of beans in my mouth.

The girl smiled and sat back down. I liked how happy that made her, and decided to stop being picky when I got home. A great relief for Vera, who dreaded my constant food inspections.

A restaurant in the mountains served fish caught from the river that flowed a few feet from our table. The closest I'd come to eating fish in Brooklyn was when I felt daring and ordered a "Whaler" instead of a "Whopper" at Burger King. As delicious as the Prizren fish was, I couldn't enjoy it. I kept wishing Fisnik was with us.

When his siblings came to pick me up for a picnic in a forest they called "a park" I prayed he'd come with them. When he walked through Teze's front gate, I didn't care where we went or what we did, so long as we were together. We hadn't even parted, and I already wondered when I'd see him again.

Was this love?

I couldn't wait to tell Arta and Jariyeh.

Fisnik's family invited us for dinner at their home. We walked through large wooden doors into an enclosed courtyard that looked like paradise. It was filled with bright pink blooms that I'd never seen before, and a stream ran through its center.

We were sitting on mats when a gray and white kitten walked over. Nana called cats the devil's pet, but I picked it up because it belonged to him.

Fisnik's mother convinced Nana to let me spend the night. I was ecstatic.

His mom was a good-looking, chubby lady in her fifties who wore a headscarf and traditional *dimija*--baggy, harem-like pants. Yet her daughters dressed modern. One had graduated college, and the other had a few years left.

How was it that they were more advanced than us in America, I wondered.

In the privacy of their fancy living room, complete with color television, Fisnik's mother lifted her blouse and rolled her stomach like a belly dancer, then challenged me to try. It was embarrassing for a young girl to expose her belly, but I did it because Jariyeh would have. As I struggled to roll my flat stomach, Fisnik's mother and sisters laughed and laughed. What a cool mother-in-law she'd make, I thought. I wanted to be a part of her family, and was sure she felt the same about me. Since mothers took the lead on marital arrangements—things were looking pretty good.

After tea with the family in the courtyard, Fisnik's mother and sisters slowly disappeared, leaving the two of us alone.

"Do you want to go to America?" I asked, not knowing how else to show my interest. I knew everyone wanted to come to America to make money. But I hoped he'd say he wanted to come for me.

"No," he replied. "I have everything I need here."

It was true. His big brother owned a store, and his family wasn't as financially strapped as Teze and the others.

"Would you stay in Kosova?" he asked.

I turned bright red. That was almost like a marriage proposal. So he did like me.

"I don't know," I said. "I'd miss my family. But I like it here a lot."

He had to figure it out from there. He was Albanian. He must know I couldn't just come out and say I like you or I love you. Those words you saved for your husband, I thought, not realizing girls in Kosova were much more forward.

When I learned Fisnik was dating someone, I was worried. In Brooklyn, our boys never married their American girlfriends. But this was Kosova—and she was Albanian. Would he marry someone who broke the rules and dated? Had they slept together? Probably not, because she would no longer be a virgin, and they would've been engaged. Maybe I should have said something different when he asked if I'd live in Kosova. But I didn't know how to play those games. I was new to making a boy want me, or showing him how I felt.

It was early morning when Jariyeh called Nana at Teze's house. Most people had to go to the post office to make or receive calls, but Nana had made sure her sister had a phone at home. Long-distance calls were expensive—so I knew Jariyeh's call was important.

"Don't do anything. Wait till I get back," I heard my mother say.

Something in her tone made me nervous.

"Is everything okay?" I asked, after she hung up.

"It's fine," Nana replied, and walked away.

"Hajde me pi një çaj"--Come have tea, my cousin Isa called from the courtyard.

I loved their courtyard, and I loved sipping tea from the delicate, tulip-shaped Turkish glasses.

"Life is more fun in Kosova," I said.

"You almost grew up here," Isa replied. "You were almost my sister."

"What do you mean, your sister?"

"When your family got permission to leave for Italy, your mom and dad came to say goodbye and brought you along. My mom always wanted a daughter but couldn't have more children, so your mom offered to leave you with us."

"What? I never knew that," I said, devastated. Had my mother ever loved me? We'd grown closer in Kosova, especially when others praised me. Did she love me now?

"So what happened?" I asked.

"Your father said no."

Of course he did, I thought. Baba loved me. I missed him so much.

"It wasn't a big deal," he said, sensing my disappointment. "People gave away their children to family all the time. It would've been nice to have you as a sister."

Would I have been happier if I'd grown up in Kosova, I wondered. Here, Albanian boys were everywhere, and they seemed to like me. Even though dating wasn't allowed, girls did it anyway. If Teze were my mother, I could've dated Fisnik. I could've gone on the evening strolls in the city center and had friends I could visit after school. I could've even gone to college. I would've been one of only two kids—not the last of eight. I would've been special. My sweet Teze wouldn't have given me silent treatments. Here, my life would've felt more like an American girl's.

But Teze's family wasn't as fun as mine.

Sitting there with Isa, I realized I was both American and Albanian—two halves that didn't quite fit together. But I'd focus on being a good Albanian girl. That would make Nana happy.

Our departure date was fast approaching. I didn't want to leave Fisnik, or Kosova. But I had Jariyeh to look forward to.

Chapter 35

Gossipy Old Woman

* * *

The deli lease expired in August, and Mehmet was jobless. One day he disappeared without a word, and returned a week later.

"I was in Canada on business," he claimed.

Jariyeh said nothing. She didn't care and didn't want to know. But shortly thereafter, during a call from Kosova, the truth revealed itself.

Elez's family usually called from the post office once a month. This time the call came early. Elez heard his brother's voice and yelled out to his wife:

"Kosova!"

Kamile rushed to the kitchen phone. "Did you see Nana and Hane?" she asked.

"Yes. They were here," Elez's brother replied, then he got to the reason for his call: "Mehmet was here too."

"Mehmet? What was he doing in Kosova?" Kamile asked.

"We don't know, but he kept putting white dust up his nose. Then he left for a few days and asked us to watch his luggage. When he returned, he opened it. It was full of cash."

Mehmet must've thought they'd be impressed. They weren't.

"He's doing something illegal," the brother said. "We're all worried for Jariyeh."

Kamile called her sister right after.

"Mehmet was in Kosova and had the nerve to leave a suitcase of cash with Elez's brother. He could've gotten him arrested."

"What can I say, sis?" Jariyeh replied, apologetic.

The sisters knew Mehmet had gone to Kosova on drug business, but not that it was just a stopover before going to buy heroin in Turkey. Back then, it was a six-hour drive to Belgrade Airport, and a two-hour flight. There were no drug-sniffing dogs or stringent customs checks. Lata later told me, "Pop said he used to tape kilos to my body."

A few days after his trip, he walked in with two large brown paper bags and set them down in the hallway.

"Apples from a farm," he announced, knowing Jariyeh would be excited.

She rushed over, but instead of apples, saw stacks of cash.

Mehmet stood there smiling. He no longer cared if she got angry.

Elez and Mehmet took turns picking up the ladies from work, and it was Mehmet's week. Kamile would've preferred taking her chances with subway criminals over sitting in a car with him. But disrespecting her sister's husband would only make things worse for Jariyeh.

"There was a woman so hot for a man that she sat on the stick shift and died," Mehmet said. Then he looked at Kamile in the rearview. "You wanna try?"

"O burr pa marre,"--Oh man without shame, she said, knowing he wouldn't have dared be so disrespectful if Nana were there. "These words you're saying to me— men are killed over."

She was right. But she also knew better than to repeat his words to Elez, who would be honor-bound to defend her. In fact, Mehmet was offending Elez, since any offense to her was ultimately to her husband.

Mehmet hated that Kamile stood up to him and decided to ruin her marriage. During another ride home, Mehmet pulled out a hundred-dollar bill, more than her weekly salary.

"Take it," he said.

"I don't want it," Kamile replied.

"Take it," he insisted.

"Give it to Jariyeh," she said.

"No, I want you to have it."

Jariyeh turned to Kamile. "Sis, just take it," she said, eager to shut him up.

Kamile took the hundred, intending to giving it to Jariyeh.

The next day, Mehmet called Roza's husband. "I gave Kamile one hundred dollars last night," he said, as if it were an exchange for a sexual favor. What other reason was there for a married woman to accept money from a man who wasn't her blood or her husband?

Word got back to Elez. Luckily, Kamile had left the hundred-dollar bill on the kitchen table when she got home and told him what happened.

Mehmet didn't stop there. Every day before Kamile went to work, he'd call and keep her on the phone for an hour, saying: "I don't know how you do it. Only you can stay with such a man. You're too good for Elez. You should leave him." Kamile wanted to hang up, but couldn't. While she was at work, Mehmet would call Elez and repeat the same nonsense: "How could you stay with such a wife?"

It reminded Kamile of Filanza. When Jariyeh first moved out, Filanza would call Kamile every day, saying, "You're too good for Elez. You're too smart for him. You should leave him." Kamile couldn't hang up on her either, so she started answering the phone in a high-pitched voice and speaking only in English. Eventually, Filanza gave up. Kamile figured Mehmet had been talking to his mother.

———

Thinking back, I could see Filanza's long game. When Jariyeh made Mehmet move out Filanza was humiliated, and wanted our family shamed too. That was why she took Kamile shopping that first day. She tried to buy her with a blouse, took her number, and kept calling to plant seeds of divorce. It hadn't worked then, but she was still trying—this time through Mehmet. Why did he listen? What was she telling him?

Frustrated, I said to Vera, "Can you believe Mehmet used to call Kamile and tell her to leave Elez?"

"I can," she said. "Mehmet became like a gossipy old woman. He listened to everything, especially women's talk, then used it to stir up trouble. When he was alone with Zogu he'd say, 'You're such a good guy. How could you keep that wife?' When Zogu wasn't around, he'd say to me, 'Zogu doesn't love you. Why don't you just leave him?'"

Jariyeh told everyone, "Please, don't pay him any mind. It's the drugs."

Was it? It sounded more like his mother.

Chapter 36

That Motherfucker

* * *

In 1979, disco reigned supreme with #1 hits like "I Will Survive," "Too Much Heaven," and "Born to Be Alive." In theaters, one found Meatballs, Rocky II, Alien, and *The Muppets*. But the movie that most resembled Jariyeh's life was *The Amityville Horror*.

When things got bad, Jariyeh normally turned to Nana, but she was in Kosova. Not wanting to worry anyone, Jariyeh kept to herself. But one night, things got so bad that she was already crying when she finally called her sister.

"What happened?" Kamile asked, panicked. Her sister never cried.

"Last night when I came home from work, Mehmet put a large black candle that looked like a penis on the bed and told me to sit on it. I told him, 'I'm tired. Leave me alone,' but he wouldn't stop. 'Sit on it,' he kept saying. Then he put a gun to my head and yelled, 'I said, sit on it!'" Jariyeh was sobbing so hard she could hardly speak. "He's been crazy before, but this time I thought he was going to kill me."

"Oh my God, sis. Then what happened?"

"I told him, '*You* sit on it!'"

Good for you, *that motherfucker*, Kamile thought, though she didn't dare say it. She feared what might happen if she encouraged her fearless sister to stand up to Mehmet.

"What did he say?" Kamile asked.

"He said, 'Okay. Okay.' You know, like he always does."

It was typical Mehmet: a weak man trying to act tough. Was it the addiction or the drug dealing that was enabling this dark side?

Kamile wanted to beat the hell out of him. Back in Kosova, they called her Hercules. She beat up boys twice her size, sometimes two or three at a time. But now she was a wife, and her husband would have to answer for her actions.

All Kamile could say was, "I'm so sorry, sis."

"Pasha Zotin, hik teqe,"—For God's sake, get away.

The words came out of nowhere. It was about a week before she died, during a daily phone call, that Kamile heard her sister cry out.

"What is it?" Kamile asked, certain Jariyeh was talking to Mehmet.

"Pasha Zotin, hik teqe," Jariyeh repeated.

The phone line went dead.

Horrified, Kamile called Vera.

"Please go to Jariyeh's and see if she's okay. But pretend you're just stopping by," she added, not wanting to provoke Mehmet. Who were *they* to check in on his wife?

Kamile waited the longest five minutes, and grabbed the phone mid-ring.

"She's okay," Vera reported. "She said she'll talk to you later."

The sisters were one train stop away, and every day at 3:45 p.m., Jariyeh entered the third car of the B train at Bay Parkway. Kamile got on at 20th Avenue.

"Shka u ba?"--What happened, Kamile asked as she sat beside her.

"I was talking to you when I saw Mehmet walking around the house naked again. Then he stopped right in front of Lata."

Albanian parents never walked naked in front of their children. The thought of three-year-old Lata at eye level with a naked Mehmet sickened me.

"I said to him, 'For God's sake, get away,'" Jariyeh continued. "But he just stood there. When I said it again, he grabbed the phone from my hand and wrapped the cord around my neck."

She pointed to the red, squiggly marks around her throat. Jariyeh didn't say how she fought back. Didn't say if the children watched. Didn't say he tried to kill her. But the marks spoke volumes.

Kamile wondered if her call to Vera had saved her sister's life, but didn't ask. Knowing would've made her feel responsible for stopping everything that followed.

"I'm going to have a talk with Mehmet," Kamile said. Maybe she couldn't beat the hell out of him. But she could still give him a piece of her mind.

"No way. Please don't get involved," Jariyeh pleaded. She was already afraid for her children and herself and didn't need to worry about Kamile too.

"If you don't want to be with him, then leave."

"Thank you, sis," Jariyeh said, tears in her eyes. "Thank you for saying that. I'm not sure what I'm going to do. But I'm glad you understand."

The rest of the ride, the sisters fell silent.

A disgraced sister was better than a dead one, but Kamile felt helpless. She knew nothing could be solved without a man's involvement, but she didn't dare tell her brothers. Men too often spoke with guns.

A dangerously delicate situation.

———

It wasn't easy for Kamile to recall these memories. She shared them only with me, and only after thirty-plus years. Her stories came in drips—too disturbing to share in one sitting. They felt like a parallel reality. I never imagined Mehmet capable of this. How did we miss the signs? If I had known, I wouldn't have spent decades excusing a murderer—telling myself it was the drugs, it was the drug dealers. There was something seriously wrong with him. I later learned from Perparim that wrapping a phone cord around someone's neck was a Bici thing.

Vera told me about the worst thing Mehmet did to her. She had just turned twenty-two.

"Come over," Jariyeh said on the phone.

Vera suspected that she wanted to give her a birthday gift. She left her two-year-old and five-day-old sons asleep and rushed next door. Jariyeh surprised her with a dozen pink roses and a pair of hot pink sandals.

"Happy birthday, my soul," she said, kissing both her cheeks. "May you dance in these."

Just then, Mehmet walked in. "Oh, you're here?" he mumbled. "I just saw someone walking back and forth in your bedroom window."

Petrified, Vera left everything and sprinted home. At her bedroom door she froze, too scared to open it and find her sons gone…or worse—dead. Finally she walked in and found them sleeping. She called Jariyeh.

"The boys are okay," she said, sobbing.

"What is wrong with you?" Jariyeh snapped at her husband.

He said nothing. He had once respected us; now all he wanted was to wreak havoc.

This was the last birthday Vera would share with her best friend.

Four days later, Jariyeh would be dead.

Chapter 37

The Building

* * *

Giving up wasn't in Jariyeh's DNA. She'd fight to live. She'd fight to escape her marriage and save her children.

"There's something important I want to talk to you about," she told Sam on the phone. "But it has to be in person."

They met at a building in Brooklyn.

"Let's take the kids and run away," she said.

"We can't," he replied. "The kids will hate me for taking them from their father. We have to do this the right way."

A clean escape was the goal. But leaving Mehmet could get messy. Selman was paralyzed for simply calling off his daughter's engagement. Ending a nine-year marriage with three children could be catastrophic. No one—not Sam, not even her brothers—could take Jariyeh from her husband unless they were ready for war. The only way out was with his permission, which was nearly impossible to get.

"Let's not rush it," Sam said. "Maybe you should get your own apartment first. If you don't leave him for someone else, he might let you go."

That would've worked if Sam were her husband. But Jariyeh wasn't married to a Sam. She was married to an insecure, controlling addict and drug dealer who kept guns at home.

The meeting didn't go as Jariyeh hoped, but now she knew where he stood.

———

When I learned of this meeting thirty years later, I understood Sam's dilemma, but wished he'd been more courageous. My father had risked everything to save Nana. He married her as a runaway knowing he'd be hunted. Sam may have been trying to do it "the right way," but I wasn't sure if he loved Jariyeh.

I was told he agreed to marry her because his little sister asked him to in a letter—but that he began falling for Jariyeh after hearing how wonderful she was. Was that true? Two years later he was briefly engaged to his friend's sister because his friend asked him to. Then he left his long-time American girlfriend and married Hasi because Jerry asked him to. Did Sam ever choose love for himself? Or did he simply go along with what others wanted—like Zogu, like Mehmet? I later learned that some of his long-haul deliveries included drugs, thanks to Jerry.

Maybe Sam wasn't all I'd imagined. Was he what Jariyeh thought? What went through her mind as she walked out of that building? Was she devastated to realize there wasn't a man alive willing to save her? Or had she not expected much?

"Sam was just a backup plan," she told people. "Because Sam or no Sam, I'm leaving Mehmet."

But why risk a meeting that could have been her end? By then, affair rumors were already swirling. Most were unfounded until someone said they'd seen Jariyeh going into a building with a man. To most Albanians, that was proof enough. How did they know? Had Tefik, the Bici spy, followed Jariyeh and told Filanza? Had Filanza told her son? Or had Mehmet himself seen them go into the building? If he had, he knew the Kanun was on his side.

> Law §920: "If two people are caught committing adultery and are killed, their blood must remain unavenged."

The Bible says the same in Deuteronomy 22:22. But Dukagjin's Kanun took it further.

> Law §924: "The parents of the adulterous pair may not seek vengeance, but must give the murderer a new cartridge with the words, 'Blessed be your hand!'"

If Mehmet caught Jariyeh having an affair, he could kill her, and not only would my brothers not seek revenge, they'd replace the bullet he "wasted" and shake his "blessed hand." Grateful to him for removing our shameful family member from the face of the earth. Even if that wasn't how we felt, that's how we'd save face. Still, our family name would be disgraced. The Bici name revered. And Mehmet hailed as a hero. Not only by us, but by every self-respecting Albanian. Someone might even write a song about him. All he had to do was catch them in the act, and shoot.

He didn't.

"Look, Jariyeh, I don't care who you sleep with," Mehmet told his wife. "As long as you don't leave me. But if you leave, I'm taking the children."

"You can't do that," she begged. "I don't need a man, but I can't live without my children."

Days before she died Jariyeh called Saranda:

"I'm working. I can take care of the kids. There's no way I'm leaving them with that father. I don't want my boys to become like him. I have to find a way to make Mehmet let me go."

Then she called her mother in Kosova.

"Mehmet is sucking the life out of me. I'm going to take the money I gave you and run away with the children."

"Don't do anything," Nana told her. "Wait till I come back."

"Okay," Jariyeh replied. What's a few more days, she thought. If she could get Nana to agree that she should leave Mehmet, then Nana could convince the brothers.

Her mother was good like that.

———

Why would Mehmet say *I don't care who you sleep with* to a wife he loved? I asked everyone. No one had an answer. Finally I turned to Xavier, a former junkie.

"He may have loved her," Xavier said, "but once he got hooked, he could no longer care what she did. Heroin gave him what she couldn't: total acceptance. It became his everything. His God. His wife. His life."

For the first time in decades, it made sense.

Heroin didn't just numb—it rewired. Like a parasite desperate for its survival, it had eaten away at Mehmet without mercy until getting his next hit was his only goal. That had to be why he stopped caring if she got upset. Why he brought home addict friends and bags of cash. Why he walked around naked in front of the children. His ability to care or feel shame no longer existed.

Mehmet didn't need Jariyeh's love. He just needed her not to leave. Fear of humiliation was still alive and well.

Chapter 38

The Dream

* * *

"I had a dream," Jariyeh said, sitting at Kamile's kitchen table. She had told Saranda about it weeks ago but hadn't planned to share it with her sister—until now. She needed a favor.

Kamile placed the Turkish coffee cups on the table and sat beside her. The two didn't look like sisters. Kamile was a light-skinned strawberry-blond; Jariyeh had an olive complexion and thick brown hair. But in their hearts, they were nearly identical.

"Hajrë e baft Zoti,"--May God bless it, Kamile said, what we always said before letting anyone share a dream. We were superstitious like that.

"Hajrë paq,"--May you be blessed, Jariyeh replied as was appropriate before continuing. "I dreamt I was on a white horse with wings. He took me high up into the clouds to this beautiful place, where there was a big celebration with flutes and drums. People were singing and dancing around a big fire."

Kamile didn't think of dreams as the subconscious solving problems or offering insight, but she believed they foretold something—and so far, so good.

"There was a handsome man wearing a blue turban," Jariyeh continued. "He was singing and beating a drum. I sat next to him and sang along. I was *so* happy there. Then someone tapped my shoulder. I told him, 'I have to go, but I'll be right back.' When I woke up, Esat was tapping my shoulder."

"What do you think it means?" Kamile asked, smiling.

"It means I'm going to die."

"Tibe stikfurulah"--God forbid, Kamile said in our adopted Turkish. "I think it means things are going to get better."

"No. I'm pretty sure the horse took me up to heaven, because I knew the entire time that I was dead."

"Stop talking like that."

"Don't worry, sis. I'm not afraid to die. It was so beautiful there, and I knew it was where I belonged. I just worry about the children. I know Mehmet will want the boys, but I want you to take Lata."

Jariyeh knew the Bicis would never give up Esat and Perparim, but hoped they'd give up the girl.

"Don't be ridiculous," Kamile said. "Nothing's going to happen to you."

"But if something does, you have to take her. She can be the daughter you always wanted."

Kamile had two sons and often told her sister how much she had wanted a girl—someone to share her worries with in her old age, because boys could never understand.

"Nama besën,"--Give me your word, Jariyeh pleaded, "that if I die, you will take her."

Kamile knew giving her besa meant keeping it—and she couldn't do that. Even if American courts allowed it, the Kanun did not.

> Law §57: "If the woman dies after leaving a son or a daughter to her husband, her parents have the right to her silver jewelry."

And only her silver jewelry. Through the centuries, silver was replaced by gold and diamonds, yet children still belonged to their father. Taking any one of Jariyeh's kids could imply they weren't Mehmet's. Kamile couldn't risk people thinking her sister was an adulteress just so she could have a daughter.

Jariyeh knew the rules. But she no longer cared what the world would think. Why would she? She'd be dead. We would have to live with the consequences.

"You know I can't give you my word," Kamile said.

"But I won't be able to rest if I know Lata is going to be raised by those animals. You have to give me your word."

"Fine," she replied, just to shut her sister up. *"Ta jap besën,"*--I give you my word, Kamile said, although she knew she couldn't keep it. But it wasn't as if her sister was actually going to die.

"Thank you, sis." Jariyeh hugged her. "And when I die, I don't want you to worry about me. It's beautiful there. I'm going to sing and dance."

III. THE BLOOD FEUD

1981 At Jariyeh's grave in Staten Island.
Top L-R: Kamile, Zogu, Vera. Bottom L-R: Saranda, Nana, me.

BROOKLYN

SEP. 1979—FEB. 1981

Chapter 39

My Hero

* * *

I search my mind for a single moment with Jariyeh after I got back from Kosova, but nothing comes. I remember looking forward to seeing her again. I remember the family meeting in our apartment. That's it.

———

It had been the best summer of my life. So much had changed. I had grown past my "Shorty" nickname. My breasts filled an A-cup. I had met a boy I wanted to marry. Nana was proud of me. And most importantly: Jariyeh had become my hero. My life was opening up in ways I never thought possible.

It was a Monday night. Nana was at work. Bekim had come over and was sitting with Zogu in the living room. He normally didn't stay late on a weekday. I figured he was waiting to ask Nana about Kosova.

Around 11 p.m., Seba and her brother showed up. They lived a block away in Jariyeh's old building. It was strange for them to visit so late on a school night. I assumed they were eager to hear about my amazing trip.

"What's different about you?" Seba asked as we entered the family room.

"I don't know," I lied. I couldn't tell her about Fisnik—not in front of Luan. Or how lucky I felt to have a sister like Jariyeh. That would've felt like showing off. So I changed the subject. "Did you know girls in Kosova date?" It was Seba's cousin I was thinking of, but I didn't want to gossip. One of Nana's rules that I liked.

"I don't believe it," Luan said.

I didn't either. I had expected the Albanians from "back home" to be more traditional. After all, they lived in Old-World Europe. We lived in the New World, among Americanized Americans. We should've been the first to change, I thought, not realizing our parents clung to our traditions out of fear that we'd forget where we came from, marry Americans, and dilute our "superior race." There was little chance of that in Kosova. Was that why Europeans were free to evolve, and we remained frozen in time?

"I'm not surprised they date in Kosova," Seba said.

Of course she wasn't. At seventeen, Seba was dating a handsome older

American with a mustache. If I'd dared to break the rules, I would've dated him too. She once told me, "One day, you'll find out the world isn't perfect." Maybe not your world, I thought. But definitely mine.

When her father Tefik found out she was dating, he beat her with a belt, dragged her to the basement, and tied her to the pipes of the rat-infested boiler room that reeked of oil. He left her there for a week. Seba would've starved if her brother didn't sneak her food.

"Are you talking about my cousin?" Seba asked.

"Yes," I said, surprised she'd admit to such shame.

"Well, good for her."

Was it good for her, I wondered in all my righteousness. Should one think about themselves and not the family name? And if it was good, wouldn't we all be doing it? Wouldn't our families have let us?

Nana came home from work after midnight. She didn't seem pleased to see Seba and her brother. Setting her purse on the dining room table, she told Vera to make her coffee, then joined her sons in the living room. Moments later, Bekim called out to Vera, and she hurried back.

She returned to the kitchen, picked up the phone, and dialed. "Hi, Jariyeh. Bekim wants you to come over."

My heart skipped. I couldn't wait to see my sister.

When the downstairs buzzer rang, Nana came out.

"Go to sleep," she said firmly.

Why was she sending us to bed? She never cared when I went to sleep. And it wasn't like she cared if I got up for school. I wanted to see Jariyeh, but Nana wasn't someone you negotiated with.

Luan usually slept in the family room, but decided to crash in the bedroom Nana and I shared. I gave Seba a pair of pajamas that barely fit over her large breasts, and we climbed onto my twin bed. The boys lay on the floor cushions below. Behind us, muffled voices seeped through the living room wall.

Seba and I were whispering about her cousin's boyfriend when Luan hurled his pillow at us—hard, the only way he knew how to play. Seba swung hers right back at him, just as hard, then turned on her brother. I jumped out of bed and joined the pillow fight, laughing.

The door creaked open.

We froze.

"Flejni!"--Sleep, Nana snapped.

We scrambled back to our places without a sound.

Nana closed the door.

Hearing her footsteps fade down the hall, we giggled quietly.

Once the boys fell asleep, I whispered in Seba's ear, "I met a boy in Prizren."

"Really?" she whispered back, delighted that I might be corrupted.

"Yeah. He's tall, with blond hair and blue eyes," I said, feeling a little guilty for being so lucky.

"Did you kiss him?"

"No, I didn't kiss him." I blushed, wishing I had.

"Are you going to marry him? I bet he wants to marry you."

"He doesn't want to come to America," I replied. "And I don't think I could leave my family and move there."

"If you love him, you should go."

Easy for her to say, I thought. Her family wasn't as loving and fun as mine.

"I have a new boyfriend," Seba admitted, knowing I wouldn't tell.

Of course she did. I smiled, baffled by her nerve.

So I wouldn't accidentally push Seba off the twin bed, I pressed up against the wall, tucked the blanket around me mummy-like, and set my mind not to move while I slept. A trick I'd mastered after watching Seba's brother do it. It gave me a sense of control in a life where others controlled everything else.

Seba kept talking. She didn't have to go to school. Her father had pulled her out, afraid she'd shame him. When she noticed I was dozing off, she got quiet.

My mind drifted off to tomorrow. I was nervous about starting my sophomore year a few weeks late, but eager to go to my classes, pick up my textbooks, and catch up on homework. After school, I'll stop by Jariyeh's. I couldn't wait to tell her she was right—I found love in Kosova. Maybe she'll call Isa and find out if Fisnik is thinking of sending a matchmaker. She'll be thrilled to make that call.

I couldn't wait to be like my sister. To sing like her. To dance like her. To be loved the way she was. I had to start paying closer attention. Why had I given my sister such a hard time about babysitting? I'll never do that again.

Oh—and on the way to her house, I'll steal her a rose.

She loves roses...

"Wake up. Wake up, Hane," I heard a whisper.

Was it morning already? Why did I stay up so late?

I opened my eyes. The room was dark. All I could make out was Vera's silhouette.

"Jariyeh's dead," her voice quivered. "Mehmet killed her."

The words don't make sense.

My sister's drama with Mehmet Bici had ended.

What I didn't know was that ours was about to begin.

Chapter 40

Our New World

* * *

I t's morning.

My sister's body is gone.

The police and detectives have left.

Vera tells me, "Esat saw Mehmet jump out the window."

Poor kid, I think, imagining seven-year-old Esat in bed watching his father jump out their first-floor window. He must have been confused, but thank God there was a witness. Now the police can put Mehmet in jail.

I hear Zogu's voice in the foyer. I step into the doorway to see what's going on. He is standing by the shoes Vera had neatly lined against the wall. Sam is beside him. The women at the dining room table are silent, and Nana's eyes are fixed on her son. I watch Zogu slide a gun into his jacket.

It's our turn. Jariyeh was dead. She'd been chased like an animal at gunpoint. She rang our buzzer hoping we'd save her. No one let her in. Our super witnessed her murder and died of a heart attack. That somehow made it easier. Another person had died. Another family was grieving—not just ours.

Still, the weight of our loss is unbearable. Seeing Nana in agony makes it worse. I don't know if she'll ever recover. If any of us will.

The visitors are a distraction. I'm surprised to see Sam; he rarely came around. But I'm grateful that my brother won't have to do this alone. Albanians make such good friends, I think.

The blood feud everyone tried to avoid had happened. At least we're not on the receiving end. The Kanun allows for the heat of the moment. The first twenty-four hours, while the "blood is hot," it's open season on any male in the Bici household. But Zogu wants *atâ*--him. Like the devil, we won't say his name. That would be acknowledging his existence.

We all want Zogu to kill Mehmet. Maybe then the pain will lessen. Maybe then, we can breathe again.

But I'm confused.

The Kanun assumes free will, Law §917: "Blood is never unavenged." Yet the Koran assumes fate, surah 57:22: "No misfortune occurs...without being recorded in a decree before We bring it into existence."

Which one are we supposed to follow? The Kanun or the Koran? Separately, they make sense. Together, they are a disaster. Weren't they built on common truths? Truths that served to create good people. Truths that helped the lost be found and the confused to understand.

If God had written who Jariyeh would marry and when she would die, didn't that make Mehmet His accomplice? So where was my brother going?

Or was this also part of God's plan?

Did God want my brother to kill Mehmet, or was He setting Zogu up for his own demise?

My beliefs begin to unravel. If only time could stop long enough for me to figure things out. Or for someone to explain. But I dare not ask. Good girls don't question. They obey. *I'll understand when I'm older,* I tell myself. Surely the adults had figured things out before they preached to us.

Or had they?

They must have.

We can't be living a lie.

I watch my brother put on his shoes. He's not perplexed. For Zogu, the Kanun trumps the Koran, every time. I'd once found comfort in those honor codes. They made me feel proud. They made me feel special. Not ordinary, like the Americans around me. What I wouldn't now give for ordinary.

Zogu opens the front door.

I'm terrified. Why doesn't Nana stop him?

She looks at her son with admiration. He is avenging Jariyeh's blood. He is honoring the family name.

Isn't she scared of losing another child?

Hasn't Jariyeh's death shown her we're not invincible?

That good doesn't always win?

That God can't be trusted?

That life's not fair?

Please don't go! *I scream inside.*

The front door closes.

Chapter 41

Therapy Session

* * *

Less than eight hours after Jariyeh's death, the traumas kept piling up. Three children were motherless. A blood feud could get Zogu killed. And Kamile couldn't breathe. What next?

I was "volunteered" to go with her to Coney Island Hospital because I was "the smart one who went to school." Kamile wasn't well enough to drive. Zogu was out looking for Mehmet. Luan had taken Esat to the police station to make a statement. So we took the bus.

Why was my sister so weak? I wondered. I was a wreck, but I was sixteen. She was thirty, fourteen years older. If Nana was holding it together, why couldn't she?

At the emergency room, they sent us upstairs to psychiatry. I was relieved it wasn't something physical. *The mind was just the mind,* I reasoned. It wouldn't kill her. I couldn't lose another sister.

A bearded, middle-aged psychiatrist welcomed us in.

"So, tell me why you're here?" he asked, looking at Kamile.

"Kallëzoj,"--Tell him, she said.

She spoke English but thought I'd do a better job. I didn't want to translate—not now, not for this. I'd been translating for Nana since I was little and never enjoyed the pressure of finding the right words.

"Kallëzoj Shka?"--Tell him what? I asked, remembering that Nana also thought I could read minds.

"Për Xharijën"--About Jariyeh, she said, turning it into my therapy session.

"Our sister died last night," I started, feeling a lump in my throat.

"How did she die?" he asked.

I turned to Kamile. She nodded for me to continue.

"She was murdered." The words felt foreign in my mouth.

"I'm so sorry."

Americans say the strangest things. What was he sorry about? He didn't kill her. But surprisingly, his words were comforting. At home, everyone was too lost in their own trauma to comfort me.

"Please, continue," he encouraged.

"Her husband shot her," I explained, my voice breaking. "He chased her from their building to our building. She was ringing our buzzer." Part of me liked telling him the morbid details; another part was hoping for sympathy. I glanced at Kamile to see if I'd said enough.

She finally spoke. "I saw my sister dead."

So that was it. I was grateful I hadn't gone downstairs—and felt sorry that Kamile had to see it. No wonder she couldn't breathe.

"That's a very traumatic experience," he said gently.

His kindness gave me pause. Was he helping her, or was he feeding her weakness?

"What you're feeling is common," he explained.

Maybe for Americans, I thought. Albanians weren't like regular people. We didn't need psychiatrists. We didn't need help. We believed ourselves invincible. What would people say if they found out about this? Of course we would not tell a soul and embarrass ourselves.

"Did they catch her husband?" he asked.

I hesitated. Should I tell him we planned to kill Mehmet ourselves? What if he reports us? Americans don't understand.

"No, not yet," I said quietly.

I wanted to ask what he thought of fate. If I told him we believed God willed it, would he think I was crazy? I said nothing. It was Kamile's session—not mine.

"Take this," he said, scribbling on his prescription pad.

Kamile seemed relieved. Maybe because someone was acknowledging her pain. I knew I felt better.

But the pills made her numb, so she stopped taking them. How was she supposed to let out all that sadness if she couldn't feel a thing? Albanians understood the importance of expressing grief. At weddings, we knocked on car trunks and called out the Nuse's name to make her cry. At death, we hired professional criers to sing about the deceased and start a crying-fest. With Jariyeh, we didn't need the extra help.

"I'm glad there's nothing wrong with me," Kamile said once we got back on the bus.

"Me too," I said, but really I was disappointed. Why wasn't she stronger?

I was a sixteen-year-old know-it-all. I had no idea Kamile knew about Jariyeh's torture. I had no idea how helpless she'd felt watching it unfold—or the guilt she carried for not being able to stop it. As we sat in silence, she stared blankly out the bus window. If she was reliving any of it, she kept it to herself, like Jariyeh. And I, like a good girl trained not to ask questions, said nothing.

It would take me over thirty years to ask her about that night.

Chapter 42

Nana's Choice

* * *

Kamile was sleeping when the phone rang. Late-night calls typically meant death, but she wasn't worried. She thought it was Kosova, so she was surprised to hear her brother's voice.

"Come over," Zogu said, and hung up.

This can't be good, she thought. She and Elez left the boys sleeping and were out the door in seconds. Less than five minutes later, Elez turned onto Bay Parkway. Two blocks away, they saw police cars and flashing lights everywhere. Kamile's stomach dropped. It was worse than she imagined. As they got closer, she saw a bus double-parked in front of our building.

She got out of the car and walked toward the entrance.

As she passed through the building archway, she saw that the vestibule door was shattered. Inside, Zogu was speaking to a detective. Kamile stepped in and saw a sheet covering a body between the double doors. One hand stuck out from underneath.

"Hane!" she screamed.

"No," Zogu said quietly. "It's Jariyeh."

Kamile's legs gave out.

Someone caught her.

She didn't remember walking up the stairs or into our apartment. What she remembered was Nana sitting in the hallway, rocking back and forth, sobbing.

"Shka t'bana moj bi? Shka t'bana moj bi?"--What have I done to you, my daughter? What have I done?

Kamile sat beside her and cried.

She remembered visitors coming in, hugging her, and saying, "Keep your head." She remembered Roza at the dining room table, staring blankly. She remembered Luan walking in with Esat, Perparim, and Lata, and how the tragedy hit even harder.

"Your mom is with the angels now," Zogu told the kids. He and Nana didn't want the children to know their father had killed their mother.

Then the police.

"Do you want the children?" one of them asked Zogu.

The question reminded Kamile that they were in America—where the parents of a deceased woman had the right to more than just her silver jewelry.

Kamile prayed Zogu would say yes, so she could make good on her promise to Jariyeh.

"Mom, let's take the children," Zogu said. "I can raise them as my own."

When Kamile told me this years later, I was surprised that my honor-driven brother had been willing to go against Albanian tradition and do right by his sister. Jariyeh couldn't have wished for anything more than to have her hardworking, honest brother raise her boys.

"My daughter is dead," Nana said coldly. "I won't raise the children of Mehmet Bici."

The belief that children belonged to their father was so deeply ingrained in her that she couldn't see them as Jariyeh's children.

"I can take Lata," Saranda offered. She had a daughter the same age.

"No," Nana said. "You can't break them up. Where one goes, all of them go. And...*he's alive.*"

If Mehmet was dead, she would've kept them.

Kamile didn't remember exactly when the police came for the children. Someone packed their clothes, sheets, and blankets. She carried three-year-old Lata downstairs to the squad car. Zogu carried six-year-old Perparim and held Esat's hand.

"You have to go with them," Zogu said, tears running down his face. "They'll take you to your grandfather's house."

"I don't wanna go. I don't wanna go!" Perparim cried, squeezing his arms tighter around Zogu's neck.

Esat just stood there.

Esat took after his father. He'd stand in front of the mirror, with his arms crossed over his chest, wearing that don't-mess-with-me face and thinking he looked cool.

Perparim was like us. He had *gjakun e ambël*--sweet blood, as we called it when someone was especially lovable. "His hair sticks up like that because he's wild," Jariyeh would say with adoration. She loved that wildness. It meant he didn't conform. When he got into fights at school, she'd laugh and blame his hair.

"You have to go, Perparim," Zogu sobbed as he gently pried his fingers loose.

Lata was too little to know her mother was never coming back, or to understand why she was going to live somewhere else. She only cried because Perparim was crying.

But not Esat. He climbed quietly into the squad car. Not an emotion in sight.

Zogu and Kamile came upstairs weeping. Everyone dreaded letting the Bicis take Jariyeh's children, but no one dared challenge Nana. She was the authority. And she was "right." We may have been living in America, but we couldn't forget where we came from.

But she regretted it.

"How was I going to keep the children?" she'd say to Vera when they were alone. "Every time I'd see them, I'd be reminded of the man who killed my daughter."

I stood in the foyer, numb. Zogu disappeared into the living room in tears. Kamile walked Nana to the bedroom, trying to stay strong.

My heart sank.

The children I had helped raise were being sent to live with the enemy—and there was nothing I could do.

Jariyeh was gone. Now so were her children.

Would this horror never end?

Chapter 43

The Dead Are for the Dead

* * *

September 21, 1979—three days after death—the simple wooden casket was lowered into the ground two rows behind Baba. My beautiful sister had made her final move. She would forever rest at Baron Hirsch Cemetery in Staten Island, where Moslems and Jews peacefully coexisted due to similar burial rites.

We all went. Women were usually told not to attend because unlike men—we cried. Crying disturbed the souls of the dead, making them wonder what they had done wrong that we weren't rejoicing at their freedom from this earth. Nana told me it was a Moslem thing. I believed her. Religion hadn't been that important to us before, but everyone needed something to believe in once they realized things were out of their control. At death, when the soul transitioned to the afterlife—the one that truly mattered—we needed religious dogmas. Even if they were made up.

I believed my sister was in *xhenet*--heaven, with the angels. Baba told us God forgave everyone, but Jariyeh didn't need forgiveness. She had to be one of His favorites. She loved all His children and brought them joy. Where else would she be?

Now that my sister was gone, every morning was a disappointment. Every day, a heartache. Life persisted when it should have come to an end. The sun rose unrelentingly. Then set. Everywhere I turned, life insulted the significance of my sister's death. People said, "How are you?" as if it mattered. As if it were an ordinary day. Didn't they understand the magnitude of the tragedy? Maybe if they'd known her, it would've been different. Everyone continued to breathe, to eat, to drink. Even I joined in on the conspiracy. But I was different. I was aware of my body as it walked and talked like a robot—a robot with one consistent loop running in the background: *Jariyeh's dead.* The life I was looking forward to was gone forever.

Seven of us lived in the apartment, but I felt alone. I lay in bed facing the wall, curled in a fetal position, and cried. Wanting to get away from a world without my sister. Wanting to understand: *How could she be dead? Who was to blame? God or man? Did Jariyeh have a choice? Did we have a choice? Did Mehmet? If everything was destined—*

what was the point?

"Get up. Go wash the dishes," Nana said, finding a chore to force me out of bed.

I didn't want to, but didn't want to wasn't an option. I dragged myself up, did the task, then lay back down and put a pillow over my head.

"Get up," Nana said, not wanting to see me sad.

I obeyed, not wanting to make her angry. She hated weakness.

On the days when I couldn't get up, I pretended to sleep. I wanted my life to be over. How long would it take? Thirty years—I calculated. Jariyeh died at twenty-six. That was old. Four extra years were plenty. Enough for me to get married. Have children. Die. Why couldn't I just die already? That's where I'd end up anyway. Dead. All this waiting was just too painful.

Nana tried to motivate me. "The dead are for the dead, and the living are for the living," she said. It meant Baba would take care of Jariyeh, which gave me some relief, and we, the living, had to take care of each other. It meant we must go on. Easy to say, but even for Nana, hard to do.

She didn't have the heart to tell her sister in Kosova what happened over the phone. Instead, she wrote Teze Fatime a letter in her second-grade handwriting: "The druggie killed Jariyeh." Nana had taught herself to write at forty-five.

My mother's belief in heaven gave her hope for the "beyond." The place where her husband and daughter waited. The place where there was no blame.

But in this world, Nana blamed herself. The only person she confessed to again and again was her sister: "It was all my fault. It was all my fault."

She wasn't the only one. All the women blamed themselves.

Kamile carried the weight of being quiet. Of not doing something. What that something was, she wasn't sure—but still.

Saranda blamed her selfishness. If only she had listened to Nana that day in Staten Island, back when she was engaged. After lunch, Saranda's sister invited everyone downstairs for coffee, but Nana stayed behind with her future daughter-in-law.

"I found a better girl for Bekim," she told her. "This is what we'll do. You're going to leave my son. It's better that way. If you leave him, you can find someone to marry much easier than if he left you."

"He asked for me," Saranda replied. "I didn't ask for him. Let him leave me."

Now, Saranda wished she'd listened. If she had left Bekim, Jariyeh could have married Sam and been alive today.

And then there was Vera, haunted by the curse. If she hadn't called her mother, she wouldn't have cast the spell that made Nana "see" and made Nana "pay" with her daughter's life. Vera never brought up the curse, but was sure Nana hadn't forgotten. Her guilt was the reason for the constant ache in Vera's chest. She couldn't cry in front of Nana, who was already in agony. Instead, after her chores, she would walk around the block in the freezing cold wearing only a T-shirt, hoping the frigid air would pierce through her chest and take away her pain. It never did. But at least outside, Vera could scream:

"Why?! Why God?! Why?!"

Nana sent most of Jariyeh's belongings to Kosova so each time someone wore something of hers, her memory could live on. I wished I could've kept Jariyeh's records, but they were probably thrown away. Music was the only thing that might have helped me heal—but music wasn't allowed.

Thirty days was how long we had to keep from turning on the radio or television. It was a time to think about Jariyeh and the certainty of our death, Nana explained, not distract ourselves with "entertainment." It was this entertainment that kept us from the most important truth of all: that we would die and should be good, so we'd have a place in heaven. Being good wasn't hard for me. But I'd forget I was going to die—*all* the time. I was determined never to forget again. I didn't know if the thirty-day rule came from being Moslem, but Nana said this was how we mourned—and that was good enough. I hoped that after the thirty days, things would miraculously get better.

They didn't.

Jariyeh's murder was the ultimate defeat. Mehmet had not only killed our sister—he destroyed our spirit. He left a massive hole in our hearts that she once filled. We would never be the same.

There were no more nights out dancing at Il Galletto. No more New Year's Eve parties at Jariyeh's. No more jogging to the Verrazano Bridge. No more weekend fun in our apartment. We still gathered on Saturday nights, but the laughing and singing had come to an end. Celebrations of any kind brought on guilt. The men gambled in silence. The women watched TV. No one joked for fear of disrespecting someone's mourning. Any joy without Jariyeh was a harsh reminder of her death—a betrayal of her existence.

Tension filled the air, and despair made a home in our stomachs. We sank into a shared depression, not knowing if we'd ever be ourselves again.

Chapter 44

Mediators of Blood

* * *

Jariyeh was lucky to have three brothers who could avenge her murder. Whether or not she wanted them to didn't matter. Of the three, Bekim was the most Americanized and would leave it to the judicial system. Luan was old enough at eighteen, but twenty-four-year-old Zogu had his heart set on it.

If life were a movie, Zogu would've starred in a cowboy film, where the good guys wore white, the bad guys wore black, and good always won. He was an avid reader of Westerns and dressed the part in his black leather trench coat. He loved anything with Charles Bronson or Clint Eastwood. We watched *Dirty Harry, The Good, the Bad and the Ugly,* but his favorite film was *My Name is Nobody.* Zogu liked to think of himself as the "Nobody" who took on the gang of outlaws—a role he'd soon fulfill.

"You never shoot a man in the back," he once explained. "One shot, between the eyes."

I didn't know he was referring to the rules of the Kanun. A book my brother never read, yet knew by heart. Zogu liked rules. They gave him things to identify with, judge others by, and most of all, put order in his life. If he didn't have the honor codes to follow, he wouldn't know who to be. For Zogu, being Albanian came first, last, and filled up all the spaces in between.

After Jariyeh died, he stopped distracting himself with movies and watched the news, waiting for a lead. He had a man to kill. Being a father wouldn't stop him. Incarceration and death were a small price to pay for teaching his infant sons the importance of avenging their family blood. For when they grew up and were asked the inevitable question, *"A je burr, a je burrec?"*--Are you a man, or are you a bug? They'd know to answer, *"Unë jam Shqiptar!"*--I'm Albanian! Implying man. Implying tough. Implying they'd stop at nothing to ensure the honor of their family name.

If you were lucky to be born a man—you should act like one.

Zogu believed himself to be the epitome of a man and would make sure his sons were too. In their teenage years, he'd take them aside: "If any of you ever fucking think of being gay, I'll ship your asses to Albania and leave you there."

Vengeance was a noble act. It wasn't sneaky. It had protocol. You were to announce your name before killing the enemy, preferably with one shot to the chest or between the eyes—never the back. Afterward, you left the body face up. No boasting. No pride in what you'd done. *Gjakmarrja*--Vendettas were the most admirable means of settling disputes. Not to be confused with punishment for murder, but rather the satisfaction of family honor.

In the old days, murder was a business. Killers paid a fine of "six purses, a hundred sheep, and half an ox," plus a fee to the council who determined cause of death. Accidental deaths were forgiven after fees were paid. Premeditated murder required an additional fine. In blood. A murderer could ask for a twenty-four-hour truce to attend the wake. Or thirty days to put his affairs in order, like harvesting crops, before his hunt began.

Mehmet had to pay for the blood that wasn't his to take.

In Brooklyn, instead of elders, the 10th District Homicide Squad sent us Detective First Class Eddie Zigo. He had earned the title two years earlier after capturing the Son of Sam. We were happy to have him. If Zigo could catch a serial killer, surely he could catch a nobody like Mehmet. The Bicis told Zigo they hadn't seen him. Yet somehow Mehmet knew to show up at the 62nd Precinct with a lawyer. He pled not guilty, his family posted bail, and he was released. I was upset, but Zogu preferred him out and available to be shot. No prison or electric chair would do.

Just days after Jariyeh's murder, the Bicis sent Mati as their "mediator of blood." An elderly man my family knew, who knew the codes of "blood for blood." Zogu welcomed the guest and told Vera to make them Turkish coffee.

"Qofsh shnosh për motren"--May you be strong for your sister, Mati said, then delivered the message:

"Mehmet did not kill your sister. After he left your house, he went to gamble on Church Avenue."

Zogu couldn't believe it. What kind of Albanian didn't own up to what he had done? Where was Mehmet's honor? Zogu would have proudly admitted to the killing and allowed the hunt to begin.

"Mehmet would like to pay for Jariyeh's tombstone," Mati added, as if it were a favor.

Do the Bicis think I'm stupid, Zogu wondered. He'd heard the stories and understood what this offer truly meant:

> When several mediators had failed to convince the family the killing
> was an accident, the murderer sent a seasoned expert. During his visit,

the expert broke his coffee cup and reached into his pocket. "What are you doing?" the victim's brother asked. "I'm paying for the cup," the mediator replied. "No need. It was an accident," said the brother. The mediator stood up and left. Annoyed, the young man turned to his father. "Why didn't he ask us to pardon the blood?" Not that he planned to give it—but he wanted to be asked. "He didn't need to ask, my son. When you pardoned the cup, you pardoned your brother's blood."

Smart Albanians listened for what was said and unsaid. If Zogu let the Bicis pay for the tombstone, it meant one thing: he accepted Mehmet's innocence. He pardoned the blood. An easy out if Zogu were afraid to kill, or had no honor.

"We don't need his money," Zogu told the mediator.

"Please, Zogu, let these things pass," Mati said.

My brother would *never* "let it pass," even if God Himself came down and told him to. Every night in bed, Zogu turned his back to his wife and cried himself to sleep. Killing Mehmet was his remedy.

"I don't know what to tell you," Zogu said. "Jariyeh wasn't just a sister. She was my friend."

Mati reported to the Bicis: "Zogu won't let you pay for the tombstone, but he never mentioned revenge. Only that Jariyeh was his friend."

The Bicis didn't know what that meant.

Mati returned the following week, reiterating Mehmet's innocence.

Zogu didn't say "boo." He wouldn't lie and say, "I'm not seeking vengeance," or show off and say, "I'm going to kill him." The Bicis knew what they'd done— let them figure it out. Preferably after Mehmet was dead. The last thing Zogu wanted was for him to go into hiding.

In the old days, murderers sought refuge in churches, safe houses, or built *kullë-*-stone homes with slits for windows. However, proud families, even mothers, would rather see their sons die than resort to such cowardly acts. They could leave the country, but with the invention of planes, trains, and automobiles, their rival would soon follow.[xvii] The other option was to simply become the enemy's guest.

> Law §620: "If a guest enters your house, even though he may be in blood with you, you must say to him, 'Welcome!'"

Nana told me the story of a man who went to his rival's house for refuge and, per law, was welcomed, given food, and a place to sleep. He never left their home and died of old age—or married the daughter. I forget which. Would we have taken Mehmet in if he knocked on our door? I wouldn't think so, but knowing Zogu's love for honor, it was possible.

The Bicis kept sending mediators to make sure Zogu wasn't planning to kill Mehmet. They didn't think anyone else from Lutfi Feza's family was a threat.

They didn't know our women.

One morning, Nana and Vera were sipping Turkish coffee at the kitchen table.

"All I can think about is how to kill him," Nana said. "So far, the best I've come up with is to throw a hand grenade in their apartment. That way, all the Bicis die."

That was brilliant, I thought. This way there was no one left to take revenge. As I imagined the explosion bursting out of their apartment door, I remembered one detail.

"What about the children?" I asked, wondering how she'd overlooked it.

"They have *his* blood," she callously said.

"But they have Jariyeh's blood too," I countered.

Nana shot me a look.

To save myself—and find out if Jariyeh's children were in danger—I asked, "Where would you get the hand grenade?"

"I don't know yet," she answered.

Nana's obsession was so great that she began to wonder if, in God's eyes, praying before bed with all that hatred in her heart was "bad." Not to be a hypocrite, she stopped praying so she could be free to loathe this man and plan his murder. But she continued listening to the Mevlud.

On the 40th day after Jariyeh's death, Imams recited the hour-long *Mevlud*--Birth of the Prophet prayer at the Albanian American Islamic Center. The Mevlud was recorded, and several copies made. Every Friday, the Moslem holy day, Nana and Vera listened to their cassette and prayed along. Kamile and Roza did the same in their homes, hoping it would bring Jariyeh peace.

Like Nana, Kamile was preoccupied with killing *atâ*--him. She thought about it all the time and looked for Mehmet everywhere.

One day, Kamile was double-parked on Albemarle Road when she saw Mehmet drive past in a car she didn't recognize. Her wheels screamed as she slammed on the gas and headed straight toward him. Her own safety didn't matter, so long as the crash would kill that motherfucker. But a parked car suddenly pulled out in front of her, forcing Kamile to a screeching halt. When Mehmet's car pulled over and the door opened, she began trembling. How could I have missed this chance? she thought. Does he have a gun? She was dreading the sight of his face—and was confused by the yarmulke.

"Lady!" the driver yelled. "Are you crazy?"

Realizing she almost crashed into a stranger, Kamile's shaking intensified. She remained parked until it subsided. After that, Kamile stopped looking for Mehmet—if only to keep her sanity.

While Nana plotted and Kamile recovered, I prayed.

"Please God, kill Mehmet."

I didn't care how God did it—I just didn't want my family to be the cause. An illness. A car accident. Anything would do. I'd fall asleep praying for Mehmet's death, only to be bombarded with nightmares. There was always lots of running. Lots of blood. Whose blood, I couldn't always tell. But Mehmet did most of the chasing, most of the shooting. Some nights he killed Jariyeh. Other nights it was Zogu, Nana, or myself. On the worst nights, there were massacres and a whole bunch of us died. I'd wake up in a cold sweat, my heart pounding, relieved to find it was just a dream.

On the rare occasion, Mehmet died.

Those mornings I'd wake up happy for a few seconds before reality set in. One morning, his death felt so real that I walked all the way to the bedroom door and placed my hand on the doorknob when the thought came: *Is he really dead?* I searched my mind for the cause of death...*he was shot*, my mind answered. But who shot him? *Zogu did*, came the reply. Who told me...who told me? I interrogated further. Someone must've told me. As I rifled through my memory, two realities coexisted: One with Mehmet dead. One with him alive. Without enough memories to support his death, a heaviness began to set in. Still hopeful, I walked to the kitchen. Nana was there. The defeated look in her eyes confirmed the reality we had all agreed upon.

He was alive.

He was out there somewhere—still tormenting us with his existence.

Chapter 45

Ivory Girl

* * *

Lafayette High School gave me a reason to get out of bed. But every time I passed the broken vestibule door, I was reminded of my sister's horrific end. *When will they change that door already,* I wondered. But the super was dead, and we didn't have the heart to ask his son. None of my teachers asked me what was wrong or sent me to see a therapist. Maybe school therapists didn't exist yet, or perhaps they had bigger worries, like gang activity that would eventually close Lafayette for good.

I still loved school, but my enthusiasm for learning had vanished. I could no longer focus. My grades began to fall, even in math, which I adored. Math had rules. Math didn't lie. Even though I could never add, subtract, or multiply in my head, I excelled in algebra and trig. There was beauty in using formulas to solve for x, and the thrill of knowing the rules would work every time. But what about the rules that didn't always work? The ones we used in life. I had trusted the Albanian honor codes and God's laws, and what did that get me? What did that get Jariyeh?

I dropped the advanced trig class. I dropped the violin and chorus.

Everything I loved.

I'd sit at my desk, pulling apart my split ends, wondering why I was going to school and wasting my time. Nana's time. Zogu's time. Everyone's time. What good was an education when college wasn't even an option? It didn't matter that I was smart.

"Husbands don't want smart wives," Nana explained.

Not smart. Not strong.

Well, wasn't that too bad. I was smart *and* I was strong. Not Luan-strong, but I believed I could beat the hell out of any man who dared hit me. Is that what Jariyeh was like? I wondered. It was hard to be submissive when you had our mother's blood running through you.

Teze Fatime told me that Nana once threatened to kill Baba.

When my parents first married, Baba had called their brother Hamdi a motherfucker. That was the worst thing you could call an Albanian. There must have been a good reason, because my father never cursed. Nana didn't respond. She waited until Baba fell asleep, then took his rifle and aimed it at his head. It was the cocking of the trigger that woke him.

"What are you doing?" he calmly asked.

"Don't you *ever* curse my brother," she warned.

"Fine. Now come to bed," he said, and didn't speak of her brother again.

I could never aim a gun at my husband, but hitting him like Luan taught me—from the hip, locked wrist—would be no problem. Everything was falling into one of two categories: destroy or be destroyed. That's what happens when your sister is murdered and you're left helpless. I needed to feel that women weren't expendable. I needed to feel safe. Was that why I was attracted to shy boys?

I had a crush on Shaun, an Irish boy who blushed every time he saw me in the hallway. He had acne, but I didn't mind others' imperfections—only my own. One day, his gym class joined ours. I was excited. First, because he'd be impressed with my athletic skills. Second, because I'd be wearing gym shorts and he'd see my sexy legs. The only problem was that they were hairy. I wasn't allowed to shave until I got married, so I wore the long tube socks and kept pulling them up to my knees.

When Shaun and I made eye contact on the baseball field, we both blushed. I knew I couldn't date him, let alone marry him. But I believed that Shaun would've wanted to marry me. *Didn't all boys want submissive girls?*

I didn't wear makeup or style my hair. It wasn't allowed. That would have to wait for my Nuse transformation. Everything good came after marriage. That was the trick to getting girls to submit to Nuse life. Parents kept you locked up, so you prayed for a husband who would take you out—maybe to the movies or the beach. Maybe he'd let you wear a two-piece. Though that might be pushing it. But if you married someone who beat you or kept you locked up, you were shit-out-of-luck. Still, at least you got to put on makeup, wear fancy jewelry, and own clothes you could wear inside those four walls you kept so white.

The kids at school called me the Ivory Girl, like the women in the Ivory soap commercials. They were the epitome of what Albanian girls were supposed to be: plain, clean, and untouched. One day, a substitute teacher said how refreshing it was to see a beautiful girl not wearing any makeup. When my classmates turned to look at me, I felt my face and back heat up. Other days, they didn't seem to notice. Maybe because I slouched to hide my tiny breasts. Maybe because I wore only sneakers and dressed modestly—except for my tight Jordache jeans and Sergio Valentes. Nana and Zogu let me wear them at school, never at home where Albanians could see.

The "cool kids" sat on parked cars, smoking pot. I never understood how addiction made one cool. I didn't need to be cool—*I was already Albanian.* But my

Albanian pride was waning, and anger was setting in. Did Albanians know what they were doing? Or did Americans? I struggled with belonging and being different, not knowing where I fit in. Maybe that's why I gravitated toward the underdogs—the rejects.

Lorraine, the chunky Italian girl. Stephanie, the frizzy-haired Jewish girl with braces. Ellen, who spoke funny because of her cleft lip. I felt the worst for her. How terrible it must be to be born with an imperfection, I thought. If only she were Albanian. All she'd have to do was be a good cleaner, and someone would surely send a matchmaker.

I loved my friends and wanted the best for them.

"Stop smoking," I said to Lorraine, as I yanked the cigarette from her mouth and stomped it out.

I didn't want her to die of lung cancer like Baba, or to chase anyone's approval—never realizing I did that all the time. Maybe because I thought the things I did were smart and brought my family honor. Not dumb, like smoking or doing drugs. You lose yourself when you do drugs, and I didn't want to lose myself. Surely Mehmet would never have killed Jariyeh if he hadn't been high.

At the end of last period, my friends proudly walked with me—the pretty one—to the bus stop.

"My sister died," I told Lorraine.

"I'm so sorry. How old was she?"

"She was old—twenty-six."

"How did she die?"

My throat tightened. Every time someone asked that, tears filled my eyes. I'd say her husband shot her—never more. Never that my brother was trying to kill him. Never that my sister wanted to leave her husband. Never that she might have been alive if we were American. Never that I was beginning to question what it meant to be an Albanian girl.

Chapter 46

Brick in the Wall

* * *

Every time Zogu left the house, I feared he'd never return. Would today be the day Mehmet killed him, or the day he killed Mehmet and went to jail? I tried to find comfort in the idea that once I married, my husband would think twice before killing me, knowing my brother would avenge my blood. But even that wasn't helping. I wished Mehmet would go to jail already, so Zogu could stop hunting him.

Except for Nana, we were all scared for Zogu. But none of us said a thing. Why would we? He wouldn't listen, and it would've sounded like we didn't care about Jariyeh, or our family name.

Zogu never told us when he went on stakeouts, and for that, I was grateful. But one day, as he and his friends put their shoes on in the foyer, I knew exactly where they were headed. While Nana beamed with pride, I watched with dread.

After they left, I went to my room and pulled out the clock radio I kept hidden under my bed so I could get lost in the music. I was always trying to get lost in the music. During the week, I'd watch Sonny & Cher, Donny & Marie Osmond, The Partridge Family, and The Monkees. On weekends, I watched American Bandstand and Soul Train with the better dancers, wishing I could be one of them.

While Nana eagerly awaited news of Mehmet's death, I lay in bed with the radio turned low and a pillow over my head.

"Another Brick in the Wall" by Pink Floyd came on. Only in America could anti-establishment bands exist. You'd never find one in Albania or Yugoslavia. When I saw President Tito's portrait on my cousin's wall in Kosova, I asked, "Why do you have a picture of *him*?" Not realizing Tito was fair to Albanians—unlike Milosevic who later tried to wipe out our entire race. Isa quietly replied, "Never say that to anyone else." That spooked me. It was then I understood the power behind freedom of speech. In America, we didn't have to hang a picture of President Carter in our house, and we could criticize him if we wanted. The people came first. No wonder America flourished.

As Pink Floyd sang about *not needing an education* or *thought control*, I sang along in my head, not quite sure what they meant. I loved school. What could possibly be wrong with education? And how could anyone control your thoughts? I was sure mine were my own.

I didn't realize I'd been brainwashed into Albanianism. A cult that groomed men to dominate and women to obey. I never questioned it and looked forward to obeying my husband. To serving his family. To keeping my mouth shut. That's how I'd honor my father's name. *It* mattered more than I did.

I didn't see the damage it was doing to my soul—or to the souls of our women. It was hard being a nobody. A nothing. In our husbands' houses we had no rights, only duties disguised as discipline. Our suffering was dismissed, but if we were killed, our fearless brothers would rise up to avenge us. I thought of that as love. As proof that I mattered, not making the connection that first—I had to be dead. Or that it wasn't me they were avenging as much as the family honor.

As I listened to Pink Floyd *beg the teachers to leave the kids alone*, I found myself wishing my family would sometimes leave me alone. I was cooped up in that house: cleaning, babysitting, not asking questions, not having friends—and I was starting to see Albanian traditions as bricks in my wall. Bricks that kept me hostage. Bricks that kept me small.

I was born under a waxing moon, which symbolized new beginnings, but I didn't yet have the courage to change a thing. I didn't know my mother had broken every rule when she married. Luckily, she had Baba to save her. Jariyeh had no one. Who did I have? It was best I kept my head low.

Still, something in me was waking up.

I thought back to when I had asked Nana, "Where do our traditions come from?" I needed to understand why honor demanded more death—why Zogu had to risk his life to kill Mehmet.

"The Kanun," she replied, somewhat annoyed, and walked away.

What was this Kanun? Was it a book of rules? How did laws work? When did humanity fall from the grace of knowing right from wrong? I didn't need the Ten Commandments. What was so hard about *Do unto others as you'd have them do unto you?* That's what Baba believed. He put goodness over the illusion of honor found in the ancient Kanun.

Albanians still clung to 500-year-old laws needed to survive the unforgiving mountains, back when there was no government, no jail, no police. But that was then. And this was America. We had come to this great melting pot, yet we didn't melt so well. Change was hard. Undoing centuries of brainwashing was harder still. That's why Zogu couldn't stay home and let the American legal system do its job. He had to avenge Jariyeh's blood to prove our family was honorable. To prove our madness worked.

Lying in bed, I waited for the front door to open. It felt like Zogu was gone forever. Just in case I hadn't heard him come home, I went to the kitchen for a glass of water. He hadn't.

I slipped back under the covers and turned the radio on.

"There's something for everyone," the Avenue I flea market commercial came on. I switched to 102.7—"Plop plop, fizz fizz..." Did all the stations play ads at the same time? I flipped back to 106.7.

Rod Stewart came on, singing that I was "in his heart and in his soul." Jariyeh once joked, "He must be Albanian," because heart and soul--*zemer* and *shpirt* was what we said to those we loved. I remembered dancing to "Do Ya Think I'm Sexy" at my sweet sixteen, and how my seventeenth birthday had passed without notice, except for the Carvel cake Kamile brought over.

It was around that time she told me about Jariyeh's dream and how Jariyeh had known she was going to die. I wanted to believe her dream was a premonition, that we couldn't have changed a thing.

"There's no escaping what's written," Nana said, then backed it up with a story:

> A mother was told her newborn baby would die in the well. Panicked, she covered the well with a heavy wooden board. When the child turned two, he tried to lift it. Unable to, he climbed on top of it, lay down, and his spirit left his body.

Fate made my sister's tragic end easier to accept. Even Shakespeare said, "All the world's a stage, and the men and women merely players." Didn't that mean everything was scripted?

I wanted to believe Mehmet had carried out God's plan, because if he had acted on his own, then we were at the mercy of flawed human beings, and so many things could go wrong. Belief in the divine organized the chaos.

How did beliefs work? Everyone had their dogmas, so who was right and who was wrong? What one called an honor killing, another called premeditated murder. What one called selfish, another called empowering. Bekim didn't think it was disgraceful to choose his own wife. Did his believing it make it so? And why did people who prayed, fasted, and dressed modestly believe they were closer to God? Believe they were more deserving of heaven? More honorable? Where was their humility?

Being a proper Albanian girl was hard, but I endured because I believed it honored my family, and that made me better.

The buzzer rang.

I jumped out of bed and cracked open my bedroom door.

"It's me," I heard Zogu's voice over the intercom.

We had made it through another day.

Now there was the worry of tomorrow.

Chapter 47

The Detroit Mediator

* * *

I knew Zogu was hunting Mehmet, but I didn't know the details, even decades later. It was too heavy a subject to bring up out of nowhere, so I gave him an early draft of this book, hoping he'd see I was trying to honor our sister.

He called me when he finished. When Zogu said he never knew Jariyeh liked Sam, I realized no one had the entire picture. Was it up to me to piece it together?

His first question was everyone's question: "Why are you writing this book?"

I choked up.

"Because Jariyeh's death changed my life," I replied.

I didn't say I needed to know why Mehmet killed her. I didn't say her death made me question God and the Kanun. I didn't say it forced me to stand up for myself.

I couldn't help but cry, and could tell he was also emotional. Her death had changed him too. Not wanting to ask too much, I settled on a simple question. "How many times did you try to kill Mehmet?"

I didn't expect him to dive right in.

"I never left the house without my German Luger..." he began.

———

Zogu never left the house without his German Luger—a gun preferred by the Nazis for the accuracy of its skinny barrel. My cowboy brother had always liked guns. After Baba died, he brought home a .38 Smith & Wesson, turned the TV way up, stood a paddle-ball racket at one end of the room, and shot at it from the other. At first, Luan and I hid behind the couch and covered our ears. Afterward, Luan took shooting lessons. I ran to a corner in my bedroom, grateful to be a girl who wasn't expected to shoot guns.

After Zogu married, he bought two hunting rifles and a reloading kit. He showed Luan and me how to make bullets, explaining that too little gunpowder wouldn't do the job, and too much could blow his hand off. We carefully weighed the powder and slowly compressed it into the cartridge shell, afraid too fast might make it explode. I was honored by Zogu's trust, but when he brought home venison and rabbit, I felt bad for contributing to their death.

After Jariyeh died, Zogu went to the shooting range until he considered himself a marksman. All he needed was to find Mehmet, so he asked a select few to be on the lookout.

One day, Ramiz, who prided himself on always packing, came for a visit with quiet Ramadan.

"Do you still want to kill him?" Ramiz asked a ridiculous question.

"Of course," Zogu said.

"I know where he is. I'll take you there."

Zogu got his Luger and gave Ramadan his Smith & Wesson.

"We'll be back," he told Nana, who smiled at her courageous son.

I watched him leave, praying it wouldn't be for the last time.

The three men parked across the street from the restaurant.

"You stay here," Ramiz said. "We'll see if Mehmet's still inside."

"Fine," Zogu replied. "But if he's there, don't come out right away or he'll know something's fishy. I'll wait half an hour, then I'll come in."

"Do you want me to kill him?" Ramiz asked another ridiculous question.

"No, I wanna kill him myself," Zogu said. "If you want to do something, cover my back."

He watched Ramiz and Ramadan go inside, then checked his watch. Half an hour was a long time. Killing a man wouldn't be as easy as killing deer and rabbits. But Mehmet wasn't just any man. He was a lowlife who didn't deserve to breathe another breath. Zogu had imagined this moment hundreds of times. He longed for his face to be the last thing Mehmet saw—and for what he had done to his sister to be the thing Mehmet thought.

Zogu glanced at his watch. Only ten minutes had passed. Looking toward the restaurant he saw Ramiz and Ramadan walking toward him. A wave of disappointment hit.

"He wasn't there," Ramiz said.

If Mehmet wasn't there, why had they stayed so long, Zogu wondered, but didn't want to question a friend who was trying to help.

A few days later, Ramiz stopped by with news: "Mehmet has been asking around why I was looking for him."

Zogu wasn't sure what to think. It was hard to know with people like Ramiz who were always trying to prove something. Did Mehmet find out because Ramiz had told someone to show off? Had Ramiz foolishly asked about him at the restaurant? Or was he lying? Maybe he was trying to sound like a hero, hoping Zogu would feel indebted? As if to say, *Look what a good friend I am, risking my life for you.* As much as Zogu hated liars, he hoped Ramiz was lying. The last thing he wanted was for Mehmet to know he was hunting him.

The truth revealed itself soon enough.

Within days, a mediator in a three-piece suit showed up. Zogu had never seen the man before, but welcomed him and told Vera to make coffee. The man introduced himself as a professional mediator from Detroit. The Bicis were spending money on mediators left and right. This one must have cost the most, but they could afford it. The Bicis had stacks of hundred-dollar bills that they kept ironed and stashed in their apartment.

Zogu figured they'd flown in a professional because they knew Ramiz was looking for Mehmet and wanted to know whether Zogu was trying to kill him. He was curious to hear what message the Bicis had sent, now that they suspected he wasn't buying Mehmet's "I didn't do it" story.

"Your sister was having an affair," the mediator began the Bicis' new song and dance.

Affair? What affair? A typical, shady Bici move. Men with no honor changed stories with the snap of a finger. Mehmet went from being "innocent of murder" to "a victim of adultery." Suddenly Jariyeh was a whore and Mehmet an honorable man. How convenient.

But Zogu wasn't having it.

"If he killed my sister because of an affair, I would've paid for his bullet. But he killed her at my door," he told the Detroit man, who surely knew the rules.

> Law §923: "The adulterous pair remains unavenged only if they were killed in the act and with a single shot."

That was the protocol. But Jariyeh was not caught in the act. She was home with her husband and children. Nor was she killed with a single shot. She was chased and riddled with bullets.

Prince Lekë Dukagjin understood the importance of details; otherwise, husbands could kill wives at their whim. Like vendettas, honor killings were dignified acts.

> Law §928: "If one of the adulterers escapes, the murderer may not kill him afterward without incurring the blood feud...."

Mehmet owed us blood. Honor wasn't flexible. It had rules, boundaries, and consequences. The Bicis would stop at nothing to end the blood feud and save their criminal son. But rumors and fantasies didn't count. The affair excuse was cowardice wrapped in custom. Mehmet wasn't following the codes. He was trying to hide behind it.

Zogu didn't say, "Mehmet owes me blood," but the seasoned mediator reported back to the Bicis: "That guy is definitely trying to kill Mehmet."

Zogu knew killing Mehmet would now be harder, but there was no question: he had to die—not just for the shame he was trying to cast on Jariyeh's legacy, but for what that would mean for us and future generations. The Bicis hadn't thought it through. If my family called off the feud, it would mean accepting both their affair excuse and the disgrace.

Now, more than ever, Zogu had to kill Mehmet and set the record straight.

Days after the Detroit mediator left, Vera filled me in.

"Mehmet said he killed Jariyeh because of an affair."

"Why would he say that?" I asked.

"I'm not sure," Vera replied. "But I know Jariyeh was in love with Sam."

Sam? How was that possible? We hardly ever saw him. But if she was in love with him, I couldn't blame her. He was so handsome.

"She wanted to marry Sam," Vera continued, "but Nana made her marry Mehmet."

That broke my heart. They would have made the perfect couple. What a terrible fate—to love another and be trapped in that marriage.

One afternoon, I came across the lyrics Jariyeh had written for me.

♪ *N'atë anë detit*	♪ Beyond the ocean
natë anë bregut	beyond the shore
Kish fillu hana me dal	The moon began to rise
Vjen nji djal	Approached a boy
por si bir mretit	like the son of a king

Was this song about Sam? I wondered. He lived across the river in Staten Island and looked like the son of a king. Was Jariyeh using songs to express what she couldn't say out loud? I pictured my siblings singing along—oblivious to her pain.

Me nji vajzë po rrin tu kja	With a girl he sits and cries
Vajza thot na kan diktue	The girl says people are talking
E pra tash duhet mu nda	And now we must part
Djali thot, jo zemra ime	The boy says, no my heart
Ti martohesh un beqar ♪	You will marry, but I will not ♪

Was that why Sam waited so long to marry?

Had they had an affair? Would it have been better for Jariyeh to be alive and "disgraced" or dead and "honorable"?

I was sure Jariyeh was happy in the afterlife, but wished she'd been happy here, with us, while she was still breathing. A part of me wanted my sister to have had love, even if it meant adultery. But if she'd been caught, it would've branded us as a family of promiscuous daughters. My Nuse status would have plummeted, and all the time I'd spent trying to be the "perfect girl" would've been for nothing. Yet even without proof, Mehmet's accusation was tainting my worth. Now I had to be extra good to prove that we weren't that kind of family. That I wasn't that kind of girl.

Up until the mediator said it, an affair was not on our radar.

The women knew Jariyeh loved Sam, but love didn't equal affair. And what Mehmet did—chasing her to our door, riddling her with bullets—was no honor killing.

Chapter 48

The Cartel Theory

* * *

After Jariyeh's death, every memory felt different.

At first, we believed Mehmet had killed her because she wanted to leave. That reason was the only one that made sense.

But then the women began to talk.

They had kept quiet while Jariyeh was alive. Now they shared what they knew, desperate to understand. With Jariyeh dead, everything carried weight.

Nana told Vera about the envelope with the $10,000. About the gun she had given her for protection. About Jariyeh's phone call to her in Kosova—and how she regretted telling her to wait.

"Mexico wasn't a vacation," Vera repeated. "It was a drug deal."

A chill ran through me.

Was I partly to blame? If I hadn't agreed to take the kids to Lulu's House, would she still be alive?

"Jariyeh started fearing for her life after the car accident at Lulu's," Vera said.

The thought that he might have been trying to kill her long before that night was unsettling. How did we miss the signs?

Kamile said Jariyeh wanted to move to Canada.

Canada? Why would she move that far away?

The stories eventually made their way to my brothers.

We all began to question Mehmet's motive. What had happened in that limo? Had he tampered with her brakes? Why Canada? Were they running from the drug dealers? Had she seen too much? Threatened to go to the police?

And finally, the unthinkable:

Did the cartel want her dead?

Three and a half years later, on March 14, 1983, we got confirmation.

"Someone sliced Mirushe's throat," Vera said. "They think it was the drug dealers."

I remembered the petite Mirushe and her three children at Lulu's House, and my blood ran cold. What kind of people had Mehmet gotten Jariyeh mixed up with?

The rumor was that while her husband Nicky was in prison, she was pressuring the cartel to get him out. So they killed her.

My family concluded they had also wanted Jariyeh dead—and had used Mehmet to do it. We believed he loved her. That he wouldn't have done it on his own.

The drug-dealer premise was easier to live with than an affair that disgraced our family. Easier to live with than admitting Jariyeh wanted to leave and we hadn't helped her. My family accepted it and moved on.

But I needed proof. Something. Anything.

———

Thirty years later, I set out to find it and began searching for the members of the Kosova Connection.

I couldn't talk to Jerry. He was killed in a shootout in Tirana, Albania, on September 26, 1982, while trying to assassinate President Enver Hoxha.[xviii] The Communist regime claimed he shot himself so he wouldn't be deemed a hero.

I tracked down Benny's pizzeria in Jersey and learned that he and his wife had both passed. Their son gave me a free slice and spoke about how devastated his parents had been when they heard about Jariyeh. When I asked why none of the Lulu's House couples came to her funeral, he didn't have an answer. I wondered if it was guilt.

I messaged Mirushe's children on Facebook. Her daughter, *Shiqere*--Candy, called me right away and told me what happened to her mother.

Her dad was incarcerated in Canada when he convinced Mirushe to quit waitressing and run his drug business. She fronted Joey Lika drugs, but he wouldn't pay up. "Give me my money. Motherfucker!" she told the man her husband used as a hit man. Weeks later, around 3 a.m., Mirushe drove friends home after a night of gambling and parked in her building's garage. She was walking toward the exit when a man came up behind her. He sliced her throat and stabbed her in the chest eleven times.[xix] Near her body, police found a cigarette burned down to ash on top of her Coke can.

"The worst part was," Candy added, "my dad said she was having an affair, and deserved to die."

I was stunned. Had "affair" become the Albanian man's default excuse for murder? I was sure Nicky said it to avoid being next, and Mehmet said it to stop the blood feud. For these selfish men, their wives' legacy and what it meant for their children didn't matter.

"My brothers will no longer talk to my dad," Candy said. "But I visit him." Nicky was back in jail, this time in the States.

She agreed to ask him about Jariyeh, then forgot and promised to do so the following week. I patiently waited, then called a few times. No answer.

Her brother told me about his lifelong search for his mother's killer. I told him I'd been waiting for Candy to ask their father about my sister.

Days later, he texted me: "My sister passed away."

He wasn't sure if it was Covid.

My last hope was Joey Lika, the hitman with a temper. I'd never met him, but I was sure he'd talk. I just needed to find out where he was doing his life sentence, but the internet was no help. A friend told me about a former convict, JR, who hated Mehmet Bici. I reached out on Instagram. He replied:

> "I don't know Joey's location. But as far as that f'ing piece of shit Bici, I crossed paths with him once. Sorry for not putting a shank in his back."

Whoa, I thought. Then again, for JR, shanking someone was probably just a Tuesday. His response made me smile. Albanians were truly either your worst enemy or your fiercest ally.

My Kosova Connection leads dried up. Like the affair excuse, the dealer theory was crumbling.

I still didn't know why Mehmet killed my sister.

Chapter 49

The Tombstone

* * *

We often went to visit Jariyeh in her new home—a lump of dirt—and took solace in the belief that she was in the best company of all: Baba. Twice a year, during the holy Bajram holidays, while other Moslems went to pray at the mosque, my entire family, babies and all, went to the cemetery. We planted rose bushes on Baba's and Jariyeh's graves, so they'd have an endless supply, and brought fresh bouquets each time we visited. On Jariyeh's grave, we'd place three blooms close together, as if they were kissing, to symbolize the love she had for her three children.

Everyone worried about the children. If Mehmet was a product of that house, what were they in for? What were the lovely Bicis saying about their mother? We ached to talk to the kids. To tell them to be kind, to stay away from drugs. To remind them of who their mother was. But rules were rules, and we couldn't call the Bici house. We prayed the boys would call us. Whenever we got a call and no one spoke, we imagined it was one of them.

"I think that was Perparim," Zogu told Vera and me one afternoon. The three of us sat at the kitchen table, staring at the mustard phone on the wall, waiting for it to ring. After fifteen minutes, we walked out—defeated.

It took Zogu a year to decide on our sister's final farewell. We all went to see the seven-foot India red marble tombstone. On top was our flag, a double-headed eagle, with roses on each side.

Këtu pushon Xharije L. Aliu   Here rests Jariyeh L. Aliu

There was no way we were calling her a Bici. It was all we could do to wipe that family's imprint from our lives. We used our clan name, Aliu, taken from Alija—the northern region where my father was born. It told others where we came from and who we belonged to.

We had to change our surname back in Italy. Getting a visa shouldn't have been a problem. We weren't criminals. Baba had money and a sponsor. But after one of his many visa inquiries, Baba learned of rumors that Lutfi Feza Alija was a spy. So he changed our last name to Selmani, after our grandfather Selman. It worked.

My father's tombstone read: Lutfi Feza Alija. I never understood how we could use Alia, Aliu, Alija, and Alijaj interchangeably until a friend explained that Albanian names behave like verbs, changing with use. It made names feel alive, somehow affirming that they were worth protecting.

Jariyeh's middle initial, L, stood for Lutfi. All children took their father's first name as their middle name. Her tombstone read:

Allah Ramet Elez	May God rest her soul
Me prejardhje nga Shqipnia	With roots from Albania
Lindi në Kosovë	Born in Kosova
me 21 Fror 1953	on February 21, 1953
Ndrroi jetë në N. Y.	Changed lives in New York
me 17 Shtator 1979	on September 17, 1979

September 17 was a curious mistake, since Jariyeh died on the 18th. Was citing the last day she was alive Zogu's way of refusing to accept her death?

The inscription continued:

E mbajm në zemër	We hold her in our hearts
Dhe se harrojm per jetë	And will never forget her
Si motër dhe nanë burrnesh	As a sister and brave mother
Fëmijt Esati Perparimi	Children Esat, Perparim
dhe Dhurata	and Dhurata
Vllhznit Bekimi Zog Luani	Brothers Bekim Zogu Luan
Nana dhe motrat	Mother and sisters

I was glad to see "sisters," even if it came at the end and our names omitted.

I was eleven when Baba's tombstone was erected. I was sad to see only my brothers' names and some male cousin in Albania we never met. There was no mention of a wife or daughters. It was the first time I realized that women didn't count. Did it take my sister's murder to earn us a place on a tombstone—even in passing? Did we matter now?

As years passed, the cemetery visits became easier. In the spring and summer, we laid out blankets, had picnics, and played soccer. In the winter, we had snowball fights and slid on the ice. Kamile snapped pictures. We wanted Jariyeh and Baba to see us happy, like in our Prospect Park days, and talked to them as if they were still with us.

"Dad, look what he's doing!"

"Jariyeh, tell him to stop!"

We left bread and sweets on their graves. Offerings for the birds and other creatures that stayed behind to keep my father and sister company.

Chapter 50

The Eagle & The Mattress

* * *

The idea that people didn't disappear into oblivion upon death, only their bodies perished, helped us deal with Jariyeh's passing. We believed the dead visited people and places they knew, and could always be found at the site where their bodies rested. When Saranda went to the cemetery, she could never bring herself to approach Jariyeh's grave. Doing so meant accepting that her friend was never coming back.

The 8 a.m. calls had stopped, but now the radio began turning itself on.

"I think Jariyeh's turning on the radio," Saranda told her husband.

"It must be a short," Bekim said.

Saranda didn't believe it. How could an electrical short cause her radio to turn on around the same time, four to six times a week? It had to be Jariyeh letting her know that she hadn't left for good. On days the radio didn't turn on, Saranda assumed Jariyeh was with someone else—probably her children.

One day, the girlfriend of Saranda's youngest brother, Ilmi, stopped by with a bottle of wine. Saranda was telling her about Jariyeh and the radio when a huge butterfly flew into the room. There were screens on all the windows, so they couldn't figure out how it got in. They curiously watched as the black-and-orange monarch flew around the kitchen.

When it landed on Saranda's shoulder, Ilmi's girlfriend stood up. "You can spend time with Jariyeh," she said, grabbing her bottle of wine. "I'm outta here."

After Jariyeh died, Saranda had recurring dreams of trying to rescue her from Mehmet. Every time they were about to escape, Jariyeh would say:

"I can't leave the children."

In one dream, Saranda managed to coax Jariyeh out of her dark, Prospect Park apartment and into the bright sunlight.

"I have to go back," Jariyeh told her. "I can't leave the children."

But the dream that disturbed Saranda most was the one where she walked into Jariyeh's Bay Parkway apartment and found her locked behind a door.

"Let's go!" Saranda begged. "Let's go!"

"I can't go. The children are here," Jariyeh said through the door.

When Saranda looked again, Jariyeh was chained to her bed.

After each failed rescue attempt, Saranda woke up in a panic.

It reminded her of the dream Jariyeh had shared a month before the murder—about a white horse with wings.

"It means I'm going to die," Jariyeh had told her.

Saranda refused to believe it. She went to see the Sufi holy man who helped couples conceive but also interpreted dreams.

"Come back in two weeks," he told her. "Tell me what's happening with your sister-in-law, and I'll tell you what it means."

Two weeks came and went. Saranda told herself she'd been too busy to go, but in truth she feared he'd confirm what Jariyeh said.

"You look beautiful in the yellow sweater," Jariyeh told her in another dream.

"How do you know?" Saranda asked. "I bought the sweater after you died."

"Hah. Dummy," Jariyeh smiled. "Just because you don't come to see me doesn't mean I don't come to see you."

Convinced her friend hadn't abandoned her, Saranda brought a dozen red roses and drove to the cemetery with her four-year-old daughter. She parked the car and bravely headed toward the grave. There, perched on Jariyeh's tombstone, was a majestic Golden Eagle, looking right at her.

Saranda froze, unable to take another step.

Birds symbolize a link between Heaven and Earth. Had Jariyeh chosen an eagle because they were known for "speaking to Spirit," or because Albanians were People of the Eagle?

Saranda didn't mind the butterfly. She didn't mind the radio turning itself on. But the eagle spooked her. Still holding the roses, she grabbed her daughter's hand and hurried away.

Once safely in her car, she said to the friend who always had a way of making her point, "Okay, Jariyeh. Okay. I get it. You're here." Then drove away.

What Nana wouldn't have given for a sign.

It was the rituals: the flowers, the weekly drive, and the prayers that helped our grieving mother stay close to the daughter she couldn't save. Every Friday, Kamile drove Nana to the cemetery on one condition—that she wouldn't cry. So she didn't. When I joined them, I tried to be strong too, so my tears wouldn't disturb Jariyeh's soul or upset Nana.

I stood next to her at the foot of Jariyeh's grave with my palms up. We prayed the *Kulhu Allahu Ahad*. A prayer I learned at the Albanian American Islamic Center after Baba died. I didn't know if prayers made it better for the dead, but I prayed just in case.

Nana's weekly visits changed the day Vera surprised Kamile with a stolen rose.

"Banma qjefin sa jam gjall. Se kur t'vdes, mos t'kosfsha fal,"--Make me happy while I'm alive, Kamile said. Because when I'm dead, all I'll need is forgiveness.

It was just a saying, but it struck Nana hard. Kamile was right. What good was visiting Jariyeh's grave now? She should have done more for her daughter when she was alive. Nana skipped the cemetery visit that Friday, and every Friday after that, eventually making it a monthly trip.

She never told Kamile why she stopped going every week, but she told Vera.

They had become closer after Jariyeh's death. Nana confided in her about her guilt and regrets, but never let Vera see her cry.

Decades later I learned that Nana cried all the time, but only when others weren't looking.

Vera told me that after I left for school, Nana would lock herself in our half bath for hours. Vera knew she'd been crying only because of her swollen eyes.

Kamile told me Nana cried at work while vacuuming because the noise drowned out the sobs, and at the end of her shift she'd find Nana crying in empty conference rooms with the lights off.

I was in my forties when Nana told me, "I cried every night when I got home from work."

"I didn't know you cried," I said. I slept in the room and never heard a thing.

"I did," Nana replied. "I knew my tears wouldn't let Jariyeh's spirit rest. But I couldn't stop. Then one night, someone sat on the mattress. I looked up to see who it was. There was no one. But the mattress was indented, as if they were still sitting there."

"Really?" I said, staring at her in excited disbelief.

"Yes." Nana smiled. "It was Jariyeh."

I believed her. Einstein said that energy changes form, but never ceases to exist. Of course we didn't disappear into oblivion when we died.

"That was when I stopped crying," Nana said, her eyes shining with a mixture of joy and pain. "Every night after that. *For a year*, Jariyeh came and sat on my bed."

I was so happy for her. "Why do you think she did that?"

"She came to tell me not to blame myself, and to let me know she was okay."

Jariyeh's visits had brought Nana peace.

But back then, the only thing that would have brought her complete fulfillment was news of Mehmet's death—and it was not coming fast enough.

Chapter 51

Two Different Animals

* * *

"I'm looking for Mehmet," Zogu told only trusted friends. "That's your business," one of them scoffed.

Zogu wasn't asking anyone to do his killing. He knew *blood was blood* and *a man was a man*. He simply needed tips on Mehmet's location. He was insulted and ended that friendship. The process of seeking revenge was teaching him a painful lesson: the friends he once cherished weren't real friends.

However, the tough guys he'd grown up with were more than willing to help. There was the good-looking Sami, who was related to Roza's husband. While he gambled with the Albanian gangsters at the "coffee houses," he quietly asked around about Mehmet's whereabouts. And then there was Zogu's oldest friend, Anton Raja, a Catholic Albanian. Back in Italy, they'd steal chickens and roast them in the woods, knowing better than to bring them home to their fathers. When Jariyeh died, Anton was doing time for "criminal possession of a weapon." He was out now and back with the Italian Mafia.

It was Anton who told me about one of their stakeouts.

The Italian Mafiosos had the Gemini Lounge in Brooklyn. The Kosova Connection occasionally did business at Benny's House of Pizza in Queens, where Mehmet once worked.

Anton told Frankie, a mob regular at the pizzeria, "Be on the lookout for Mike Bici." On the streets, Mehmet went by his American name.

The moment Anton got the call, "Mike is here, and he's armed," he phoned Zogu.

They raced to Benny's House of Pizza, parked across the street, killed the engine, and with eyes glued to the pizzeria door they waited.

Half an hour later, five men walked out. One of them was Mehmet.

"Oh shit! I know these guys," Anton said. "That's Bata. That's Joey Lika. If we kill Mehmet now, it's gonna be a shootout."

Anton didn't recognize the other two men.

Decades later I'd learn from Lata that they were Mehmet's bodyguards. They went everywhere he went. One was six feet tall and quick to pull the trigger. Were they hired to protect him from Zogu, or did other people want Mehmet dead?

Zogu wasn't there to kill anyone other than the man who owed him blood, and couldn't risk Anton getting shot. Then he'd not only lose a friend—he'd also have to avenge his blood.

Was this when Zogu began to realize it wasn't a typical blood feud, and Mehmet wasn't a typical brother-in-law, but a member of a cartel?

Anton's friend Frankie, like a good rat, told Joey Lika, "Anton Raja and some other guy are trying to kill Mike Bici."

Joey knew of Anton, but needed to find out who "the other guy" was. Was it a rival, or the brother-in-law seeking revenge? He started asking around at all the cafes. Jerry heard and immediately called Zogu.

"Don't rush it with Mehmet," Jerry said. He respected Bekim's family and understood Zogu's need to avenge his sister, but knew that Zogu was in way over his head.

"I told you. It's gonna be handled."

Was Jerry helping because a part of him blamed himself for Jariyeh? What was taking him so long? Was he trying to find a hitman outside the Albanian circle—someone the Kosova Connection couldn't trace back to him?

Zogu didn't respond, and continued his hunt.

When he wasn't on a stakeout, he lay on the couch watching the news and waiting for a lead. He'd have one ear on the television and the other listening for the kitchen phone. Not that he'd pick up.

Vera begrudgingly walked into the living room. "It's for you."

Zogu jumped off the couch and rushed to the phone.

It was Sami's older brother, a devoted Church Avenue gambler.

"I know an Albanian guy who does these things," he said, careful not to say too much in case the phone was tapped. "You want me to see if he'll take care of it for you?"

Zogu had not expected revenge to be this difficult. In the criminal world, the odds were stacked against a plumber who drove a checkered cab, no matter how many cowboy films and cop shows he had watched. Albanians weren't supposed to pay to have a rival killed. Zogu preferred to do it himself, but it no longer mattered who pulled the trigger—as long as Mehmet was dead.

"Sure, find out," Zogu told him.

The following day, Sami's brother called back. "The guy said he doesn't do Albanians."

Zogu respected that. Real men didn't get involved in another man's feud.

The next call came from Jerry.

"Didn't I tell you not to rush it? It's gonna be handled."

A simple fact that had escaped Zogu was that criminals knew one another. If the Albanian hitman knew, Jerry knew. If Jerry knew, Mehmet knew. And that meant killing him would only get harder.

"Yeah, you'll handle it," Zogu said. "But she was *my* sister."

He didn't know why Jerry wanted Mehmet dead and didn't care. Jerry's reason and his reason were two different animals.

Chapter 52

The Terror

* * *

"Zogu and Bekim are in jail," Nana tells me as soon as I walk through the door.

"Why?" I ask, scared for my brothers, but grateful they're still alive.

"I think Mehmet is dead," she says the sweetest words I've ever heard. Followed by the most terrifying.

"The Bicis might try to kill us."

A feeling of pure terror creeps into my bones. What does she mean—*us?* If Mehmet is dead, wouldn't we be even? Isn't it one for one? Eye for an eye? Blood for blood? The laws on vengeance were meant to limit the killing and prevent entire tribes from being wiped out, though some feuds still lasted generations, as one story explained.

> A seasoned mediator was once asked, "How hard is it to reconcile blood feuds?" He replied, "If both families are smart, there's no problem—it's one for one. If one family is stupid, there's still no problem. I tell the smart family to let the other slide because they don't know any better. But if both families are stupid, well, may you be the mediator, not me."

"Will the Bicis kill women?" I ask Nana.

"They have no honor. We can't put anything past them," she says.

Unbelievable. According to the Kanun, those safe from vendettas are the elderly and sick, because they are helpless. Priests and Imams, because they'd given their lives to God. And women, not because we're fragile, but because our blood wasn't worthy of cleansing a debt.

What cowards the Bicis are, I think. I'm a seventeen-year-old girl. If they kill me, they should be ashamed of themselves. I don't know how much more I can take. I'm already in constant fear that Zogu might die, and now it could be *any one of us?* This "blood feud" thing was becoming a free-for-all. No rules. No integrity.

Just madness.

"Can I stay home from school tomorrow?" I ask Nana. There were a few days left, and I wouldn't be missing much—not that she'd care.

"No," she says, like a general speaking to her soldier. "We must do things as we always do. We don't want the Bicis to think we're scared."

I didn't realize how ruthless my mother was until that moment. She had no problem endangering her teenage daughter to prove a point. Sure, we were the children of the war hero, Lutfi Feza, and must honor his name, but I'm doing my part. I stay home after school. I babysit when Vera fills in at 1 New York Plaza. I serve my brothers. I clean. Why am I being drafted into a feud women have no place in? Isn't anything sacred? I want to be brave but feel like crying. How was a chicken like me born into this fearless family?

I do an inventory in my head of the access points. The front door is double-locked, metal, possibly bulletproof—good. Our windows face a busy street where there'd be witnesses—good. We have two fire escapes—not so good, but at least the one in Zogu's bedroom has gates. I used to hate how that looked. The kitchen fire escape though has easy access via the crisscross storefront gates below.

One time Luan's friend, Crazy Nicky, decided to surprise him and climbed up the fire escape. The kitchen window was locked, so he leaned over and stuck his head into our family room window, where Zogu was napping, and was greeted with a Luger to the temple. Nicky never did that again. At the time, Luan and I laughed so hard. Now, it isn't so funny.

The family room is vulnerable, and Nana says we're sleeping there tonight. Before bed, Luan and I make sure to lock the windows by reaching over from behind the wall in case a sniper is waiting.

Afterward, I lie on a floor cushion between my mother and brother, afraid to fall asleep. Past my feet, I see the open doorway. I wish it had a door, but maybe it's better to see them coming?

I sneak a look at Nana and Luan. Their eyes are closed. Are they sleeping? Am I awake all alone? My body becomes one loud heartbeat. I hope Nana can't hear it. I try to calm myself by thinking that Bekim and Zogu are safe, and Mehmet is dead, but it doesn't work. I keep looking toward the door. My eyes burn for sleep and begin to close. I force them open. If I sleep, like when Jariyeh died, I won't hear them.

A short story from junior high comes to mind. "Being hunted is the worst feeling in the world," the writer claimed. At the time, I could think of a thousand other things, but now I totally agree. How did he know? He wasn't Albanian. Had he been hunted?

I wake up, unable to believe I'd fallen asleep, but relieved to still be alive.

Is everyone?

I hear normal talking in the kitchen. Relieved, I walk over to find Nana and

Vera drinking Turkish coffee.

"Miremengjes,"--Good morning, I say, surprised to see them so at ease, almost happy.

"Miremengjes," they respond, calm as can be.

Picking an outfit for school usually took time, but not today. I look in my closet and wonder: What do I want to be wearing in case I die? I choose the best of everything. Without question, the light blue slacks I had perfectly taken in. My newest white blouse with the puffy sleeves—angels wear white. I remember someone saying in a movie or something, always wear clean underwear in case of an accident. I pull out my newest cotton panties, so the ambulance drivers don't see me in my old ones. That would be embarrassing, I think. Even though I'd be dead, I opt for leaving a good impression.

I'm not hungry but pour myself some Cheerios to postpone my departure. Nana and Vera talk like nothing happened. My brothers are in jail. I'm about to walk outside into possible death—but they're not fazed.

Not wanting to be late, I force myself to get up. Slipping on my blue Pro-Keds, I remember: *I can run fast.* This gives me hope. Then I hear a movie line in my head: "You can't outrun a bullet."

Will I die today?

If so, I'm not going down easy. I feel somewhat prepared, thanks to all the cowboy films and cop shows I watched with Zogu. I'd seen Bibles stop bullets in westerns, so I grab two hardcover books. But if God had willed it, is there anything I can do to keep from dying? In case I can change fate, I clutch the books in front of me. I used to hold them like that to hide my underdeveloped breasts. *This* was a better reason. As a late bloomer, I'd spent years worrying I'd never get my period and couldn't have children. Now my life might be cut short, and all that worrying would've been for nothing.

Should I hug my mother goodbye? I wonder. I don't on regular days, so maybe it's best not to, or she'll think I'm weak.

"Ditën e mirë,"--Have a good day, I say from the foyer.

"Ditën e mirë, bija nanës"--Have a good day, mommy's girl, she replies.

Mommy's girl? That's nice. A good final memory if I die.

What if the killer is waiting outside the front door? I think. I look through the peephole. No one. What if he's down the hallway? In case he's aiming for my head, I squat down, slowly open the door, and quickly scope out the hallway.

All clear.

The stairs or the elevator? The stairs or the elevator?

I imagine taking the stairs, and a man jumps out from our hide-and-seek spot under the stairwell—not good. I imagine taking the elevator down. The doors open to a man aiming a gun at my head. There's nowhere to run.

The stairs it is.

Like a ninja, I reach the stairwell without a sound. I press my back against the wall, and make my descent. Thank God it's just one flight. In the lobby, I look through the glass vestibule doors at the clear, sunny day—and it hits me:

I can't see.

"If you wear glasses, it'll be hard to get a good husband," my mother told me in elementary school. I agreed, and squinted ever since. I now wish I hadn't listened. Being ugly is better than being dead. How will I know when to run? Or is it better this way?

The bus stop is only fifty feet away and across the street, but feels like miles. I step outside, clutch my books tighter, and go on high alert. I feel the breeze brush against my face. I hear tires rolling on the pavement and people talking—as if it's a normal day. What I wouldn't give for another one of those.

I make it to the corner.

The crossing light flashes:

DON'T WALK!

Shit!

I see the blurry kids at the bus stop in front of the Exxon station and have never been happier to see them. Normally, I'd think I was better than these Americans. Now I wish I could trade places. They wouldn't be in a blood feud. They wouldn't be contemplating their death.

Will this light ever change?

WALK.

I want to run, but hear my mother's voice in my head: "We can't let them think we're scared." I walk to the bus stop, proud of my fearless display, and hope Nana is watching. I maneuver into the center of the crowd, using the kids as a shield. They should be safe if the shooter follows the rules. The Kanun demands one person from the intended family. No more. And definitely not strangers.

> In the northern mountains, a man hid in the fields for two days, waiting
> to avenge his family's blood. Just as he took aim at his target, he noticed
> a boy in a tree. Realizing the gunfire might startle the child and cause
> him to fall, he lowered his rifle and went home. He returned the next
> day to complete his task.

The chatter around me is loud. So much talk about nothing. Even my worries now feel senseless. I'm no longer sad about Jariyeh. I'm not worried about her children. I'm not even scared for Zogu. I just want to live.

Am I selfish?

If I die, I could be with Jariyeh and Baba. That wouldn't be so bad. But I don't want to die. I must live! Will I still be alive by the time the bus comes? I hope so, but I can't think about that. I can't think about tomorrow, or yesterday. None of it is real. Only this moment—and here I am.

Now where is the goddamn bus?

I glance up at our kitchen window across the street, hoping to see Nana watching over me. I see no one. She's standing away from the window, so the Bicis won't know she's worried, I tell myself. But that's probably not the case. Careful not to stick my head out too far, I look for the bus.

Finally—the B64 pulls in. I push onto the packed city bus with schoolkids who act so tough. They don't know what tough is. Nana could teach them a thing or two. Their noise makes life feel normal. Safe.

Unless the killer is on the bus.

I scan the blurry faces.

Damn those glasses.

Chapter 53

The Hitman

* * *

A week later, Vera told me why Zogu and Bekim were in jail. "Nana hired a hitman."

I was shocked, but not surprised. Of course she did. The hand grenade had been a heat-of-the-moment fantasy. She'd never risk killing Jariyeh's children. Naturally, she made other plans.

I wouldn't learn the details about the hitman until decades later. Sitting on the brown leather couch in her office, Vera told me, "I helped Nana get the hitman."

I believed her, just as I had believed her when she'd said she found Jariyeh still alive in the vestibule. But Zogu later told me that Jariyeh had no pulse. I wondered if Vera imagined it. Now she claimed she'd helped Nana hire a hitman. Was she trying to sound important?

I didn't know how much of Vera's story was true, but this is how she told it.

———

"I found a hitman," Nana told her favorite son. "Can I hire him?"

A year and a half had passed since Jariyeh's death. In the old country, having her son pull the trigger would've been preferable, but Nana understood this was America. Instead of respect, they'd give him twenty-five to life. She'd been asking around and got the number of an Italian hitman from a janitor at her cleaning job.

"Yes," Zogu said, having long accepted that this feud might not be per code.

Nana was eager to begin. Only one problem—she didn't speak English.

"Duhet me sos nji punë"--I have to finish a job, Nana told Vera. "I found someone to kill Mehmet and need you to call him for me. But you can't tell anyone, especially Zogu."

Nana knew the police would suspect him, so she figured the best way to protect Zogu was to keep him in the dark. No one would suspect a fifty-five-year-old grandmother. And if they did, she'd accept her fate. She'd already lived her life. Jail was nothing compared to annihilating her daughter's killer.

Vera happily dialed the number.

Having a hitman kill Mehmet meant her husband wouldn't have to.

"I don't make arrangements on the phone," the hitman said. "Do you want to meet, or not?"

Vera turned to her mother-in-law. "He wants to meet."

"Fine," Nana said. "We'll go when Hane gets home." They needed a babysitter.

Nana wore a brown flowered headscarf, and a striped greenish dress. Matching wasn't her thing, as long as it was spotless. Vera wore a silk top, A-line skirt, and pumps. It was 3:30 p.m. when they walked into the deli on 86th Street and looked around for a pasta-bellied middle-aged man. To their surprise, a handsome Italian in his twenties waved them over.

"Vera?" asked the man with eyes like arrows, who reeked of cologne.

Some hitmen dabbed aftershave under their nose to keep from smelling their victim's blood.

"Yes," she answered, mesmerized. She would never cheat on Zogu, but would've loved to get lost in his eyes. If only she weren't scared to look at them for more than a second.

"I'm Giovanni," he claimed, shaking Nana's hand first, then Vera's.

Italians knew respect.

They gave him a picture of Mehmet.

I thought we'd thrown out all his photos. Luan and I went through the albums on the bedroom floor and jabbed Mehmet's eyes out with scissors, then sliced him out of every picture, like we were slicing out his soul. We wanted no record of his existence. Then we chopped Mehmet to pieces and shoved him to the bottom of the garbage where he belonged. Burning him would've felt like black magic, and we'd never mess around with that. Nana must have saved a photo of him. She was strategic like that.

"Why do you want him dead?" Giovanni asked in a hushed voice.

"He killed her daughter," Vera explained. "She was my best friend."

"It'll be eight thousand dollars."

Nana heard five thousand was the going rate, but she wasn't about to haggle. She'd take it from the ten thousand Jariyeh had given her. The very money Mehmet made from his first kilo sale—the very money Jariyeh planned to escape with—would now be used to end him.

"We'll pay when it's done," Nana told Vera to translate.

"Fine," Giovanni replied, not worried that they'd stiff him. "It'll be done soon. I need to know where he lives and who lives with him."

After Vera gave him Mehmet's information, he asked for hers.

"This is the first time I've been hired by women," he said with a smile as he shook their hands. "I'll call you when it's done."

Feeling empowered, Nana and Vera walked to the train and headed to their cleaning jobs.

One morning the phone rang. Naturally Vera picked up.

"Hello," she answered.

"It's done," Giovanni said.

"Hold on," she interrupted, rushing to get her mother-in-law.

"Tell him I need proof," Nana said, like she'd done this before.

"My mother-in-law says she needs proof."

"I don't have proof."

"She won't pay until we have proof," Vera translated.

"I'll give you twelve hours. You should know something by then. But if you say anything to the police or do something stupid, I know where you live. You will be gone, and your children will be gone."

Vera now understood why he wanted her information and was terrified for her little boys.

"Okay," she said. "I'll call you when we hear something."

Nana wasn't intimidated. Let him come. She wouldn't give him a penny until she knew that *the devil* was dead.

Vera stayed busy in the kitchen, where the phone was, growing more anxious by the minute. Three hours passed with no confirmation of the kill, and she had the scariest thought: what if it never came? What if no one found the body? What if Giovanni hadn't killed Mehmet and was just trying to scare them into paying—because they were women? If it were up to her, she'd give him the money just to get rid of him. But she knew Nana would never agree.

What had they gotten themselves into?

When the phone rang, Vera dropped the dishes and grabbed the phone with wet hands. It was Kamile. She asked to speak to Nana.

Nana told her she'd call her back.

Not five minutes later, it rang again.

"This is the Bronx Housing Authority Police," said an officer who handled crimes in the Bronx projects. "We need to speak to Zogu Selmani."

Vera smiled at Nana, then rushed to get her husband.

"It's for you," she said, acting cool.

"This is a courtesy call," the officer told Zogu. "Are you and your brother Bekim willing to bring yourselves in, or do you want us to pick you up?"

"For what?" Zogu asked, hoping to hear—murder.

"We can't tell you over the phone."

"Fine. We'll bring ourselves in."

"Good. I suggest you both bring lawyers."

Zogu hung up. He figured it had something to do with his mother's hitman, but didn't want to "know" until he beat this thing.

"It was the police," he told his mother. "They want me and Bekim to go in, but they didn't say why."

Oh, the joy, the joy.

For the first time since Jariyeh's death, the three of them were happy. Vera and Nana couldn't help but smile as Zogu put on his shoes and walked out the door. Justice had finally come.

"Mehmeti ka cofë"--Mehmet has died, Nana said to Vera, her heart so full it could burst. Albanians had two words for "dead": *vdek* and *cofë*. Vdek referred to human death. Cofë was only used for animals—like Mehmet.

"Call the Italian," Nana said. "I'll watch the kids. You go give him the money."

Vera happily agreed.

Nana was impressed that her daughter-in-law wasn't afraid to meet the Italian alone. This was a Nuse to be proud of, even if her cleaning was not up to par.

Giovanni was at the deli, looking even more handsome in his three-piece suit. His unbuttoned shirt revealed manly chest hair and a gold chain with a cross.

"Hi," Vera said like a giddy schoolgirl, then sat across from him, smiling uncontrollably.

Amused, Giovanni smiled back. "You're sick," he said, shaking his head. "You weren't scared to come alone?"

"No," she grinned. Was he kidding? Going to him was a dream, compared to the terror of having him show up at her door. She handed him the envelope.

"Do I need to count it?"

"No. It's all there."

Sliding the money into his inside pocket, he stood to leave.

"Wait," Vera blurted. "My mother-in-law wants to know how he died."

Giovanni shook his head at the nerve of these crazy Albanian women, and sat back down.

"My guy climbed in through the fire escape," he said in a hushed voice, "and shot him in the head while he was sleeping. He was about to shoot again, but he heard the father coming in his wheelchair. So, he jumped back onto the fire escape and got away."

Giovanni stood, kissed the brave girl on both cheeks, and left.

Vera rushed home to report every detail to her partner.

Nana was *ecstatic.*

They had done it. They were only women—but they had done it.

The only problem now was Bekim and Zogu. What if they were found guilty of murder?

Chapter 54

Shot in the Head

* * *

"What happened when you went to jail?" I asked Bekim.

"Which time?"

"You were arrested more than once?"

"Yes."

"Huh. Okay, tell me about the time you and Zogu had to turn yourselves in."

"That was ridiculous," he replied, meaning insane, meaning it never should've happened, meaning he was pissed. "Zogu told me we had to bring a lawyer, so I called Fred Krantz."

———

Krantz was a police captain turned lawyer who lived at Plaza 100, where Bekim worked concierge. The two men respected each other. Years back, when Bekim worked two jobs, porter in the morning and manager at night, he sometimes slept at the Skytop Lounge between shifts. One night, he overheard Fred's daughter fooling around with her boyfriend. Bekim stayed quiet, not wanting to get caught and lose his job. But when the yelling started, he looked and saw Mr. Krantz with a gun. Bekim jumped out.

"Fred!" he yelled. "You know better than this."

Mr. Krantz was grateful he stopped him. But what impressed him most was when the immigrant who worked two jobs found his gold watch and gave it back. Krantz told him, "You're stupid," knowing he could've used the money.

When Bekim called and asked, "Will you represent me?"

Krantz didn't hesitate. "I'll be at your arraignment first thing in the morning," he said. "And I'll bring the best attorney I know to represent your brother."

Bekim and Zogu drove to the 40th Precinct, eager to hear the charges.

"You're under arrest for attempted murder," the officer told the brothers.

Murder? Bekim was shocked.

Attempted? Zogu was disappointed.

"Whose murder?" he asked.

"Agim Bici."

Zogu was confused. Wasn't Mehmet's brother away at college?

"What happened?"

"He was shot in the head," the cop said.

"And the guy lived? Let me tell you, I don't miss," Zogu boasted.

"Well, whoever shot him didn't miss either. I guess it just wasn't his time."

"Just so you know, I have a rifle at home."

"We know." The officer smiled. "We have witnesses who say you guys went into the apartment and shot him."

"That's funny," Zogu sneered. "Have you *been* in their apartment?" Having lived there for two weeks, he knew the place was a fortress. There were four or five deadbolts, latches, and an assortment of contraptions that got locked every time someone came in or out. Zogu assumed it was because of the gold. But maybe it was also because of the cash Jariyeh was made to iron.

The police *had* been in their apartment and saw the locks. The break-in story seemed farfetched, but the Bicis swore to it. So Bekim and Zogu were patted down, fingerprinted, and officially put into the system. The large holding cell had one phone, one toilet, three benches, and thirty or so detainees.

This place is for animals, Bekim thought. It wasn't until he heard the heavy clang of the door locking behind him that reality set in—*he* was one of those animals. Zogu had been preparing for prison, but not the "smart brother." He was above these things. Even in Bekim's dreams, some of which were premonitions, he never saw this coming. He was so pissed about having a police record that he stretched out on one of the benches, folded his hands behind his head, and crossed his legs—daring anyone to *fucking* say something. Maybe then he could get some of his frustration out. Still, it bugged him that his sneakers were dirtying the bench.

"What are you in for?" one detainee asked another.

"I was arguing with my girlfriend and threw the TV out the window."

"What are you two in for?" he turned to Bekim, assuming the only white guys must be together.

"Attempted murder," Bekim replied, not trying to impress. He was simply stating a fact.

No one talked to them after that. They knew better than to mess with two white boys in the middle of the Bronx charged with attempted murder. Those guys, you left alone.

Hours later, the prisoners were handcuffed, feet chained, and then led into a police van. On their way to Rikers Island, they sat on parallel benches facing each other. Just for kicks, the driver slammed on the brakes at every red light and sent the men crashing forward.

At Rikers, the men were handed overalls and put into a bullpen. Bekim tried to sleep, but he was so angry there was no way. Zogu, however, was feeling pretty good and ready for some shuteye. Even though it wasn't Mehmet who got shot, and even though Agim was not dead, a message had been sent.

At the arraignment the next morning, Mr. Krantz personally guaranteed that Bekim wasn't a flight risk and asked that no bail be set. The judge granted the request. Hearing Krantz vouch for him almost made the arrest worth it.

The lawyer Krantz brought for Zogu, Mr. Adler, had a mouth like a machine gun that words came shooting out of. Without even knowing his client, he got Zogu minimal bail.

Adler asked the brothers if they'd be willing to take a lie detector test, which he'd offer as evidence if they passed. They agreed. Bekim, because he had nothing to hide. Zogu, because he was sure he could outsmart a polygraph. Though he usually told the truth, he had no problem lying to a machine. How hard could it be?

"Answer only in yeses and nos. Were you in the Bronx last night?"

"No," Zogu confidently replied.

"Did you break into Mr. Bici's apartment?"

"No."

"Did you shoot Mr. Bici?"

"No."

"Do you know who tried to hurt Mr. Bici?"

Not me, my mother. Not me, my mother, Zogu repeated to himself, trying to convince his own mind.

"No."

The results came.

"You passed with flying colors," Mr. Krantz told Bekim. "But stay away from your brother." He knew Zogu didn't shoot Agim, but was guilty of something.

At home, Zogu broke the news to Nana.

"Mehmet's alive. Agim was shot, but he's still alive."

Nana was *pissed!*

When she was alone with Vera, she said, *"Shka kum ba moj Nuse"*--What have I done, my Nuse? "I never should have paid him."

Vera panicked. What if her mother-in-law wanted her money back and Giovanni decided to come for a visit?

"Call him. Call him now," Nana demanded.

Vera reluctantly obeyed.

"You made a mistake," she said to Giovanni, almost apologetic. "You didn't shoot Mehmet. You shot his brother."

"You didn't tell me about a brother," he snapped.

"We didn't know. We thought he was in college. But still, you didn't kill him,"

Vera said, nodding at Nana to show she was handling it.

"Che cazzo"--What the fuck. "Lady! What do you want me to do?" Giovanni yelled, then hung up.

Nana made her call him back. To Vera's relief, there was no answer. But Nana wouldn't stop. Two, three times a day, she kept urging Vera to call. Still, no one picked up. The phone rang and rang. Then one day came the message: "The number you have reached is not in service or is temporarily disconnected."

"Don't worry. I'll get his number from the janitor," Nana said.

"Please don't," Vera begged, remembering the soulless look in Giovanni's eyes. "All our heads will be gone, including the children."

Injuring Agim and instilling fear into the Bicis was rewarding, but nowhere near what Nana wanted. She wouldn't be happy until the Bicis suffered as she had. But Nana saw the terror in her Nuse's face and let it go.

For now.

Chapter 55

The Good Hostess

* * *

While Zogu and Nana were doing their thing—trying to kill Mehmet—I was doing mine: preparing to be a good Nuse. I'd been cleaning the house since I was eight and had that part down pat, so I focused on my dowry. Between homework and babysitting, I finished embroidering the cross-stitch doily set Jariyeh and I had started. It was only meant to be a practice piece, but it came out so well that Nana said it was dowry-worthy.

In Kosova, Isa's wife taught me how to crochet. I chose a serving tray cover with spiral designs as my first project. I loved how repeating stitches formed patterns that fit perfectly together to reveal a grand design—never realizing that patterns were also forming within me. Ones that started even before my time.

My mother was molding me to be a good Nuse, as her mother had molded her. They say I look like my grandmother. Did I act like her too? Was she spiteful like Nana? Was that a pattern I couldn't help but learn?

But the worst type of learning came from trauma: like Baba's death and Jariyeh's murder. They caused deep-rooted patterns, like constrictor knots, intertwined with love and panic. They existed simultaneously, neither canceling the other out. Unlike crocheting knots that fell away with one pull of the string, trauma knots stayed forever. Time softening their grip was the only hope.

The love I received from Baba and Jariyeh stayed with me, playing in the background—filling me with compassion. Like my sister, I masked pain with humor. Like my father, love echoed in my laughter. Like them, I loved people. But loving too much triggered the panic.

What if they left me? played in my head. *I'll leave them first* became the answer that would sabotage my relationships. The fear that anyone could be taken from me at any time was debilitating. I imagined worst-case scenarios ending in death. I exhausted myself trying to stay in control, thinking maybe, just maybe, I could keep them safe. No one had saved Jariyeh, so I tried to save everyone else.

Never imagining I also needed saving.

How was I to know I had inherited my ancestors' scars? Or that my beloved culture had set me up to fail? No wonder my feelings of helplessness turned to rage. It would take a lifetime to untangle those debilitating patterns. Maybe then my descendants will inherit my strength.

Meanwhile, I lived in that uneasy mix of love and panic as I prepared for marriage.

Nana bought me dowry pieces when we were in Kosova. It was a new world, really, one where women could work and buy embroideries for their daughters. Buying felt like cheating. I didn't like cheating. But I'd rather go to school than stay home to embroider.

Serving was also a Nuse requirement. My family was always happy at the sound of the buzzer, eager to be good hosts and hostesses. But with it came responsibility.

> Section XXXI: "For two acts, a woman may be shot in the back: a) For adultery; b) For betrayal of hospitality."

I didn't know that was a thing, and I'd never heard of it happening. But I'd also never met a disrespectful hostess. Was that why?

Vera was visiting her parents when Ramiz came by with his wife and mother. I took on the server role, buzzed them in, opened the door, and waited—as we always did to show guests they were welcome.

Luckily, they were longtime friends, so mistakes would be forgiven. Zogu escorted Ramiz to the coveted spot farthest from the door, indicating that we didn't want him to leave. His mom got the seat next to him, followed by his wife. Though the mom was older, the oldest male was always first—and with that came perks. You were the first served. The first addressed in conversation. And the one whose opinion mattered most.

I stood in the middle of the living room with Nana and Zogu as the greeting mayhem began. There was a litany of questions we had to ask one another, all at the same time—or else we'd be there forever.

"How are you?" Zogu asked Ramiz. Nana asked his mom. I asked his wife.

"Good, how are you?" they practically replied in unison.

"I'm good. How's your mom?" Zogu asked Ramiz.

"I'm good. How's Ramiz?" Nana asked the mom about her son.

"I'm good. How's Ramiz?" I asked his wife about her husband.

Although they were right there and we could've waited to ask them directly, that's not how it worked. We had to ask each person about every family member in seniority order preferably by name. I found it hard to remember names and preferred the "how's the family" catch-all that strangers got to use. But that showed laziness, and laziness wasn't respected. Questioning a guest was an art. You were judged by what you asked, how you answered, and authenticity.

If anything was festering inside, it was bound to come out after being bombarded with "how are you's" by every person in the room. There were only so many "good, goods" you could say. It was therapy for a people who didn't know what therapy was or consider themselves broken. There weren't any Albanians lying on some couch blaming their mothers. You never complained about the woman who gave you life. Ever. No matter what she did or said, you cherished and obeyed her.

Work inquiries came next.

"How's work? Do you get tired?" Which, of course, no one ever did. What Albanian gets tired or admits to it?

Once the greeting ritual was over, I politely asked Ramiz, "Would you like a soda?"

"You never ask a guest if they want something," Nana corrected me. "That's an American thing."

I turned red. I hadn't even started and was already wrong.

The "always serve and never ask" rule began back when people were very poor. Giving a guest options would put them in an awkward position. If they said no, the host would be denied the honor of serving. If they said yes, they risked seeming insensitive to the host's hardship. Even in America, with its abundance of food, where yes or no hardly mattered, we stuck to the tradition of never asking.

"You only ask a sick person," my mother continued. "They might have a special diet to follow."

That made sense, because once something was served, it had to be accepted. That's also why you avoided visiting the homes of people you suspected of practicing witchcraft. What better way to cast a spell than through food or drink your guest was obligated to consume? In America, we were too busy chasing money to think about black magic. Still, there was one old woman with mischievous eyes we visited only when absolutely necessary—after a death, an engagement, or a wedding.

Like a good hostess, I headed to the kitchen and prepared a tray of sodas. I served each person in gender and age order, then respectfully walked backward a few steps before leaving the room. This was acceptable for an unmarried girl. A Nuse would have to make her entire departure without turning her back, at least her first few months. I returned with nut assortments, an American addition, placed them within everyone's reach, then sat quietly on the couch.

Sitting with elders was a treat. Typically, they told teaching stories and shared funny anecdotes. But visits after Jariyeh's murder were different. We had gone from being the joyful family to the one in a blood feud. No one spoke of it, but it loomed over us. Everyone patiently waited to hear the *mizhde*--good news that

Zogu had killed Mehmet. Maybe then we could joke and sing once more.

"How are Jariyeh's children?" Ramiz's mom asked Zogu.

People didn't usually bring up the children or anything that would *trazu*--wake up those memories for us, especially for Nana.

"We don't know much," Nana answered, because Zogu couldn't.

For him, the children were a sore subject. When the family gathered, someone always tried to lighten the mood, but if anyone said something like, "Dhurata was such a good dancer," or "Perparim's lisp was so cute," Zogu would cry and cry and cry like a baby.

I felt Nana looking at me, and turned to her. She eyed the empty glass in front of Ramiz. Embarrassed at not having noticed, I quickly retrieved it.

"Të baft mirë"--May it do you good, I said.

"Të baft mirë," Nana repeated.

"Për t'mirë,"--For good things, he replied, wishing we'd serve only for happy occasions.

Zogu poured Ramiz a shot of *raki*--moonshine, while holding his left hand over his heart.

"None for me," Ramiz said, with his hand over his heart. But we all knew he liked a little begging.

"Për hatrin tem,"--for my sake, Zogu insisted.

Even if Ramiz had been in AA for years, not that an old-school Albanian would attend, he couldn't say no. After someone said *for my sake*, you had to do it out of respect. Ramiz happily accepted.

"Make us coffee," Nana directed. There was no need for "please" or "thank you." We all knew our roles, and no one took offense.

I simmered the Turkish coffee on a low flame, like Baba taught me, lined the tiny cups perfectly on the tray, and filled them to the top. Then I walked slowly into the living room, and placed a cup in front of each guest, making sure the handle faced their right hand—"God's hand"—for easy pickup. I felt Nana watching and hoped I was making her proud.

"Remember Qemal's wife?" Ramiz's mom broke the silence. "She had eyes like the butt of a coffee cup."

She meant to say, "eyes like a coffee cup," which was supposed to be a compliment. I never understood how that was flattering, but she had messed up, as usual, and everyone laughed.

"Thank God I made a mistake and made you all laugh," she said, smiling.

Making us laugh was *sevap*--a good deed. Everyone wanted to see us happy again.

"They were never a good match," the now tipsy Ramiz said what people normally whispered behind Nana's back. "He wasn't for Jariyeh. He was a wimp. Who would have thought he'd kill her?"

No one thought. Or it never would've happened. It was the very people no one thought anything of, who did what no one could imagine.

The room fell silent.

There was nothing to say. Mehmet had to be killed. That was all. And Zogu never stopped trying. I was happy not to be a boy who had to avenge blood. I preferred serving people to killing them.

I liked being a good hostess. I liked making sure visitors always had something to eat or drink and that empty glasses didn't sit in front of them. I picked up the last coffee cup and headed to the kitchen, ready to prepare the fruit.

Fruit was another American addition to our serving protocol. Back home, a piece of fruit was a precious gift brought to the sick. But here, everything was overdone. Nana made sure we had plenty of goods on hand in case visitors came. I ate only softened apples or shriveled grapes to save the best for them. Luan, on the other hand, snuck the good stuff. When Nana found out, she'd do her infamous pinch-and-twist, which I never got because I always listened.

I had to fill the fruit plate with enough for everyone, but all I could find were some grapes, two apples, and lots of carrots. We never served vegetables, but I couldn't show up nearly empty. I peeled and cut the carrots into bite-sized pieces and arranged them on the sad-looking fruit plate. Red-faced, I walked into the living room, placed it on the table, then set a dish, knife, and napkin in front of each guest so they could help themselves.

Nana looked down at the carrots, then up at me.

My heart dropped. It wasn't my fault they had come before she went shopping.

"Good girl," she said, meaning: you've done your best to make our guests feel welcome, and one day you'll make a good Nuse.

I was so happy.

No matter how much Nana and Zogu begged our visitors to stay for dinner, they didn't. We walked them to the foyer and waited while they put on their shoes. Nana shook Ramiz's hand with both hands, to show her deep gratitude for his visit. A gesture too forward for most women, but Nana wasn't an ordinary woman. They called her a *burrënesh*--a manly woman.

I gave everyone a firm handshake just as Nana had taught me—to show I was a hard worker. Other girls were taught to keep their hands limp, a sign of submissiveness. Nana hated that.

The men of the house always accompanied visitors to the sidewalk, and sometimes all the way to their cars. Zogu walked our guests outside. Having done such an excellent job, I decided to join my brother for what I called "the long goodbye," not knowing this custom was Kanun inspired. If a guest is killed in your home or courtyard, the host is responsible for their blood.

Violation of Hospitality Law §651: c) If you do not avenge the murder of your guest… you remain dishonored for the rest of your life.

I didn't realize keeping guests safe was part of the job.

An Albanian guest was thoroughly cared for. The good hostess fed them. The good host made sure they didn't die. If either failed, it could cost them their life.

That seemed fair.

Chapter 56

Top of his Class

* * *

Decades later I sat at Perparim's table as the guest. His American wife was a good hostess, but Perparim had an Albanian upbringing and couldn't help but go above and beyond. After dinner, he made tea for Lata and me, then went to help his wife with the kids.

"I was just writing about the hitman who shot Agim," I said to Lata. "I heard he climbed in through the fire escape, and your grandfather came out in his wheelchair."

"That's not what happened," Lata said. "I was little, but I remember. There were no fire escapes in those projects. And at home Selman used crutches."

Had Giovanni made it up? I wondered. Did he invent the story just to appease the crazy women so he could go home? Or had Vera filled in the blanks herself?

"So how did it happen?" I asked Lata, leaning in.

"We lived on the second floor of the Mitchel House projects," Lata began the story. "A much higher second floor than usual. Our windows were oversized and had no guardrails. Kids fell out all the time, especially in the summer. Danny Boy, the son of the only other white family, was nicknamed "The Star" of the projects. He was always catching the babies."

I didn't understand where this was going but didn't want to interrupt. Lata explained that she was four and wasn't allowed to go outside. So, she'd sit at the window and watch her brothers play below. Selman sat with her, holding her shirt so she wouldn't fall. He was always watching over her and the boys.

"Pop was never around," Lata explained. "But he warned my grandparents not to let anything happen to us."

Her tone made me wonder if she thought that somehow made him a good dad.

"Why wasn't he around?" I asked, curious if Mehmet blamed his parents, at least in part, for Jariyeh's death. "Was he mad at them about something?"

"No. When Selman and Filanza realized what Pop was doing, they let him know how disappointed they were. Filanza would say to Selman in front of Pop, 'Why did we come to America? So our son could become a gangster?'"

I didn't think to ask: if he wasn't already a gangster, where did the cash Jariyeh was always ironing come from?

"Pop didn't like being called a gangster, so he stayed out," Lata explained.

"So, how did Agim get shot?" I put her back on track.

———

Agim was going to be a lawyer. He went to John Jay Law School in Manhattan, and had come home for a visit.

"I was top of my class," he proudly announced.

The boy who once pulled a gun on Bekim was becoming a man his parents could be proud of.

Since Mehmet wasn't home, Agim stayed in his room. It was a hot summer night, so he opened the window hoping for a breeze.

After nightfall, the hitman stationed himself in the courtyard below and located the Bicis' second-floor windows. He waited for a dark-haired man in his thirties. He'd be easy to spot, since the only other male was old and crippled. Just as the sun began to rise, he saw his target.

Agim was walking past the window when a bullet tore through the open frame and struck him behind the ear. He didn't feel pain—only a sharp, high-pitched screech, like metal on metal, followed by a deafening buzz. Warm blood slid down his neck as his legs gave out. Before he could grasp what was happening, he pitched forward straight out the window and into the open air.

His seventeen-year-old sister heard the shot and ran to see what happened. Following the trail of blood to the windowsill, she saw her brother lying on the grass below.

"No!" she yelled.

Selman and Filanza rushed out, followed by Lata, who'd been sleeping beside them.

"Agim! Agim!" the sister yelled, reaching out for her brother.

"Stop! Stop!" Filanza shrieked.

Selman grabbed his daughter and pulled her in.

If Nana had known how Agim was shot, it would've given her some joy.

Good that the Bicis had suffered. Good that the bullet couldn't be safely removed from his head. So what if he had to drop out of law school? So what if he'd never be the same again?

So. Fucking. What.

He was alive.

Her Jariyeh was dead.

At Bekim and Zogu's next court date, the only Bici to show up was the sister who hadn't been home that night. She had snuck out to go clubbing. When Zogu spotted her in the back, he let out a long, cold, diabolical laugh—"Ha. Ha. Ha. Ha."—making sure she knew exactly how pleased he was that her brother had been shot.

During the hearing, a number of things worked in Bekim and Zogu's favor: the police verified that the Bicis' front door was a fortress, and with no fire escape, there was no way they could have gotten in. The lie detector test confirmed that neither brother had been in the apartment or in the Bronx. It didn't matter that Zogu knew "who tried to hurt Mr. Bici."

If they hadn't lied about a break-in to get an attempted murder conviction, but had simply said they suspected the brothers, Zogu might have been arrested and possibly found guilty of conspiracy. The Bici lies worked against them.

When Zogu came home and told us the judge threw out the case against both brothers, I exhaled for the first time in weeks. Mehmet wasn't dead—but at least my brothers weren't going to jail.

With the courtroom drama behind us, I tried to go back to being seventeen. Tried to feel normal. Tried to focus on things that didn't involve revenge, being hunted, or jail.

Chapter 57

Izzy & Rich

* * *

I discovered the cutest boy while testing out Zogu's hunting binoculars, which hung alongside his rifles. Feeling bored and trapped in the apartment, I decided to explore the action outside. At the corner Exxon station, the attendant ran from car to car, pumping gas and washing windows for tips. At the Bay Parkway pizzeria, customers lingered out front, talking and eating their slices. At the Bath Avenue liquor store, a woman stood at the register. When I focused in, I saw the cutest boy ever ringing her up and immediately called Arta.

On the weekend her dad let her sleep over, I couldn't wait to show her the hunk. Zogu and Luan were out, so we waited for Nana and Vera to go to bed, then snuck into the living room. I turned off the lights so no one could see in, a trick Luan had taught me, and grabbed the binoculars. I focused on the liquor store and waited for him to pass by the window. After five frustrating minutes, it hit me: the phone was by the register.

I grabbed the Yellow Pages and found the number.

"You call," I said to Arta. "I'll look for him."

She rushed to the kitchen while I zoomed in on the phone. It almost felt like a date. My heart raced as I watched him answer, then hang up, looking confused.

Arta ran back. "Did you see him?"

"Yeah," I whispered with excitement, handing her the binoculars. "Now I'll call, and you watch him pick up."

Nervously, I dialed.

"Hello… hello," he said. I loved hearing his voice.

The moment he hung up, I ran to Arta. "Did you see him? Isn't he a hunk?"

"Yeah. He's cute," she agreed, but wasn't all that impressed. No boy interested her except for Izzy, her fiancé.

Arta met Izzy at a relative's house in Jersey. The romance began when one of the women said, "You guys would make a good couple." And just like that, Arta started looking forward to Jersey visits, hoping she'd run into him. After a few stolen glances, she was crazy in love and hoped he was too. Every weekend she waited for him to send a *Shkus* as confirmation.

When Arta's father said "yes" to Izzy's matchmaker, she and I cried. We were happy she'd get to marry someone she loved, but sad that she'd be leaving. Once married, the only time we'd see each other would be at weddings, funerals, births, and when she visited her parents. Unless, of course, I married into Izzy's family, or one of his close friends.

When my sixteen-year-old niece got engaged, it should have put pressure on Nana and Zogu to engage me, the seventeen-year-old aunt. But they turned matchmakers away with, "She needs to finish school." In truth, they were too busy trying to kill Mehmet to think of anything else.

It was fine by me. I wanted to graduate high school. Some girls weren't even allowed to finish junior high. The more modern parents said yes to matchmakers only after they were assured that their daughters would be allowed to stay in school. But girls often wound up pregnant. *"You don't need an education—your husband will provide everything,"* they were told. So they stayed home.

Arta and Izzy didn't date, but when her parents weren't home, he'd call from the pizzeria. My niece was in heaven.

Izzy and her dowry. Izzy and her wedding. Izzy and his phone calls—that's all she talked about, in person, on the phone, and in her letters that I excitedly looked for in our mailbox. Not that anyone in my house could read English except Zogu, but he wasn't nosey.

> *Dear one and only, Hane-kapane,*
> *My mother wanted to buy me that picture, but it cost $100. She thought it was too expensive and that my father would refuse. Well, he didn't. He said for Arta, anything.*

The "picture" was a Victorian tapestry needlepoint of a woman in a garden placing a wreath on a man who looked at her adoringly. Arta imagined it to be her and Izzy. She had wanted to embroider it for her dowry and hang it over their bed.

> *God Hane, it always seemed like my father didn't give two shits about me, but deep down inside, he cares. He's just too proud to show it. And you're not going to believe this. At night I usually cry about missing Zogu, Samir, my mother, etc., but last night I cried for my father.*
>
> *When you asked what I was doing for spring break, I said Jersey, because I was hoping to run into Izzy. But now I feel guilty. Soon I'll see him for the rest of my life. I want to spend my remaining time with my Brooklyn family. New Jersey people aren't so closey close, so you better come, cause I need help with the picture.*

For eight straight pages, Arta went on and on about her wedding, and naturally, music came in.

All these songs played while I was writing this book. Now read how I figured out their meaning: Izzy says <u>Don't Be Afraid to Love</u>, although it's been a <u>Cold Love</u> so far. But <u>When We Get Married</u>, Izzy will feel like a <u>Macho Man</u> and tell me <u>I'm in Love with a Plain Old-Fashioned Girl</u>. He'll kiss me and say <u>You're My Lady</u>, and <u>I Love You More Than I Can Say</u>. Then we'll sleep happily ever after.

THE END

All her letters ended with "the end."

"I hope Izzy will be happy with me," Arta said during spring break at her house as we cleared the table after dinner.

How could she doubt it, I wondered. My niece was beautiful, funny, tough, smart, and had the most amazing long hair. And though she was younger than me, she was more developed and much sexier.

"Of course he'll be happy with you," I assured her.

"I mean about sex," she clarified.

"Oh, don't worry, he'll teach you," I said, as if I knew what I was talking about. "But when he wants to, don't fight or turn him off."

Turning him off meant turning him away, and that you never did. It was the one lesson mothers imparted on their daughters before marriage. Everything else we learned from TV, friends, sex-ed, and Nuses. Vera happily shared little details, but never anything gross.

"Okay," Arta replied. "I guess that will probably make him happy. So no fights from me."

Feeling like I had just saved a marriage, I was proud of myself. All marriages needed saving, and it was up to us women to make sure we did what we could to keep our husbands happy. Affairs and beatings we had to overlook, but hopefully, we wouldn't get one of those husbands.

I helped Arta clean the kitchen, then we embroidered her large Victorian picture. She sat on one end of the couch, I on the other. When her father walked in, we froze. Everyone was afraid of him. Not sure what to do, we got up to leave.

"No, no, stay. Keep embroidering," he said sweetly, then went into his bedroom so we could relax.

After 11:00 p.m., her father left to pick up Roza from work in lower Manhattan.

"Wanna go upstairs and hang out with Rich?" Arta asked. "He's Izzy's best friend. Who knows, maybe you'll like him, and you guys can get married. Then you and I can always be friends."

Rich was related to Arta's dad and lived with his mother and brothers. His eldest brother left his wife at home to clean and take care of their mom while he gambled on Church Avenue. His middle brother was Zogu's friend, the good-looking Sami. Of the three, Rich was the youngest, the nicest, and his mother's favorite. He worked at a pizzeria and brought his paycheck home, but was no pushover. One night, two muggers with knives tried to rob him. Rich fought them off and ended up in the ICU with multiple stab wounds. No one thought he'd make it.

I hoped to like Rich, and that he'd like me.

Arta and I sprinted up the three flights. Before she knocked, we tried to compose ourselves. But there was nothing casual about two girls hanging out with a boy in the middle of the night, or anytime, even if he was related. Our saving grace was that his mother was home, though she was probably already sleeping.

Rich opened the door. He wasn't as good-looking as Sami or my liquor store guy, but there was something about him even more attractive.

"Hi Rich. This is Luan's sister Hane," Arta said.

"I know who she is," he smiled, shaking my sweaty hand.

I was so embarrassed. Of course, he knew Luan, but how did he know me? Had he been interested?

"Come in," he said, leading us into the living room and closing his mother's bedroom door so as not to wake her. "What would you ladies like to drink?"

Ladies? Well, isn't that nice, I thought.

"Nothing," said Arta, my spokesperson.

"Don't be ridiculous. You're my guests." He went to the kitchen and—opening the fridge—called out, "Orange juice or soda?"

"Soda," Arta replied, looking at me, all smiles.

I liked the feeling of being served by a man.

"Your brothers are good men," Rich said as he sat on the couch.

So, he approved of my family, I thought. Then realized that Zogu trying to kill Mehmet improved my ranking as a potential Nuse. Families wanted to be related to fearless clans.

"Are you going to school?" Rich asked, though I felt he already knew the answer.

It was the first time a man showed interest since Fisnik in Kosova, and it felt good. I loved the way Rich looked at me. With such sweetness. Such attention. Like I was the only person in the world.

"Yes, I'm going to school," I said, hoping he didn't think girls belonged at home.

"That's good," he replied, although he himself had dropped out in order to work. "But you know Albanian men don't want smart wives," he added teasingly.

"I know, 'cause then we'll be telling them what to do. And we know how much

Albanian men like that," I said, hoping he'd know I was joking.

Rich laughed. "Well, it depends on the woman."

I had been blushing from the moment I walked in, but now my face was burning, and I was speechless.

Arta and Rich spoke about her favorite subject: Izzy. I listened to the stories and laughed at their jokes. Before I knew it, it was time to go. I didn't want to leave, but if her parents came home and found us missing, Arta would be in big trouble.

Rich walked us to the door and shook our hands. The moment he closed the door, we sprinted down the stairs, terrified her parents might have come home early. My heart pounded as we reached her front door and checked for their shoes.

No shoes—*thank God.*

"So, would you marry him?" Arta asked the moment we got inside.

"I don't know. I think so," I answered excitedly.

Now our daily phone conversations turned to Izzy and Rich. We talked about all the places we'd go to as couples: movies, the park, and their pizzerias. That would be so much fun. Rich was becoming a great distraction from my worries about Zogu.

"Do you think Rich likes me?" I asked Arta. But what was there not to like? I was submissive. I was pretty. My father was an honorable man. And my brother was trying to kill Mehmet.

"I'll find out," said my matchmaker.

"Rich said he likes you," she reported a few days later. This meant he wanted to marry me because there was nowhere else for liking to go.

On weekends, I'd ask Nana if I could sleep over Arta's just for a chance to see him again. She always said yes, since I was helping with the dowry.

In the afternoons, Arta and I went upstairs and hung out with Rich's sister-in-law and his mother. She was a kind, thin old lady with a raspy voice who smoked cigarettes and drank Turkish coffee nonstop. I knew she'd make a wonderful mother-in-law and would love to serve her.

At night, Arta and I impatiently waited for Rich to get home. Every time we heard someone walk into the building, we'd rush to the peephole to see if it was him. Some nights he wouldn't come home. Some nights he'd leave before we got the chance to sneak upstairs. I wondered if he was meeting a girl. It wasn't fair that boys could date, but I understood they didn't have to prove virginity on their wedding night.

When I saw Rich, I acted as if I didn't know he liked me. Liking me meant marrying me, and marrying me meant sex—and that was embarrassing. As much as I tried to act cool, it must have been obvious that I knew. My face felt like it was on fire, and I couldn't look him in the eye.

"My mother likes you," Rich said.

I blushed even more.

I knew this meant she blessed the union, and there could very well be a matchmaker in the future. Rich was waiting for his older brother Sami to get engaged before telling his family. I couldn't wait.

Life was thrilling again, like it was with Fisnik, whom I never heard from. I couldn't believe I would get to marry someone I really liked, and get to hang out with Arta all the time.

All I had to do was wait for his brother to get engaged, and my brother to kill Mehmet.

Chapter 58

Mustache Mix-Up

* * *

Mehmet was charged with criminal possession of a weapon and murder in the second degree. I looked it up; it meant murder with intent but without planning, typically after a fight. The District Attorney offered him a lesser charge—first-degree manslaughter—if he pled guilty. Mehmet turned it down. He had other plans.

On July 24, 1980, he sent a mediator to Zogu with a new message:

"Mehmet killed your sister, and says that if you and Bekim value your lives, you will not testify."

That same mediator was sent to 1 New York Plaza to speak to Nana.

"Mehmet has plenty of money," he said. "If your sons testify, he will get rid of them just like he flicks his pinky."

Didn't the Bicis know my mother? She would *never* tell her boys to back off. In fact, if Bekim and Zogu didn't testify, she'd disown them.

Less than two weeks later, the Bicis came up with another plan.

———

"Why were you arrested the second time?" I asked Bekim, pen in hand.

"The Bicis hired an eyewitness," he said, then laughed through the entire story.

"When was that?"

"I don't remember, but it was raining hard. I remember that because it never rains hard when I'm outside."

Years later, Lata's son would tell me the same strange thing about himself.

"Do you remember the detective's name?"

"Detective Stevens, I think. Ask Zogu—he knows."

I called Zogu.

"Was the detective's name Stevens?"

"No. His name was Detective Simon. Definitely Simon," Zogu said, *definitely* being one of his favorite words.

Bekim called me back. "I found the arrest papers. It was August 6, 1980."

———

It was pouring tigers and wolves on August 6, 1980, when an eyewitness pointed to Zogu's mug shot and said, "That's the guy. The one with the mustache."

He claimed to have seen the man hold up a gas station in the Bronx with a rifle, then drive away in a white Malibu Classic. Zogu owned a rifle and Bekim owned a white Malibu Classic. Mehmet knew that. And thanks to the "attempted murder" case, the brothers' mug shots were available for the picking.

Zogu was home watching the news when Vera said, "It's for you."

Hoping it was a lead, he rushed to the phone.

"This is Detective Simon from the 40th Precinct in the Bronx. I'd like to meet up with you when you have a chance."

"Just say when and where," Zogu replied.

"All right. I'll get back to you," the detective said.

Half an hour later, Simon called again.

"I'd like to meet up with you."

"Okay. Just say when and where."

"I'll get back to you," the detective repeated.

But he never called back. Instead, he gathered two plainclothes detectives and drove to Plaza 100—Bekim's work address on file. Not only had Zogu agreed to come in too easily, he was a plumber who owned a checkered cab and didn't need the money. His brother was the better fit. He worked the concierge desk and lived in the Staten Island projects. Though he didn't have a mustache, he could've grown one.

Bekim was sitting at the front desk when the manager called him into the office. Unfortunately for Detective Simon, he walked in without a mustache.

"When was the last time you were in the Bronx?" the Detective asked.

"When I ran the marathon. You could say I was just passing through." Bekim chuckled. He always got a kick out of himself.

He had been in the Bronx qualifying for the New York City Marathon after a sportswriter in his building told him it was hard to come in under three hours. Bekim took it as a challenge and finished in 2:52. My big brother had mastered the physical world—the emotional one, not so much.

"You have to come with us," the detective said.

"Why?"

"We'll let you know when we get there."

"Whatever this is, it's a setup," Bekim said, keeping his cool, as always. "But no problem. First, I'm going to the locker room to change." There was no way he'd walk out of the building in his uniform, looking like a criminal.

A detective escorted him, then waited while he put on his spotless clothes, white sneakers, and stylish Corvette jacket. Back in the office, Bekim made more demands.

"I'm not going through the lobby. We'll use the service entrance. And no handcuffs. That would be embarrassing."

He walked with one officer on each side and one behind him. In the stairwell, a big-bellied detective walked backward down the steps ahead of him.

"Guys, why are you doing this? I'm not going nowhere," Bekim said.

"You just told us you ran the marathon," the big-bellied detective replied. "If you run, you think I can catch you?"

Bekim wanted to laugh, but didn't.

Outside, they ran through the unforgiving rain and into the car. Bekim slid into the backseat, a detective on each side.

"Listen," Bekim said, "whatever this is, my brother-in-law set it up. He lives in the Bronx. He had my brother and I arrested before. He knows I'm going to testify against him and wants to make me a bad witness."

"If it makes you feel any better, we're just bringing you in for a lineup," Detective Simon explained.

"There's no point. The guy has my picture. He's going to pick me in a second."

Hungry, Simon pulled over and ran through the rain into a diner for burgers to go. When he returned, he flashed his police light on Bekim's face, blinding him.

"Did you ever have a mustache?"

"No," Bekim said.

He wanted to say, *No, but my brother does. You should arrest him.* He loved teasing his little brother. Once, at a coaching conference, Bekim asked Zogu, who barely used a hairbrush, "Did you bring your blow-dryer?" knowing it would piss him off. "Get the fuck outta here," Zogu said, only realizing he was being teased when Bekim started cracking up. But he knew this was no laughing matter.

"Tell you the truth, guys," Bekim said, "I tried growing a mustache once, but I shaved it because it looked ugly." Bekim didn't do ugly.

At the precinct, Simon asked, "Do you own a white Malibu Classic?"

"No, I own a brown and beige Malibu Classic."

It had been white, but he had it painted two-tone at Jerry's autobody shop, per the latest fad. Luckily, Mehmet didn't know.

"Where were you last night?"

"I was home with my wife."

"I have an eyewitness who says he saw you rob a gas station in the Bronx."

"I have no clue what gas station you're talking about. I'm not a thief."

Bekim never stole a thing in his life. He believed only peasants stole—and he was no peasant.

"Let's see if your wife confirms your story."

"If you call her, she's going to think someone's playing a joke."

"Hello, ma'am. This is Detective Simon. Your husband has been arrested."

"*Really?* What did he do this time—pick up a blonde?" Saranda laughed. "Oh no, wait, does he need me to drop off his hair gel?"

"Ma'am. Your husband has been arrested for armed robbery."

After Saranda verified the alibi, Bekim was placed in a holding room with six white male lineup fillers—college students doing it for a few extra bucks.

"Listen," Bekim said to them, "you don't have to worry. The guy has my picture. He's going to pick me in a second. So, do any of you guys play soccer?"

In the lineup room, it happened exactly as he predicted.

On their way out, the students told the detectives, "We don't know what they say this guy did—but he didn't do it."

"You see? I told you," Bekim said to Detective Simon as he was being led into his cell. "He's got my picture. You can't get better than that."

Simon drove to the eyewitness's house and pulled out the mug shot.

"Just checking," he said. "Is this the man you saw rob the gas station?"

"Yes. I'll never forget that face."

Simon nodded. "Okay, buddy. You just picked the wrong guy."

He had shown the eyewitness Zogu's mug shot—the brother with the mustache—yet at the lineup he instantly pointed out Bekim.

Back at the precinct, Simon asked Bekim, "Where's the one place you want to be?"

"Home."

"That's where you're going."

Bekim called Zogu to pick him up.

"Oh shit! They got you?" Zogu said, unable to stop laughing.

Afraid they'd arrest Zogu when he walked in with a mustache, Bekim kept telling everyone, "My brother's picking me up. He's a plumber. He makes lots of money."

On the drive home, the brothers laughed at how lucky they were. If Detective Simon had asked Zogu to come in, he would've driven himself. There wouldn't have been a car ride with the detectives, and no chance to create doubt. Unlike Bekim, he wasn't calm under pressure and wouldn't have put the college kids at ease with nonstop soccer talk. He would've been picked out of the lineup on the spot. And if Simon had gone back to the eyewitness, there wouldn't have been a mix-up. Zogu had the mustache.

———

When I heard this story years later, I wondered how the Bicis managed to set up a gas station robbery. Much later, I learned about Mehmet's connection to Nicky and the gas station business.

Chapter 59

The Wig

* * *

After nearly a year and a half of waiting for a lead, Zogu knew exactly where Mehmet Bici was going to be—at the courthouse on Lafayette Street in Brooklyn. That year, New York State was ranked number one in violence and twelfth in murder. Courts were busy and convictions weren't easy, but Zogu preferred Mehmet dead to incarcerated anyway. Killing him at a government building was risky, but there was no way he'd pass up this opportunity.

His other leads never worked out.

One time, while visiting Vera's family, her nephew walked in and said he had just seen Mehmet at Benny's House of Pizza. They rushed over, but he was already gone. Later, Zogu went back and told the young Albanian pizza man, "I'll pay you if you call me when Mike Bici comes in." The kid took his number. When Zogu left, he called the Bicis, figuring they'd pay better.

Naturally, Jerry heard and called Zogu: "I told you. It'll be taken care of."

As a friend, Zogu was unsurpassed. As a murderer, he was way over his head.

But this time—it was a sure thing.

Zogu put on his black leather trench coat and a long, curly brown wig, then went to pick up Anton, whom he now considered a blood brother. Zogu went to Anton's for Christmas, and Anton came to our house for Bajram.

In the elevator, Anton's dapper father ran into Zogu in his ridiculous wig.

"What are you doing? You vagabonds!" he playfully asked. "Up to no good?"

Not wanting to worry the old man, Zogu said nothing. But Anton's father knew what no good they were up to, and would never stop his son from being a good friend. Even if it meant jail. That's what real men did for each other.

Anton disguised himself with his father's tan fedora and matching trench coat before heading out. Their plan was simple: Zogu would shoot Mehmet. Anton would stand watch in case a shootout began. Afterward, they'd run in separate directions, tearing off their disguises as they went. If they got caught, Zogu would take the fall and swear Anton wasn't there.

Then came the best part. Zogu would send a mediator to the Bicis' to let them know we were even—blood for blood—one for one. Then everyone could go about their business.

Not knowing the trial time, the blood brothers arrived before the courts opened. They waited, armed and ready, by the courthouse stairs, watching everyone who passed. *Is that him? Is that him?* They didn't realize Mehmet suspected an ambush and slipped in through the back entrance.

The brother who fancied himself a cowboy had done his best to avenge his sister's blood. It was time to see what justice looked like in America.

———

Zogu never got to look Mehmet in the eye. I did. Almost twenty-five years to the day that he killed my sister, Mehmet stood before me.

In September 2004, Perparim invited me to his Fire Academy graduation.

"I want you to come in my mother's place," he said, then added, "But Pop might be there."

My family would be furious if I knowingly put myself in Mehmet's presence. But Perparim lost his mother when he was six and asked me to come in her place. I wrestled with it for days. But what decision would my soul be happy with on the day I died? My father taught us that was what mattered most—so I went.

Seeing Mehmet alive while my sister was dead by his hand was painful. He could attend his son's graduation. She couldn't, and I was a poor substitute for a mother like her.

"This is my aunt," Perparim introduced me to everyone. "My mother's sister," he'd always add, smiling big and breaking my heart each time.

When Mehmet shook my hand, he was distant, like he always was. He looked away, clearly uneasy in my presence.

"How's your mother?" he asked.

"She's good," I said, feeling strange to be talking to him about the family he destroyed.

"She's one tough lady," he added, knowing tough was a compliment.

If only you knew she paid to get you killed, I thought.

I was supposed to ask about his family, but this was a situation with no set protocol. Knowing his father had died of a heart attack, I asked, "How is your mother?"

"Good," he muttered, looking away.

Perparim called us to watch him do a "single slide." In full firefighter gear he rappelled down a two-story wall like a champ.

"You must be proud of him," I said, wanting Perparim to have a parent who was proud, even if that parent was his father.

"Yeah, he's a good kid," Mehmet said, smiling weakly.

Because he didn't take after you, I thought.

Perparim walked over knowing he'd aced the move. Jariyeh would have beamed at her son, hugged him hard and called him, *"Djali Nanës,"*--Mommy's boy. But all he had was a vacant father, and me. In a letter years earlier, he said, "It feels good writing to you. Feels like you're the only one who understands."

"Wow, That was awesome, Perparim," I said.

He grinned. "Pretty good, right?" He placed his hands on his hips, superhero-style, unconsciously like his mother.

"Yeah, that was good," Mehmet said, trying to fulfill what was expected.

"Let's go outside," Perparim said. "You can see how we work the fire hose. It looks easy, but it takes a lot of us to keep it steady. You can try if you want."

Mehmet said he had to go right after. Perparim told me this was the first graduation his dad ever attended, so I felt bad he'd be leaving him. Was it probation? Work? A need for a hit?

"That's okay, Pop," Perparim said before heading toward the gushing hose.

I began taking off my heels to join them, as Jariyeh would have, when Mehmet asked, "How are your brothers? How's Zogu?"

"He's good," I replied, surprised he'd ask about the brother who tried to kill him, not knowing they'd once been friends.

"I have nothing to live for."

It felt like a confession. I felt sorry for him. Perparim had told me his father never remarried because he still loved his mother. Over the years, I often thought about forgiveness. How much free will could he have really had—as an addict and as an Albanian male desperate to prove himself? But who was I to forgive? I hoped he would one day forgive himself, but maybe not just yet. I wasn't ready for him to be off the hook. After all, he had pulled the trigger and ruined our lives. Did he feel remorse?

Mehmet looked at me, and I felt his pain—a deep heaviness in the heart I knew all too well. But was it his—or was it mine?

He looked down. "I wish your brothers would have killed me."

IV. THE NIGHT OF

August 1979: In front of our building the month before she died.
Jariyeh and her children (L-R: Perparim, Lata, and Esat.

BROOKLYN

SEP. 17, 1979 - 1981

Chapter 60

9:30 PM: The Phone Call

* * *

"What happened that night?" was the hardest question to ask. That night, which began the evening of September 17, 1979, and ended at 2:35 a.m. That night which changed us forever.

My family couldn't bear to relive the horror all at once. They slowly shared bits and pieces. Bits and pieces they'd kept to themselves. Bits and pieces that opened old wounds. It was up to me to gently ask the questions, give them space, and fit the fragments together.

"What happened that night?" I asked Bekim, expecting him to start with the family meeting.

"I got a phone call," he said.

"A phone call? What phone call?"

———

The sound of the phone ringing annoyed Bekim. He thought people already talked too much, and this invention had made matters worse. Phones were for small talk. Small talk was for small people. Bekim was never small. He grew up around men. Even when he was young, he was old.

It was around 9:00 p.m. when the phone rang.

As always, Saranda answered.

"It's Jerry," she said, handing the receiver to her husband.

Jerry hardly called, so Bekim knew it must be important.

"I saw Mehmet at the Café," Jerry said. "He's saying that he's going to kill you guys."

Bekim knew that by "you guys" he meant the brothers. It wasn't the first time Jerry relayed that message. The other times, it felt like Mehmet was trying to act tough in front of his friends. But this time Bekim sensed something different. Something cold. Something sinister. He could almost taste it.

"Okay," Bekim replied and hung up.

He never liked Mehmet, but neither he nor Zogu ever showed their brother-in-law disrespect. Why would he want to kill them? *It must have something to do with Jariyeh,* he thought. Had she threatened to leave? Was Mehmet planning to kill her?

Section XXVIII: "Her husband purchases a woman's labor and cohabitation, but not her life."

Although a girl was sold for the price of her blood, it didn't mean her husband could spill that blood without good reason. If Mehmet killed her, the brothers would avenge her—so he had to kill them first.

The more Bekim thought about it, the more pissed he became. First at his mother, for having chosen Mehmet. Then at his sister, for not knowing her place. Thanks to them, they were all in deep shit. Marriage was a fragile life-and-death agreement that too easily involved the spilling of blood. Bekim wasn't interested in getting caught in a game of vengeance that left no winners. He was civilized— for an Albanian.

He picked up the dreaded phone, dialed Zogu, and said the only words necessary: "Come over."

Zogu, the middle brother who preferred to be the oldest, respected his place in the bloodline. He hung up the phone, jumped into his checkered cab, and raced to Staten Island.

The brothers had four years between them, but in some ways were worlds apart. Bekim lived for soccer. Zogu lived for honor. Bekim didn't care what people thought. Zogu cared too much. If the integrity of the family name was in question, Bekim would seek intelligent means of setting the record straight. Zogu would consider it an honor and a privilege to pull the trigger. That's why Bekim chose his words carefully when his brother arrived.

"Jariyeh and Mehmet are having problems," he said.

Zogu was shocked. Why didn't they say anything? They were friends.

He and Jariyeh were inseparable back in Kosova. As children they herded sheep, worked the fields, and played together. Zogu was two years her junior, but as the boy felt in charge, and like a good sister she let him think so. As teenagers in Italy their friendship faded when they found new friends. He had Ali, she had Saranda—but in Zogu's mind, they were still tight.

He and Mehmet were also friends. After Jariyeh's engagement, Zogu stayed with the Bicis for two weeks and shared a room with Mehmet. During that time, Mehmet got him a job at Benny's House of Pizza in Queens, taught him how to spin pies, and navigate the NYC subway maze. In March 1979, when Mehmet got arrested for shooting a man at Benny's Pizza, he called Zogu, not his new Lulu's House friends. Zogu posted bail and drove him home, no questions asked.

So why hadn't either of them told him they were having problems? Zogu was sure he could have helped. What he didn't understand was the pressure he put on others when he judged anything that defied his "honorable Albanian" infatuation. He placed friends on high pedestals, and when they fell—as they inevitably did—he felt betrayed. To be Zogu's friend, you had to be flawless, as he believed he was. Not to disturb his fantasy, friends hid things.

Jariyeh never told him that she had fallen for Sam in Italy and didn't want to marry Mehmet. Or that she wanted out of her marriage. Mehmet never told him he was part of a drug cartel, or that his new love was heroin. Zogu's fantasies were now crumbling, for truth had a way of rearing its ugly head.

"What do we do?" Zogu asked, like a soldier awaiting orders.

"We must get them to make up," Bekim said.

A family meeting was in order. American laws did not apply. There was no need for judges, policemen, lawyers, or therapists. They were strangers. This was family business. In the old country, village elders would have resolved such matters, but this was Brooklyn, and the burden fell on him, the eldest son. Bekim would do his best to handle it as his father would have—peacefully.

The meeting would be held at our apartment, since Jariyeh and Mehmet lived next door. Bekim grabbed his keys, and they headed out.

Zogu followed behind in his car. As they approached the Verrazano Bridge, he wondered if anyone's life was in danger. Nah, he thought, *that I would've definitely known.*

Chapter 61

12:00 AM: The Last Song

* * *

"What do you remember about that night?" I asked Kamile.

Kamile hesitated, as she always did before delving into something painful. Even good times were sometimes hard to recall.

"During the drive home from work, Jariyeh told us she had a bad feeling," she finally said.

I hated hearing that. I wanted her to feel only good things on her last day.

"What kind of bad feeling?"

"She didn't say. Just a bad feeling."

Interesting—Saranda told me she also had a bad feeling that night. Was their gut trying to warn them? Why didn't they listen?

———

"This is it. I'm leaving Mehmet tonight," Jariyeh had told Saranda on the phone that morning.

"Okay," Saranda replied, not knowing what else to say.

But when Jariyeh called her from work later that evening, Saranda wasn't as agreeable. "Please don't do it," she begged. "I've had a bad feeling in my stomach all day. Don't do it. Not tonight."

"It's gonna be tonight," Jariyeh insisted. "Don't worry. It will all be over, and I'll finally be free. You'll see."

Jariyeh tried to sound confident, but deep down, she also felt something was off, but couldn't tell her sensitive friend.

After work, Jariyeh sat in the backseat with Kamile. Nana sat up front with Elez. She was grateful it wasn't Mehmet's week because all he did was talk nonstop and gossip *si gru e keqe*--like a bad woman.

Jariyeh had counted the days to her mother's return from Kosova, hoping things would be different—good-different. But her gut told her otherwise.

"I have a bad feeling," she said.

That disturbed Kamile. Jariyeh was the type to joke rather than complain, to laugh rather than cry. It was unlike her to say such things.

As Elez took the ramp onto the Brooklyn Bridge, Jariyeh looked up at the waning moon and began to sing, trying to lift the heaviness she had caused.

♪ *Ti moj hanë shkilqim argenti*	♪ My blushing golden moon,
Mos din gja	Do you know
per timen vash	where my girl has gone?
Ka shum koh	It's been so long
se kam pa un oj shkreti	since I have seen her
Per tej zemra	For you, my heart
mdixhet flak	still burns strong

Jariyeh sang all the time: during car rides, picnics in the park, while embroidering, cooking, and every family gathering. Anytime was a good time for a song. Even when life was hard—especially when life was hard. She didn't know it, but this song would be her last.

♪ *Ishin tri*	♪ We were young
edhe te lumtun	and we were happy
Qe te'dji androjshim	Both of us had dreams
Tash ka tretun	But that was then
vetmin m'ka lanun	now I'm all alone
Per te zemra	For you my heart
me'dixhet flak	still burns strong

Kamile wanted to join in, but a heaviness in Jariyeh's voice gave her pause. She sat quietly and listened, hoping her sister could sing away her bad feeling.

♪ *Prandaj hanë*	♪ That's why dear moon
un ti pot lutna	I beg of you
T'mi dhojsh vashes po e pres	Tell my girl I am still waiting

Jariyeh's voice began to crack.

Se me te	For with her
kam kujtime t'amla	I have sweet memories
Per te jetoj	For her I live
Per te dot vdes ♪	For her I die ♪

She finished the song and the car got quiet.

"I don't know, Jariyeh." Elez broke the silence. "It's just not working for you tonight."

"You're right, Elez," she replied.

Kamile looked at her sister, who stared blankly out the window, and tried to say something to lift her mood, but couldn't quite find the words.

The twenty-minute car ride began to feel like days. As streetlights passed overhead, Kamile took a deep breath and let her mind drift to a happier time in

Kosova when Jariyeh was eight. She, Jariyeh, and Zogu were among the children chosen to recite a poem in front of the entire elementary school. She and Jariyeh wore dresses Nana had sewn for them. Kamile had red sandals and Jariyeh black. Jariyeh's was a socialist poem. She had practiced for weeks and couldn't wait for her recital. When the day finally came, Kamile proudly watched her little sister take the stage in her braided hair and tailored dress. Jariyeh reveled in the attention for a few seconds, then recited loud enough for all to hear:

Republik, a ndjeve oj	Republic, have you heard,
Dy trima, dy heroj	Two warriors, two heroes
Me ty, O flamurtar	Are with you, O flag-bearer

She lifted one hand toward the heavens, as she had rehearsed and raised her voice for the final stanza.

Nën yllin qlirimtar	Beneath the savior star
U ngrit I ulti rob	The lowest slave rose up
Puntorë katundar!	Into a working farmer!

The memory made Kamile smile.

Pulling up in front of our building, they exchanged goodbyes.

"Natën e mirë,"--Good night, Jariyeh said.

"Natën e mirë," each replied.

Kamile watched as Nana walked toward 8747 Bay Parkway and Jariyeh turned toward 8735.

Tomorrow will be a better day, Kamile assured herself. Her sister could never stay upset for long. *Surely the next time I see her, Jariyeh will be singing and laughing again.*

Chapter 62

Bullet Wound Entry

* * *

I had been gathering "night of" stories from my family for years, but the biggest clues came from the court transcripts. It took years to find them and nearly a month's salary to have transcribed.

The email hit my inbox on April 5, 2013. I stared at it, my heart pounding. There was no way I could learn how my sister died—after thirty-four years—and go to work the next day. My vacation was coming up. I'd wait until then.

On May 1st, my fiftieth birthday, I treated myself to a five-star bed-and-breakfast in the Berkshires. There, in a quiet room, I opened the nearly 800 pages of testimony on my iPad—a gift from my children—and braced myself.

THE PEOPLE OF THE STATE OF NEW YORK
-against-
MEHMET BICI

The thought that the People of New York were seeking justice for my sister brought tears. But the sight of Mehmet's name brought rage.

The trial commenced on February 6, 1981, a year and a half after Jariyeh's murder. I couldn't wait for Mehmet to go behind bars, like the animal he was. None of us went to court. There was no way we could stomach seeing the Bicis, let alone listen to their lies. For they would surely lie. My brothers would testify, but not Nana. I thought that was because she didn't speak English and wouldn't have much to add—not knowing she knew much more than my brothers.

The courtroom was filled with a new cast of characters. Characters whose roles came to life when crimes occurred. The District Attorney (DA), Wayne Roth, sought justice for Jariyeh. Mehmet had eight lawyers. The lead defense attorney, Lawrence Barse, stopped at nothing to free his client. Running the courtroom stage was the Honorable Judge Lentol, who did his best to give my sister a fair trial.

First to take the stand were the detectives and police officers who responded to the 10-10 call. They described what my sister's entire existence had come down to: "the crime scene." They didn't call her Mehmet's Nuse, Lutfi's daughter, Lata's mother, or my sister. She was simply "the deceased." There was no talk of Jariyeh's love for people, for singing, for dancing, for roses or her children. In that courtroom, there was no talk of Fate. Free will was the premise.

The DA's opening statement caught me by surprise and catapulted me back to that fateful night, when I was sixteen. This time, I wasn't sleeping.

Then, too soon—on page 52, Detective Kane was asked to describe her cause of death. I recalled writing in an old journal: *He shot her five times; one struck her hand.* I always thought another pierced her heart—because that's how people died instantly in the movies, and instantly was how I wanted her to go.

THE COURT: Tell us what you observed.
A(Answer): Yes, sir.
A bullet wound entry of the left forearm. And a bullet wound exit, just on the opposing side of the arm.
A bullet wound entry beneath that arm in the trunk of the body on the left-hand side, beneath the armpit.
A bullet wound of the right rear upper back, closer to the spinal cord.
A bullet wound entry of the inner right upper leg.
A bullet wound to the right breast, showing what we call a bullet wipe mark, which is left by the projectile as it enters the body.
And a bullet wound entry on the left breast.
A bullet wound entry on the left upper chest.

I cringed with each bullet wound entry he cited, then read his testimony again. And again. Trying to count. Was it six shots? Seven? It couldn't be eight. Didn't guns only have six bullets?

Did my sister feel every hit?

I drew a body outline, front and back, marked the entries, and imagined the wounds. In her leg. Her back. Her chest. Her breasts—were they shaped like mine? What did that exhibit photo look like?

"What's a wipe mark?" I asked AI. "The impression or discoloration left on the skin around the entry wound when the projectile strikes the body."

Why did I find this detail so disturbing?

When did each wound happen? Was there a trail of blood? How close was he?

All I had was questions.

Detective Kane gave more details. "Wound number two had an angle of descent from front to the back, and upward."

Which one was wound number two? Was it the one in the chest? Did he shoot her while she was lying on the floor? Did he go inside the vestibule?

Kane continued: "The medical examiner's opinion on the immediate cause of death was multiple gunshot wounds of the chest wall, entering the lungs, heart, and thoracic artery; gunshot wounds of left thigh and right arm, massive internal and external hemorrhage."

Massive hemorrhage? Didn't someone say there was hardly any blood? Why did the medical examiner say left thigh? Kane said *right* thigh. Why couldn't things just make sense?

It wasn't the best way to spend my 50th birthday, but the truth had always been important. I imagined my sister running for her life. I imagined her fear. I imagined her short, sloppy husband shooting her. And I became *livid.* To think I had excused him all these years. He was high. The drug dealers were to blame. He loved my sister. Was this love? All I felt now was hate.

Fuck him!

Fuck Mehmet!

I wanted him to hurt like I was hurting. I wanted him to read what he had done. I wanted him to SUFFER.

I went to bed sobbing.

In the morning, the inn owner gave me a free upgrade. I thought of it as a birthday present from my sister. Upstairs, in an exquisite room I couldn't afford, I prepared a luxurious bubble bath. I felt Jariyeh smiling down at me—proud of the woman I'd become.

"I love you, sis," I said out loud. "I promise to tell your story."

Under the covers of my plush bed, I reached for my iPad. There were several mysteries to unravel. DA Roth had said:

"My opening statement to you will be brief, brief because it is an outline of the case that I intend to prove, and brief because the evidence of the defendant's guilt is overwhelming."

It sounded like an open-and-shut case. So why were there so many pages?

And why did Mehmet only serve eighteen months?

Chapter 63

12:35 AM: The Family Meeting

* * *

It was one thing to hear stories, another to read what was said under oath. Most times the versions complemented each other. Other times the testimony caught me by surprise. Then there were details that never made it into the courtroom—things lawyers didn't know to ask, and things witnesses didn't bother to tell.

Like Jerry's phone call. Why didn't Bekim think it was relevant? Wouldn't it have shown premeditation and raised the charge to murder in the first degree? Or did Bekim not want Mehmet to know Jerry had betrayed him?

Bekim did tell the DA about the family meeting. What happened in our living room that evening ended up on full display before the jury.

———

We were proud of our large guest-worthy living room, which was created by knocking down a wall. Everything was in *kuq e zi*--red and black, the colors of our flag. Three long velvet couches covered in plastic and piped in gold wrapped around the room, and a black carpet with large red flowers engulfed the floor. On our walls hung Zogu's hunting rifles. A photo of Nana's brother in his white felt hat. A painting of Baba on the white stallion that he had sold for the price of a house. A photo of Nana and her seven children from New Year's Eve at Jariyeh's. And of course the Albanian flag: a double-headed black eagle on a red background. Ours was cross-stitched and framed. Everything important was on display: homeland, bloodline, family—was there anything else?

The color TV brought us into the twentieth century. The world we had joined nine years earlier. Still, we believed we were the superior race.

Around 12:30 a.m., Nana got home from work. She wasn't pleased to find Luan and me talking to Seba and her brother—Tefik's children.

"Bekim's here," Vera told her.

"Make me a coffee," Nana said, setting her purse on the dining room table before heading in to join her boys.

"Things are not good with Jariyeh and Mehmet," Bekim told his mother. "We have to fix things."

Nana couldn't tell Bekim she knew about the troubles. She had kept it from her sons because involving men was risky. "Children fight, women argue, and men kill," the saying went. Now that he knew, she could only hope he'd fix things without bloodshed.

Bekim called out for Vera, who had stationed herself in the kitchen in case her in-laws needed something. She rushed in.

"Call Jariyeh and tell her to come over," he directed.

"I'll be right there," Jariyeh told Vera on the phone.

Was she hoping this was the family meeting that would put an end to the madness that had become her life? That this would be the night her mother convinced her brothers to stand beside her?

I heard the downstairs buzzer and got excited—Jariyeh was here. Then Nana sent us off to bed.

Vera greeted Jariyeh at the front door.

"A më kan thirrë mem ba pash?"--Did they invite me to crown me king? Jariyeh joked, but Vera didn't get it—only men got crowned king.

At the trial, a year and a half later, Bekim was asked about the family meeting. DIRECT EXAMINATION BY MR. ROTH:

Q: What time did Jariyeh come over?

A: It must have been five minutes after we called, like 12:35 or something.

Q: What happened when she came over?

A: As an older brother, I tried to convince her, you know, to have no trouble and to stay with him, because it would affect the whole family. In our tradition we try, you know, to be on the husband's side, so, the wife won't do something that would make us look bad.

I was surprised Bekim had admitted to not supporting his sister because of our traditions. Didn't he care that the Americans might think us animals?

"I know you're having problems with Mehmet," Bekim said to his sister.

This was Jariyeh's chance to make her brothers understand. She wasn't an American wife. She wasn't asking for alimony or child support—just her freedom. If she and her children could live with her mother, she'd consider herself the luckiest woman in the world.

"Yes, we're having problems," she replied. "I can't stay with him anymore. I don't want to live with haram." *Haram* meant evil, forbidden, and everything else that sent one to hell. She wanted no part of Mehmet or his sinful life.

Zogu looked at his sister in disbelief but said nothing. He let his big brother do the talking.

Noise from our pillow fight seeped through the wall. Nana got up and headed toward us.

"You don't want to live with haram?" Bekim said. "But don't you understand that if you leave Mehmet, you are affecting me, your brothers, your sisters? All of us. It's not just you."

It wasn't just her. It was everyone who carried our name—in America, Kosova, and Albania. Seven generations' worth. But Bekim wasn't worried about ancestors or shame. He was worried about Mehmet killing Jariyeh and the brothers.

"But he's a drug dealer," Jariyeh replied.

"You have to find a way to make up," Bekim said. "You have three children."

"And he's putting their lives in danger," she said, fighting back angry tears. "He leaves drugs around the house and leaves the children home alone."

"Do you want to keep your children?" he tried to appeal to her maternal side. "Then stay with him. Make up and stay with him."

At the trial, Bekim tried to explain those words to the jury:

"I told my sister, I said, it's not just you because when we get married we don't, you know, divorce that easy. But she told me that you are not in my shoes, and you don't know what I am going through."

Bekim knew he wasn't in her shoes, but what could he do?

"Stay with him and make up," he told her. "In the name of family. In the name of God."

Bekim thought of religions as cults that turned people into sheep, but he did believe there was some kind of Intelligence out there. He knew his sister was a believer.

Jariyeh had placed her faith in the Almighty. She tried everything: got a job, gave her mother runaway money, took Nana's gun, called Bekim when Mehmet left the kids alone, lit the gypsy's candles, even tried making plans with Sam. There was nothing more to do and no one else to turn to. So she prayed to God at every turn: *"O Zot i madh, me ty përpara."*--Oh great God, lead my way.

Had she thought this meeting would be an answer to her prayers?

In court, Bekim testified to what happened next:

"After I spoke to her, I don't know how long, we kept repeating things. I told my sister-in-law Vera to tell Mehmet to come. I thought maybe we can talk it over and maybe between them they can figure something out."

Did Bekim think that if Mehmet agreed to change, Jariyeh would stay—and Mehmet would no longer want to kill them?

Inviting him over was risky. Bekim knew Mehmet would come armed. Like a fine leather belt or Italian shoes, guns were an accessory that accentuated Albanian manhood. Bekim didn't own a gun, and Zogu's .38 was in his bedroom. He didn't know about Mehmet's threat, not that he'd pull it on a guest, but he would have kept it close.

With both brothers unarmed, Mehmet could shoot them one by one, including Luan, leaving no one to avenge their blood. No one, that is, except me—the virgin daughter. I didn't know the "Sworn Virgin" rule at the time, but I'm sure Nana would have enlightened me.[xx] Despite our lowly status as Albanian women, gender equality was possible if we were willing to become men. An excellent solution for families cursed with the dreadful fate of not having sons. By swearing to remain celibate, a daughter could wear men's clothing, go to men's meetings, carry a gun, and take vengeance. She could kill and be killed. *It didn't get better than that.*

Would I have been able to take revenge? I had killed roaches before, but I couldn't hurt a soul. Still, with the shock of losing my brothers, and the chance to finally earn Nana's love, which would surely follow such an honorable act—there was no telling what I might have done.

Did Mehmet know I qualified to be his assassin? If he did, would he have killed me too? Would he have killed Nana? She wasn't a virgin, but she was dangerous. More so, I believed, than my brothers.

Chapter 64

1:00 AM: Speaking Into the Void

* * *

"Listen," Bekim said to Vera. "When Mehmet comes in, look to see which side he has his gun on."

Vera nodded. The downstairs buzzer rang and she let him in.

Bekim waited at the door, as we did with all our guests, and watched with caution as he shook Mehmet's hand.

"How you doing, Mike?" he said in English, using his American name to keep things light.

"Good, good," Mike said.

As Mehmet removed his shoes, Bekim noticed the gun in his left pocket.

"Make us a coffee," Bekim told Vera, then respectfully waited for Mehmet to walk ahead into the living room before glancing back at her.

Vera pointed to her left, confirming his assessment.

Zogu and Nana stood to greet Mehmet.

The custom of waiting for your guest to sit first worked to Bekim's advantage. After Mehmet sat across from Jariyeh, Bekim took the seat to his left, in case he needed to stop him from drawing his gun.

"So, how you doing, Mike?" Bekim repeated, trying to distract from his awkwardly close proximity.

"Good. How you doin'?"

"I'm doing good," Bekim replied.

"How are you?" Nana asked Mehmet first, followed by Zogu.

"Good," Mehmet answered to both.

"How are things with work?" Bekim said, knowing the deli had closed.

"I want to open a sandwich shop," Mehmet replied.

Vera walked in with a tray of Turkish coffee for all.

Bekim waited for her to leave, then said, "I know you and Jariyeh are having some problems."

"Well…yeah…" Mehmet hesitated. "You know, she gets angry at me."

"I get angry at you!" Jariyeh snapped. "Just look at you."

And there he was: disheveled, slouching, glassy-eyed, with saliva glistening at the corners of his mouth. But wives weren't supposed to get angry at husbands, or God forbid, point out their failings. To keep this unspoken rule intact, men stuck together. Women enforced it too, making it harder for those like Jariyeh who refused to conform.

Bekim glared at his sister, wondering why she couldn't control her temper and listen for once.

"Listen," he said. "We have to work this out."

Mehmet nodded like a little boy as he wiped his nose.

"There is no reason why you guys can't be happy. You have three children, and those children need you," Bekim continued, disgusted with himself for having to appeal to such a man, but knowing he had to.

"Yes. Yes," Mehmet agreed. He liked to agree. It was easier that way, and he liked easy. Or was he just saying what Bekim wanted to hear until he got his chance to kill them?

Persuading him was easier than expected, but not surprising. Mehmet wasn't the toughest or the most intelligent—a dangerous combination. Weak and stupid men did dumb things to prove they weren't weak and stupid.

"Your children need their parents," Bekim said, driving the point home to Mehmet, who quietly looked at his wife from time to time. "They need you both," he added, as if his words could stop Mehmet from killing the mother of his children. Then he turned to Jariyeh, knowing she was the one he had to convince.

"Do you understand?"

At the trial, DA Roth asked Bekim to recall what happened next:

Q: What did your sister say?

A: She said, "I cannot live with him no more." She said, "I cannot take these things, he takes drugs."

MR. BARSE: Objection, your Honor, he is testifying to something someone else is saying.

THE COURT: I will sustain the objection insofar as the conversations of every other person is concerned except as far as the deceased is concerned.

Q: Tell us what Jariyeh said.

Bekim's reply caught me off guard. Everything he testified to that day he had already told me—except this. Maybe he forgot. Maybe he regretted saying it. Maybe he omitted it out of shame.

A: Jariyeh said, "He takes dope." I said, "Listen—

THE COURT: He takes dope?

A: That's right, that's what she said.

I said, "Look, if he takes dope, you are his wife, the hell with it, you take dope too, why don't you take dope and as long as you live together, it will affect no one else."

She said, "I won't take dope, never in my life will I take dope."

Bekim wouldn't have said something like that unless he was desperate. He knew how stubborn and fearless his sister was. If she knew Mehmet had threatened to kill the brothers, she'd confront him—and ignite the very blood feud Bekim was trying to prevent.

Jariyeh knew Bekim wouldn't want her to leave Mehmet—but this, she didn't expect. Though the words left her mouth, it was as if she were speaking into a void. No one seemed to hear her.

Not her brothers.

Not her mother, who sat there in silence.

Not even God.

The meeting reeked of injustice. Its only message was: *You are a wife and must accept your drug-dealing, drug-using, lying husband.* But Jariyeh would NOT listen.

"You know how many times he said he was going to stop taking dope? He is a liar!" she said.

She needed her brothers to understand the kind of man she was married to. Worse than an addict, he didn't keep his word. How was she expected to live with such a man?

Bekim's testimony continued:

"In the meantime, Mehmet didn't say nothing. The only words that he spoke were, 'I know I lie. I know I take dope,' but he says, 'The money is no problem.' She says, 'I don't care for your money.'"

I wondered if the jury understood that my sister didn't want to raise her children with his dirty money.

"I don't need a man," she said. "I will become a nun and live by myself before I raise them with a drug addict."

She didn't need Mehmet. She didn't need Sam. She needed sanity, and all around her was madness.

"It's not just about you!" Bekim said.

It was fine when he put himself first—got engaged, moved out, married on his terms. He was a man. She was a woman.

She *had* to listen.

It was 2 a.m. Bekim had been at it for over an hour and a half. No matter how hard he tried, he couldn't talk sense into the sister who was putting all their lives in danger. All he wanted was for her to say she'd stay with Mehmet—for now.

Later, he'd figure something out. Jariyeh was intelligent, but at times she could be such a mule. He lost his cool.

Bekim told the court:

"I stood up. I said for my sake, the sake of my mother and my brother, I said for the sake of God, I said go home and settle this between you two, and I left. I didn't say nothing, I just left. I left."

Years back, Baba had begged Jariyeh to leave the Bicis. Now Bekim was begging her to stay. And like Baba, he walked out without a goodbye—never imagining those would be the last words he'd ever say to his sister.

Chapter 65

2:00 AM: A Mother's Prayer

* * *

Nana was surprised Bekim handled the meeting according to the codes decreed by the Kanun so many moons ago. Codes she didn't think her son respected. Codes Nana had once broken, but now obeyed with a vengeance. But these rules of man didn't hold the answer to her daughter's predicament. So she turned to the only one truly in charge, *Zot*--God, and prayed the only way she knew: in Arabic.

Bismillahi	In the name of Allah
e-Rahman e-Raheem	the Beneficent, the Merciful
Al hamdu lillaahi	Praise be to God
rabbil 'alemeen	Lord of all the worlds
e-Rahman e-Raheem	The Compassionate, the Merciful

My mother didn't use a prayer rug or bother to face Mecca. She worshiped as she had since Baba died five years earlier, in bed before sleep. Tonight, she recited the salah with rare enthusiasm.

Maaliki yaumid Deen	Ruler on the Day of Reckoning
Iyyaaka na'abudu	You alone do we worship
wa iyyaaka nasta'een	and You alone do we seek help

Nana learned the prayer phonetically, like I did. Neither of us knew what the words meant—which made them feel more mystical. More powerful. She prayed in Arabic to get Allah's attention, but she revealed the reason for her prayer in Albanian, so there'd be no confusion.

"*O Zot i madhë*"--Oh great God, she said. "Help Jariyeh."

Nana desperately needed His help with the daughter she loved so dearly. It was the stubborn part of Jariyeh that she wished she could change. The tough part. The part that was just like her.

Life had brought Nana from a farmhouse in the mountains of Albania with dirt floors, outhouses, and oil lamps to an apartment in Brooklyn with carpeting, indoor plumbing, and electricity. No longer would her guests sit cross-legged on itchy goat-hair rugs, but on fancy velvet couches. To relatives and friends back home, Kadire Kola had made it. But those were outward things. Inside, where it mattered, her world was the same.

Nana recalled Jariyeh's phone call to her in Kosova.

"Mehmet is sucking the life out of me. I'm going to take the money I gave you and run away with the kids."

Instead of giving her permission, she said, "Wait till I return." And she had returned. Nana was the wise elder others called to reconcile their marriages. Yet when her daughter needed her most—she said nothing.

Growing up, I assumed we didn't help Jariyeh because our traditions were rooted in Islam. I didn't know they had been decreed by a Roman Catholic prince, or that Islamic law recognized a woman's right to seek divorce more than biblical law. [xxi] Surah 2:228 says a divorced woman had to wait three menstrual cycles, and surah 65:6 instructs the husband not to make her stay unbearable. It wasn't the Koran that suppressed women. It was men who invented these customs and claimed they were God-sent. I never thought to check.

My mother didn't push for Jariyeh to live with us because she feared shaming Baba's name—or worse, owing Mehmet blood and losing her sons. She wished she could take away Jariyeh's pain, but didn't know how. Nana let Bekim take the lead. The resolution he proposed was right according to the Kanun, but not according to Jariyeh.

Nana turned her back to the streetlamps that lit our bedroom windows and faced the bed where Seba and I slept. With the occasional car humming up and down Bay Parkway, she drifted off to sleep.

Chapter 66

2:36 AM: The Bullshit

* * *

Bekim pulled out of the Exxon station still reeling from the family meeting. He wasn't ready to go home, so he drove past our building—just to see. As he approached, he saw Jariyeh and Mehmet come out and head toward their building. She was yelling at him, so Bekim followed to see what would happen. He pulled up in front as they stepped into their block-long hallway. Through the vestibule doors, he saw Jariyeh waving her arm in frustration while Mehmet walked behind her like a reprimanded child.

He's going to kill her. The thought came to him like a premonition. Helpless was not a word Bekim would ever use to describe himself, but in that moment, he felt like the thief in the Albanian tale.

> A man caught a thief stealing apples from his tree. He aimed his rifle at him and said, *"Hip, se t'vrava. Zhdrip, se t'vrava"*--Go up, or I'll kill you. Come down, or I'll kill you. The thief was stuck on the tree with no way out.

Bekim had tried all he knew. He didn't think to call the police. He didn't think to get an order of protection. He didn't think to send his sister and her children to a shelter. He didn't even know such options existed, and neither did we. Bekim was powerful in many ways, but he couldn't think beyond his upbringing. In that sense, he was blameless.

He watched Mehmet and Jariyeh disappear into their long hallway, then made a U-turn toward the Belt Parkway. The light turned green as he approached the intersection, as if confirming his need to move on. Bekim watched himself drive toward the Verrazano as if he were in a film. A film he'd seen the ending of, and like an actor following a script, he couldn't change the ending.

"All you women are is trouble," he said the moment he got home, dropping his keys on the table.

Bekim didn't throw things. You felt his anger even in silence. He always seemed a little mad at God for placing him in a world full of idiots. All Bekim wanted was a simple life that revolved around soccer. But thanks to Jariyeh, life got complicated.

Saranda had never seen her husband this angry. She knew he was talking about Jariyeh, her fearless friend who knew women should keep their mouths shut but never held back. Saranda was dying to know what happened in Brooklyn, but to avoid becoming the "trouble" her husband was referring to, she held her tongue.

In court, DA Roth asked Bekim, "What happened when you got home?"
A: I told my wife, I said, The things with Mehmet and Jariyeh don't look good. She said, "Don't worry, nothing is going to happen."
THE COURT: Get some water, please.

Bekim had told his wife, "Nothing is going to happen? This guy is going to fucking kill her." But he didn't get to say that in court. After the drink of water, the DA moved on.

Q: What happened next?
A: I was not even five minutes in bed when the phone rang. My—
THE COURT: Would you like to take a break?
A: Yes, I would.

What was happening? My brother never took breaks. He looked down on any display of weakness. But there he was, in a room full of strangers, unable to go on.

I called him at work. "Why did you need a break?"

"Because I couldn't stop crying," he admitted.

That broke my heart. I'd never really thought about other people's pain, let alone that of my fearless brothers.

After the short recess, Mr. Roth asked Bekim to continue.

"I was not even five minutes in bed when the phone rang," he testified. "And I said to my wife, I said, 'Oh my God, he killed her.'"

Bekim wasn't psychic, but at times he had feelings. And if he ever dreamt of you, you paid attention.

"Hello," he said, with dread.

"Mehmeti e ka vra Xharijën," his mother told him, confirming his fear.

Not knowing what to say, Bekim hung up and looked at his wife, who sat up in bed, holding her breath. Then a thought came to him. The word *"vra"* had a few meanings: hurt, shot, or killed. Had Mehmet "hurt" Jariyeh, or had he "killed" her? Bekim picked up the phone and called his mother back.

Luan answered.

"Is she dead?" Bekim asked.

"Yes."

Bekim hung up and turned to his wife.

"Shit! Mehmet shot her."

"Maybe she's not dead," Saranda replied.

Bekim didn't bother explaining. It was too many words. Too many feelings. He quickly dressed and headed for Brooklyn. There was no reason to take Saranda or wake the children. "Men matters" were at hand. In a blood feud, the eldest son was the chosen instrument of revenge, but he would not participate. It was beneath him. He had always tried to get away from the Albanian bullshit.

But the bullshit followed.

Saranda locked the door behind him and cried, and cried, and cried. Till she could cry no more. She paced around the apartment. Numb. Lost. Constantly looking at the time. Looking at the phone. Waiting for it to ring. Hoping her husband would say Jariyeh was hurt—not dead.

But inside, Saranda knew. She had known all day long that something terrible was going to happen. She tried to warn Jariyeh. But no, she wouldn't listen. She said it had to be tonight.

Had to be.

Saranda looked at the phone, and like her husband, now dreaded its existence—for she knew that when it rang, her worst fear would be confirmed.

During the cross-examination, I wasn't sure if Barse was trying to make Bekim look stupid or just piss him off. After a series of convoluted questions, Barse said:

"Don't you understand me?"

A: Yes, I understand. I understand you very well, but you are not coming to the point. I don't know what word to answer.

MR. BARSE: I ask the Court to direct the witness to answer the question.

THE COURT: Ask the witness a specific question, he will answer it.

Q: Do you know Mehmet Bici?

A: Yes, I do.

Q: Were you at the wedding?

A: No, I was not. We have a law that we don't go to the wedding of the sister.

Q: You know he was married to your sister though.

Reading my brother's testimony, I could hear his anger and was sure he wanted to rip Barse apart with his teeth.

I know I wanted to.

Bekim said the hardest part of the trial was being asked to point out Mehmet— then have to see his face.

"Did you know Jariyeh dreamt she was going to die," I asked him. "Do you believe it was fate? Could we have changed anything?"

"I don't know if it was meant to be. Sometimes you write your destiny," he said. "After Jariyeh died, I read book after book, trying to understand why she couldn't see that her actions could lead to murder."

Unlike Zogu, who read westerns, Bekim read the New York Times from cover to cover every day and preferred books about soccer and psychology. He had been looking for answers.

"Why couldn't she see that her actions could lead to murder?" I asked.

"It's because women don't think in violent terms," he explained. "They can't know how men will react."

I wondered if that was my brother's way of forgiving Jariyeh—or himself.

The fact that he'd wrestled with her death for so long touched me. It confirmed his love for her—and the guilt he may have carried for not knowing how to stop it. Maybe all that introspection was what made Bekim so approachable. In the years to come, he became the brother I turned to.

Chapter 67

2:34 AM: Between Two Doors

* * *

The family meeting was a nightmare Zogu hadn't seen coming. He was shocked to learn of his sister's struggles but stayed silent and let his older brother do the talking. After Bekim left, he and Nana walked Mehmet and Jariyeh to the door and waited for them to put on their shoes.

That's when Zogu finally spoke.

"Edhe mos harro. Ajo asht motra jeme,"--And don't forget. She's my sister, he said to Mehmet in a tone that made Vera shudder.

(The meaning was clear: if anything happens to her, he was dead.)

It was 2 a.m. when Vera and Zogu got into bed. Their two-year-old and newborn sons were sound asleep in their cribs.

Zogu tossed and turned, unable to escape the night's conversation that played over and over in his head. Vera knew the meeting wasn't any of her business, but hoped her husband would say something—anything. But nothing came.

From their second-floor window, they heard the occasional car roll up and down Bay Parkway as they tried to sleep. Thirty minutes passed, and no sleep came. Then Vera, with her bionic ears, caught the sound of a scream.

"Oj Nanë! Oj Nanë!" Jariyeh was calling out for her mother.

Vera shot up.

"It's Jariyeh!" Zogu said.

Then the sound of gunshots.

Four of them—maybe more.

Zogu bolted out of bed, pulled on his pants, sprinted barefoot to the front door, and flew down the stairs.

In the lobby, he found the Polish superintendent dead of a heart attack, his wife crying over him.

Zogu rushed into the vestibule. There, lying in a pool of blood and broken glass, was his favorite sister. The smell of gunpowder still in the air.

He dropped to the floor beside her.

If only she had told him. He would have stopped it.

Then blood gurgled from her mouth.

Weeping uncontrollably, he checked her pulse.

Nothing.

He ran upstairs to call the police and tell Nana.

In court, the jury heard a truncated, pain-free version of what Zogu experienced. The dead superintendent was not mentioned. Despite Mehmet's role in causing his heart attack, Barse made sure it was ruled inadmissible.

Q: What happened after Bekim left?

A: A couple of seconds later, Mehmet left with my sister. I shook their hand, which is our tradition, I said good night, and they went away. Then I went to sleep, but I couldn't sleep.

About twenty minutes later, I heard the scream, and I said to my wife, It's Jariyeh.

Right after the scream, I heard shots. I heard more than three shots.

I got up, I put my pants on, and I ran downstairs. The first door of the building was all shattered. I opened the door, and she was dead between the two doors. I checked for her pulse, and I found none. I ran upstairs and I called the police.

In the stairwell, Zogu had passed Vera but couldn't bring himself to speak. She'd have to see for herself.

Vera rushed into the vestibule and knelt beside her best friend.

There's not enough blood for her to be dead, she told herself, not knowing how much was too much or too little.

She wiped the blood from Jariyeh's lips and tried giving her mouth-to-mouth, like she'd seen on television.

"I felt her breath brush against my face," Vera told me decades later. But Zogu said there was no pulse. Had she imagined it?

"Stay with me," she whispered. "Stay with me."

Weeks earlier, Jariyeh had told her, "I wish I could take my children, go far away, and live high up on a hill. Only then could I be happy."

Now, she said nothing.

"I love you," Vera whispered. "I love you."

She heard Nana screaming as she ran down the stairs.

"Jariyeh! Jariyeh!" Nana cried out to her daughter.

"Oh Zot!" she cried out to her God.

Rushing into the vestibule, Nana's knees buckled at the sight of her little girl. She didn't see the bus outside. She didn't notice the flashing police lights.

Nana pulled her daughter's lifeless body into her arms.

Hugging her.

Holding her.

Wailing.

"*Unë ta kam ba, moj bi. Unë ta kam ba.*"--I have done this to you, my daughter. I have done this to you.

Chapter 68

2:30 AM: The Chase

* * *

I was told a bus driver had seen what happened. I didn't know there was another witness.

At about 2:30 a.m., Michael Patino, an auxiliary police officer who lived in Jariyeh's building, was returning from work when he heard gunshots—followed by screams. Through the vestibule doors, he saw a woman in a white nightgown running down the hallway toward him.

He wasn't trained for this. He didn't carry a gun. He wasn't taught to apprehend criminals or stop murders. He was taught to observe and report suspicious activity.

The woman pushed through the door, frantic.

Trembling, he asked, "How can I help?" as if reciting from his auxiliary manual.

"She ran past me," Patino told the jury. "I turned around and came face-to-face with a man armed with a gun. A white male, five foot five, 150 pounds, dark brown hair, approximately thirty-two years of age. The man pointed his gun at my stomach.

I was stuttering. I said, 'I didn't see anything. I don't want to get involved. I'm just leaving,' and started to back up.

I charged right through the door and ran upstairs and called the police. Twice."

At the corner of Bath Avenue and Bay Parkway, Paul Nissenson sat in his empty B6 bus, waiting for the light to change. He had begun his first shift at 12:19 p.m. and his second after only eleven minutes of recovery time. He could've done the route with his eyes closed, if it weren't for the construction detour. Had it not been for the detour, he wouldn't have seen the woman in white running toward him. Was she running for the bus? he wondered.

The light turned green. He made the wide right turn in her direction. Then he heard a loud noise, like a gunshot, and slammed on the brakes.

The bus screeched to a halt in front of our building, 8747 Bay Parkway, as if placed there by the hand of God to bear witness. Not that Nissenson would think it a blessing.

From his driver's seat he could see everything. The area was flooded with light—the bright interior of the bus lit the sidewalk, the entryway lamps glowed overhead, and the fluorescent vestibule shone through the glass. Nissenson saw a short man in brown pants and a dark shirt, maybe blue, chasing the woman as she turned into the building's archway.

DA Roth asked him, "How far was the shooter from her?"

A: He was behind her, about ten, twelve feet.

Q: What happened next?

A: She was trying the door, looked like she was reaching for bells, you know, in panic.

In the time this was happening, I was on my radio calling for help.

I saw the woman being hit several times, you know with bullets. She was trying the door in pain, I think trying to get in—

I had to stop reading. I had ordered the transcripts because I wanted to know—and now I wished I hadn't.

Q: Was the man inside or outside of the vestibule?

A: Outside. He had his back towards me, and I heard approximately three or more shots. The glass got blown out of the door.

Q: Describe to us what happened to her as you heard these gunshots.

A: She was trying the door, as the gunshots were going off. The man just kept firing shot after shot at the woman.

You could see her clutching her body. Her body was contorting in all different ways. She was bending over and twisting around, you know in pain. Then she proceeded to fall down. And the last thing I saw was her fall backwards.

I never could have imagined such a gruesome death.

Q: Referring to People's Exhibit. Is this the position that you finally observed her in?

A: Yes, sir.

What did that photo look like?

When I try to imagine my sister in that vestibule, the scene is peaceful. There is only one bullet hole in her wrist. No blood. Even when I try to imagine blood and broken glass, it disappears. Jariyeh's long hair softly frames her face. Her eyes are closed, as if she were sleeping.

It hadn't been that.

Q: After the man stopped firing, what did he do?

A: He turned around and started walking fast out of the building entranceway and headed straight towards me. He came up to the curb, picked up a revolver in his right hand and pointed it at me.

I was sitting there just petrified, frozen. There was nothing I could do. Then he turned to his right and proceeded to walk rapidly up Bay Parkway. He started to run in a slow trot and tucked the revolver into his waistband, then ducked into the next building entranceway.

Why didn't Mehmet shoot him? Had he run out of bullets or was he saving them in case my brothers followed?

During cross-examination, Barse tried to discredit Nissenson:

"How bright were the lights?"

"Was there a car parked between you and the shooter?"

"Was it five feet, or twenty-five feet, like you stated at the Wade trial?"

What is a Wade trial? I looked it up. It's a pretrial proceeding held to determine whether a witness's identification of the defendant, often during a lineup, is reliable. It had taken place just a week earlier, on February 3.

At that Wade hearing, the District Attorney had asked Michael Patino:

"Can you point out the individual who you saw on September 18, 1979?"

Patino pointed to the wrong man.

Twice.

How was that possible?

I recalled the police described Patino as "shaking and stuttering," and figured he didn't make a good witness. Surely Nissenson got it right. He was described as "nervous but cool."

Barse turned to Nissenson:

"Did you point to the defendant at the Wade Hearing?"

"No."

Shit. He had pointed to that same wrong man—Sabri, Mehmet's brother-in-law. I looked Sabri up. Same height. Same build. The man looked more like Mehmet than Mehmet's own brother.

I remembered meeting Sabri many years later. He was a chef at an Italian restaurant that Zogu frequented. Whenever he heard Zogu was there, he'd come out to say hello, then send complimentary dishes. We thought he was a good guy.

Mr. Roth asked for a redirect:

Q: Mr. Nissenson, when I asked you if you saw the individual in court whom you saw on the evening of September 18, 1979, what happened?

A: I recognized the defendant in the hallway prior to him coming into court, and when you asked that question, I tried to visualize the clothes he was wearing.

MR. BARSE: I move for a mistrial.

THE COURT: Overruled. You may continue.

A: I saw a man who looked similar to the defendant, wearing the same jacket and shirt the defendant was wearing in the hallway, and pointed to him.

But told the judge I made a mistake.

I then walked over to the defendant, who was sitting way in the back, and pointed him out.

THE COURT: Are you telling us that this man had on in the courtroom what you saw the defendant had on in the hallway?

A: That is correct. They had switched clothes.

Mehmet stood in the hallway just long enough for both witnesses to clock his clothes, then switched outfits with his look-alike brother-in-law before entering the courtroom. I never imagined him to be that clever.

When Mr. Roth credited Mr. Barse with the scheme, that made sense.

At the Wade hearing, two eyewitnesses had four chances to point out Mehmet—and got it right only once. The people's case was hanging by a thread.

Esat was the DA's last hope.

Chapter 69

2:25 AM: The Little Witness

* * *

Esat was nine at the trial, but only seven the night his mother died. He was just a little boy in race car pajamas, trying to sleep, unaware that what he'd see would one day decide his father's fate.

While Jariyeh and Mehmet were at the family meeting, their children slept soundly. Three-year-old Lata lay in her princess canopy bed with Cinderella sheets. On her walls, big-faced girls in oversized hats adorned with feathers and flowers watched over her. Next door, her six- and seven-year-old brothers slept in mahogany beds, tucked under their Star Wars sheets and matching blankets. Sailboats and compasses surrounded the boys—meant to inspire them to see the world and find their way.

Their mother had wallpapered the rooms herself. She wanted her children to have the best. To be the happiest. To not have a care in the world.

Weeks earlier, Esat had found a stash of heroin in the refrigerator door and asked, "What's this?"

"Nothing, my soul," his mother said. "Take your brother and sister and go play in your room."

Esat marched off holding their hands. He saw himself as their protector, especially when his parents fought. And they fought a lot.

"Are you crazy?" he heard his mother scream. "How dare you leave drugs around the house!"

Esat knew his mother wasn't supposed to yell at his father. He was the man. He carried guns. Esat planned to be tough like his dad when he grew up, not knowing what that really meant.

A year and a half later, on February 11, 1981, DA Roth had Esat pulled from school and placed with Social Services on Long Island. He didn't trust that the Bicis would bring him in to testify against his dad. Judge Lentol appointed a Law Guardian and ordered that Esat be placed in protective custody.

"Judge, for the record, I object to the separation from his family," the Law Guardian said.

"You wouldn't want to take it upon yourself to let him go home," Lentol said. "And take responsibility for something happening to him. I'm not concerned about the family talking to the child. I'm sure they've already done that. I'm concerned with what will happen to him when he goes back."

On the stand, Detective Zigo testified to being present at the precinct the afternoon Esat Bici gave his statement. Judge Lentol dismissed the jury and called the lawyers into his chambers.

"Mr. Roth has wrestled with whether or not to call the child," Judge Lentol said to Barse, "He knew the trauma it could cause. But he felt he had no choice."

He handed Barse Esat's statement to read.

"I have spoken to this child," Barse said. "And at no time did he reveal the information I just read. What troubles me, Your Honor, is that I have to live with myself. I know defense counsel is often asked: what do you do if you know your client is guilty?"

I had hated Barse all this time, thinking he knew Mehmet was guilty—but now I felt sorry for him. Mehmet had lied to him too.

"If I had been given this statement earlier," Barse added, "there wouldn't have been a trial, but a plea taken."

Mr. Roth apologized for the late notice and put the original plea offer of first-degree manslaughter back on the table. And Judge Lentol granted Barse forty-eight hours to speak to his client. Keeping the child off the stand was the goal.

Two days later, Barse returned to the judge's chambers and said:

"Let the record indicate that I have just discussed this matter with the defendant, the defendant's father and mother, and several sisters, for approximately twenty-five minutes. The defendant wishes to proceed with this trial."

I was stunned. Barse had asked for forty-eight hours, yet waited until he was back in court to consult the Bicis. At first, I assumed the family wanted the trial to continue because they were confident they'd brainwashed Esat during the year and a half he'd lived with them. But if that was the reason, why did Barse then start filing motion after motion for a mistrial? The judge denied every one, but he kept going.

"The family requested a psychiatrist examine the child to determine if it will do irreparable harm to place him on the stand to testify against his father. For the welfare of the child, Your Honor."

"Motion denied," Judge Lentol replied. "What else? Let's get on with it. You're racing the clock again, aren't you?"

"I am not, Your Honor. Please don't say that to me. I am trying to defend a client!"

"Don't shout at me, Mr. Barse. Shout at me again, and I'll hold you in contempt and put you downstairs with him."

Barse dragged them into lunchtime, just as the judge suspected—a stalling tactic lawyers use when they need time to talk to their client. Was it Barse who convinced the Bicis to continue the trial? Did he tell them that he could keep Esat off the stand, or that he could keep the statement from being read?

Before Esat could testify, Judge Lentol had to make sure he knew the difference between the truth and a lie. The Bicis were removed from the courtroom so the boy wouldn't be intimidated, and Mehmet was told to sit still.

Q: Do you know the difference between telling the truth and telling a lie?

A: Yes. Telling a lie is—it's a wrong thing.

Q: Do you believe in God?

A: Yes.

Q: Do you get punished if you tell a lie?

A: Yes.

Q: What punishes you?

A: Who?

Q: Who would punish you?

A: My aunt and my uncle.

That was a dagger to my heart. Esat feared his father's brother and sister more than he feared God. Perparim told me Agim had a short fuse, but after being shot in their father's place, he took it out on Jariyeh's boys—especially Esat. One time, he repeatedly threw him against the concrete walls so hard the apartment shook.

Judge Lentol was satisfied that Esat knew what the truth was and brought in the jury. After several objections by Barse, the DA began his questioning.

Q: Esat, do you remember the events of September 18, 1979?

A: No.

Q: Do you remember speaking to an Assistant District Attorney, Brendan Lantier on that day?

A: Yes.

Q: Did you tell Brendan Lantier the truth?

A: Yes.

Because Esat said he remembered telling the truth that day, the DA moved to admit his statement into evidence.

"I object," Barse said. "The statement is hearsay."

"It's past recollection recorded," Judge Lentol corrected. Then he invited Barse into his chambers and read *People v. Raja.*

I looked it up. Ironically it was Anton Raja, Zogu's friend. His gun possession case set the precedent that a witness who didn't recall an event could still have their statement read, if they remembered telling the truth when they gave it.

Back in the courtroom, Mr. Casciorizzo took the stand. After many objections, he was asked to read the statement he had transcribed that day. I became a fly on the wall of my sister's apartment and watched it all unfold through the eyes of her seven-year-old son.

Question: What woke you up this morning?

Answer: The racket they was making, they was screaming all day.

Question: Who was screaming?

Answer: My mother and father.

Question: Did you know what they were saying?

Answer: My father said, "Stay still, or I'll shoot you."

He heard that? I'd thought the only thing Esat witnessed was his father jump out the window. No wonder Barse fought so hard to keep the statement from being read.

Question: Then what happened?

Answer: My mother ran into my sister's room, he shot and it went through the window, it's broken, the window.

Question: You heard that?

Answer: I didn't see, I heard that.

Then she ran into the hall and tried to get help, and she tried to open the door, and it was locked, and then he shot her.

I put down the iPad and went for a walk.

Poor Jariyeh. Poor kid. I assumed Esat had followed his parents, but later learned he was scared and hid in the closet. I pictured him crouching in the dark, shuddering, building a wall around his heart. Trying not to feel. Trying not to care.

Question: What went on in the hallway?

Answer: I just heard shots.

Question: Had you ever seen your father with a gun?

Answer: Yeah. Five times, because my grandfather has some, he gives it to his son.

Question: You said you got some pills, is that right?

Answer: Yeah.

When the shots in the hallway stopped, Esat came out of hiding and walked around the apartment looking for the pills. On the table, he found the small red ones and went to his schoolbag, which he called his briefcase. He pulled out his *Happy Days* lunchbox—the one with The Fonz on his motorcycle giving a thumbs-up—and stashed the pills inside. His father wouldn't find them there.

Question: How do you know they were your father's?

Answer: Because he was like drowsy when he shot her.

Esat heard the door open. The click of the lock. Footsteps. The dialing of the kitchen rotary phone.

Question: Did you hear your father on the telephone?

Answer: Yeah.

Question: What was he saying?

Answer: He said, "I have four bullets."

Question: Who was he talking to?

My heart beat wildly. Finally—proof. He must've called the drug dealers to say it's done.

Answer: He was talking to his father.

What? Why, of all people, would he call Selman?

Question: The police came through the window?

Answer: Yeah.

Question: Your father went out a different window?

Answer: Yeah.

Esat didn't say which window his dad jumped out of. But all of Jariyeh's windows faced Bay 31st, the block behind the building.

During cross-examination, Barse tried to suggest that my family had beaten Esat or frightened Esat into lying, but the stenographer testified that the boy had no marks, and no fear.

"What impressed me most," Mr. Casciorizzo said, "was how calm the boy was for his age."

Barse had no more questions.

Judge Lentol excused Mehmet and the jury.

Esat's Law Guardian told the judge that the child wanted to go back to the place on Long Island, and not be sent back to the Bronx.

Then Mr. Michelman said he'd been hired by the Bicis to represent Esat, and insisted that he be allowed to take the child home; otherwise, he would file a writ of habeas corpus—a petition demanding the judge justify why Esat was being held in custody.

After hearing both sides, Judge Lentol said:

"Mr. Michelman has been retained by the defendant's sister, the wife of the man who exchanged clothing with the defendant at the Wade hearing. Michelman has made himself a pawn by using this child to protect a man charged with murder. Rather than act as counsel for the child, he coached Mr. Barse throughout the child's cross-examination.

I have determined that allowing the child to live with the defendant's family would not be conducive to his safety, and placed him in the custody of Social Services. Apparently, I was right. The child asked to go back to that place, not his home. I find nothing illegal about his detention as a material witness.

Your writ is therefore denied."

Judge Lentol turned to Mehmet's lawyer, "Do you want the child back here for any reason?"

"First, I'd like to speak to the child," Barse said.

"The child doesn't want to speak to you. The only reason I will bring the child back is if you want him on the stand. The child doesn't want to speak to you. He doesn't even want to speak to his father. Is that clear?"

"No."

"It's not?"

"No."

"How do I make it clear to you—take a chisel and hammer and drive?"

"No, by giving me the right to speak to the child."

"You don't have the right."

I loved this Judge.

Barse said he did not want to cross-examine Esat. But after watching Esat's videotaped interview in the judge's chambers on the day he was pulled from school, he changed his mind.

The next morning, Barse put Esat on the stand and called him by his American name, Eddy.

Q: Eddy, when the Judge asked what happened, do you remember saying, All I heard was screaming, that's all?

A: Yes.

Q: When he asked if you saw your father, do you remember saying, No, my head was against the wall, I was sleeping?

A: Yes.

Q: You never heard your father tell your mother to lie still. Did you?

A: Oh, no.

Q: Did you hear your father shoot your mother?

A: No.

Q: So if you ever told anyone on September 18th that you saw something different, that wasn't the truth, was it?

Esat shook his head. No.

"For the record, that's a no," Barse clarified.

Judge Lentol asked Esat questions.

"Did you hear somebody arguing that night?"

"Yes."

"You know your mother's voice, don't you?"

"No."

"Did you hear your mother screaming?"

"I heard somebody scream."

"Do you want to be here today?" he asked gently.

"No. I don't like court."

"I didn't call him, Your Honor," Barse interrupted.

But he had.

Chapter 70

2:35 AM: The Crime Scene

* * *

Police Officer Gatto and Detective Cataneo were two blocks away, at 86th and Bay Parkway, when the call came in: "Auxiliary police officer in need of help, possible shots fired at 8735," followed by: "Man with gun at 8747 Bay Parkway." By the time Zogu dialed 911, the officers had already switched on the sirens and made a U-turn. Less than two minutes later, they were at the scene.

Outside 8747 was a bus with its flashers on and a bus driver waving them down. The man was nervous but cool as he described what he saw, then pointed toward the women in the vestibule.

Detective Cataneo testified:

"I ran to the lobby of 8747 Bay Parkway where I found a female lying face up with multiple gunshot wounds in her body. I felt for her pulse, at which time I didn't find any. I called for a backup unit and an ambulance to come to the scene as soon as possible."

Zogu came downstairs, surprised to see the police already there. He told them that it was his sister, that her husband killed her, and that they lived next door. Cataneo taped off the area and secured the crime scene.

Officer Gatto went to search the bushes in the front gardens of both our buildings. Finding nothing, he approached Michael Patino, the Auxiliary Officer who came outside visibly shaken. He stuttered as he reported on all that he had seen.

Zogu went upstairs, then downstairs, upstairs, then downstairs. He didn't know what to do with himself. The night was becoming a blur. He spoke to so many officers and was constantly repeating: "Family meeting… my sister… her husband…shots…the buzzer…the kids…"

Officer Gatto told his superior, "I'm going to look for the shooter in the building next door."

"No. Let's wait for backup," Cataneo instructed.

Was the scene so gruesome it made him hesitate?

One ambulance, three police cars, and twenty minutes later, the search for the shooter began. Cataneo remained with the deceased. The rest of the officers spread out. Some headed to the rooftops, others to the alleyways, and a few went with Officer Gatto to Jariyeh's apartment.

The DA asked Zogu:

Q: Did you go someplace with the police?

A: I went with them over to where my sister lived.

Q: What happened there?

A: The police officers told me to stand on the side. They knocked on the door and called Mehmet Bici's name and told him this is the police, to open up. Nobody responded. Then police from inside opened the door.

The officers in the alleyway must have seen the lights on, and possibly spotted Lata's broken window, and climbed inside.

The officers searched the apartment. They found nothing.

No Mehmet.

No drugs.

No money.

Just three children in their beds and an Iver Johnson .38 in the master bedroom—"not the gun used in the homicide."

Was it the one Nana gave Jariyeh to defend herself?

Five minutes later, Zogu left. There were things to do—he wasn't sure what things exactly, other than setting out to kill Mehmet. But for that, he'd have to wait until the police were gone.

"I went back home," Zogu told the jury. "I told my younger brother, Luan, to go over to the apartment because the kids will wake up and they will get scared when they see only the police and nobody that they know."

At 4 a.m., Detective Kane of the Crime Scene Unit was called in to collect evidence. He was greeted by Cataneo, who was with the deceased and would stay with her until 7 a.m. Kane measured the location of a deformed piece of lead and its copper jacket. He took photos of the victim, and waited for the doctor before inspecting the body for cause of death.

Kane removed Jariyeh's heart pendant necklace and diamond ring—pieces she'd bought herself after her jewelry went missing—and gave them to the brother who was in the hallway.

———

"Do you remember signing for Jariyeh's jewelry?" I asked Luan years later.

"That's a lie. I never went downstairs," he said.

"But you went to get the kids."

"No. I didn't get the kids. And no one gave me any jewelry."

How could he not remember? Maybe he had sealed off the memory of seeing Jariyeh dead to protect himself. That wasn't the same as what Mehmet and his family were doing.

Mehmet told Perparim we stole Jariyeh's jewelry. I tried explaining that his mother had complained that her jewelry went missing when his father started taking drugs. Perparim didn't seem to believe me.

Mehmet told Perparim that when Zogu went to the apartment with the police that night, he stole $100,000 and bought a building with it. I explained that everyone in our house worked at least one job except me. I stayed home to babysit so they could work.

I had never thought of Mehmet as a liar before. Did he need to make us look bad in front of the children so he could be like the victim?

He told Lata he owned several buildings in Manhattan and had opened the first belly-dancing club, but his sister and girlfriend stole everything while he was in jail. I believed it for years, until Nicky's son told me his father had opened the club, and that he and his brother used to sweep up the cash people threw at the dancers and pocket it.

But the worst lie was the one Filanza told Lata about how Jariyeh ended up between the double doors of our vestibule. Detective Cataneo had secured the scene, but couldn't stop not the lies that followed.

"When I was little," Lata said, "Filanza told me your family was to blame for my mom's death. She said your mother controlled everything, and was always telling my mom what to do. That night, Pop convinced my mom to get away from her. We were all in the car, ready to go back to the Bronx, but my mom jumped out of the car and ran to her mother's. That's why Pop killed her."

The cruelty was astonishing. Filanza lied to a child, as if it justified what her son had done. According to her, it was all my mother's fault.

Lata was in her forties when she told me this and still believed it. I reminded her that Esat saw Mehmet shoot Jariyeh in her room and that window broke. I told her police found them asleep at home, not in a car.

Lata shook her head. "I'm not surprised Filanza lied to me. She hated your family. Especially your mother.

God, what had we done? We sent the kids to live with *these people?*

Chapter 71

The Unreliable Witness

* * *

It was Barse's turn to present his defense. He wanted to put Selman on the stand but had to convince the judge his testimony would contribute to the case. *What could that possibly be?* I wondered.

MR. BARSE: I am making an offer of proof that Zogu Selmani spoke to the father at approximately 2:45 to 3 a.m. on September 18, 1979, and told the father that Jariyeh, the deceased, killed the defendant.
THE COURT: Very interesting.
MR. BARSE: It certainly is.
THE COURT: It sounds like a lie, and Jariyeh is dead.
MR. BARSE: That's right.
THE COURT: I will let you do it.

On the stand, Selman was asked to explain the phone calls to and from his house that evening. I was sure he'd tell the truth. Instead, he lied under oath through an interpreter.

Selman claimed that at 3:00 a.m., Zogu called him and said, "Jariyeh killed Mehmet." I knew Zogu would never have said that.

Selman said he was so shocked to hear his son was dead that he called Mehmet's house. Luan picked up and said, "Mehmet killed his wife and three children. Be careful—close your doors and windows, because he's bound to come and kill you too."

That, I believed. I could see Luan saying it. He was probably there to pick up the kids and wanted a moment of satisfaction. He couldn't get his sister back, but at least he could instill some fear in Selman.

At about 3:05 a.m., Selman said he called our house to see if Mehmet had killed his children. According to Esat, Selman knew his son had four bullets left. Did he think Mehmet used them on his kids?

As Barse questioned him, Selman grew confused. He kept changing who called whom, and which brother said what, until it became impossible to track. I didn't understand why Barse had put such an unreliable witness on the stand until Selman said, "I was so worried my son was dead. I called around the coffee houses and found him at the one on Church Avenue."

Ah…so Barse needed Selman to set up the alibi.

DA Roth began his cross-examination by asking about the phone call Esat mentioned in his statement.

Q: Mr. Bici, isn't it a fact that you spoke to your son when he called you from his house, at approximately 2:40 in the morning?

A: (In English) No.

MR. ROTH: Your Honor may the record reflect that the witness has answered the question without it ever being translated into Albanian.

Selman was so eager to deny Esat's statement that he forgot to pretend he didn't speak English. He answered again, this time through the interpreter.

A: My telephone rang but I didn't answer.

MR. ROTH: Your Honor, would you please -- I am hearing comments from the audience.

THE COURT: If the audience doesn't stop, I will clear the courtroom.

The outburst had to be from Filanza and her daughters. Why right then—never before, never after—as if on cue? Were they trying to distract from Selman's lie? The Bicis were a shifty lot.

Q: Mr. Bici, weren't you the one who originated the phone call to Zogu's house at approximately three o'clock that morning?

A: Yes.

There it was. He had called Zogu, not the other way around, as the offer of proof claimed. But the damage was done. Selman had planted the seed that his son was gambling on Church Avenue.

Three phone calls stood out that night:

First, Jerry's call to Bekim around 9:30 p.m., saying, "Mehmet is going to kill you guys."

Second, Mehmet's call to his father at around 2:40 a.m., saying, "I have four bullets left."

And third, Selman's call to our house.

I asked Zogu if he spoke to Selman that night.

"Yeah," he said. "He called me around three o'clock."

———

When the phone rang Zogu had just returned from Jariyeh's apartment.

"Hallo," said a man with an Albanian accent.

Zogu hadn't heard that voice in years—not since the two weeks he'd spent at the Bicis' when Mehmet got him the pizzeria job.

"Djali jot e ka mbyt motrën teme,"--Your son killed my sister, Zogu said.

"Who did he kill her with?" Selman asked.

This implied Mehmet had found her with a lover. The cruelty of his words left Zogu stunned. His sister was dead, and this man had the nerve to imply that she deserved it?

"He killed her at my door," Zogu snapped.

There was no need to explain further: *N'kofsh Bektesh, mere vesh*--If you're smart, figure it out. Everyone knew honor killings happened "while in the act," and with a single bullet. Not gunned down at your mother's door.

Selman hung up.

Was it because he was shocked to learn his son had shamed the family? Or because he understood that his son now owed blood?

Had Selman called to gloat? To let Lutfi Feza's family know that the Bicis— the honorable Bicis—had "killed an adulteress" and were now owed respect? Was he proud?

Would he have been proud if he knew his son left heroin around the house, endangering his grandchildren? Or that he pressed a gun to his wife's head and demanded she sit on a penis-shaped candle? Or that he wrapped a phone cord around her neck when she told his naked son to get away from Lata?

If the Bicis knew any of this, would they have cared? Or had spite been festering inside their stomachs ever since Jariyeh told Mehmet to move out, that caring was out of the question?

———

My first clue that the drug dealers weren't to blame was that Mehmet called his father after the murder—not them.

I asked Lata years later, "Why did your father call Selman after he killed Jariyeh?"

"Pop called him because he was upset and needed his dad," Lata replied. "Selman loved Jariyeh."

I wasn't surprised Selman loved my sister. What surprised me was Lata's explanation: *He was upset and needed his dad.* My sister—her mother—was dead, yet Mehmet was the one who needed comfort?

"Pop was hearing rumors, and Selman would talk my dad off the ledge. He'd tell him, 'You have to stop listening to people. That's what they do. They talk about what they don't know.'"

Chapter 72

The Liars Club

* * *

One by one, Barse called the members of the "Liars' Club" to the stand: Andy, Mehmet's former deli boss, Jusuf, Rahim, and Pajazit, one of Mehmet's bodyguards. Three swore he was gambling at the Church Avenue Café "around said time of murder."

DA Roth asked if they'd been coached by Barse. They said no.

I was disgusted. How could a jury find him guilty beyond a reasonable doubt when all these men did was lie? Yes, it's better for a hundred guilty people to go free than for one innocent person to be put away—but Barse knew his client was guilty. If not before Esat's statement, then certainly after. Yet, he defended Mehmet as if he were the Messiah.

I couldn't stand the "It's his job" mentality, as if the law expects lawyers to have no conscience, no integrity, no heart. It wasn't about who did it, but whose lawyer was best at motions, objections, theatrics, and coached alibis. Grief was a sport. The courtroom a contest. Barse argued with Mr. Roth every chance he got.

Judge Lentol asked, "You fellas want me to give you boxing gloves?"

It felt like Barse was killing my sister all over again. Not with the pull of a trigger, but with hundreds of calculated shots. If I could have jumped through those pages and choked him—I would have.

Lawrence Barse didn't care that Mehmet massacred my sister. Though he often said, "For the welfare of the child, Your Honor," he didn't care about traumatizing a nine-year-old boy. Would Barse have been this ruthless if Jariyeh were his daughter? If Esat were his grandson?

Was this American justice?

Blood for blood seemed much more humane.

The Kanun may be barbaric, but the politics of American courts weren't much better. No wonder Lady Justice wore a blindfold—she didn't want to see.

———

As a final Hail Mary, Barse called his "Messiah" to the stand. Did he suspect the alibi wasn't working? Had Esat's testimony all but sealed his fate?

Barse asked him about his marriage. Mehmet painted a pretty picture: "I loved her very much." "I took her on vacations." "I bought her lots of jewelry."

Nothing about the drug deals in Mexico and Kosova. Nothing about the jewelry he stole. Nothing about the phone cord around her neck or the gun to her head. Or was this what the Bicis called love?

The DA began his cross-examination:

Q: Isn't it a fact that you are considered a drug dealer?

BARSE: Objection.

THE COURT: Overruled.

A: No, sir.

Q: Were Joey Lika, Dujo Seljanin and Bata business partners of yours?

BARSE: Your Honor, could we have an offer of proof as to why this questioning is allowed.

THE COURT: An offer of proof is not in order during cross-examination. You should have thought of that before putting your witness on the stand. You may answer the question.

A: No, I don't know them, sir.

Q: Isn't it a fact that on January 4th, 1981, you shot and killed Dujo?

A: It's not true, sir.

A month before the trial, Dujo Seljanin short-weighted Joey Lika and was shot thirteen times at the Park Avenue South restaurant he managed. Before he died, he gave up names. Bata was killed with a shotgun. On the stand, Mehmet denied any involvement, but would later take a plea and put Joey away for life.

DA Roth asked about the family meeting.

Q: Did Bekim tell you and your wife that he wanted the two of you to continue living together? Isn't it the Albanian way to side with the husband?

A: I wasn't in Albania. I grew up in this country.

Q: But, isn't it a fact that your marriage was arranged according to Albanian customs, Mr. Bici?

A: Yes.

Q: Isn't it a fact that you went to the apartment with a gun, Mr. Bici?

A: No.

Mehmet claimed he had no gun and no marital problems. He said he went to play cards. They discussed a sandwich shop he was planning to open. Then he walked his wife to their building hallway—where Bekim testified to seeing them last—and left to play cards on Church Avenue.

Q: Isn't it a fact that you bragged to the Albanian community, that you'd never spend a day in jail? That you are going to buy yourself an alibi?

A: I never told anybody.

Q: Was it your idea to change clothes with your brother-in-law at the Wade hearing?

A: No, sir. I don't remember, sir.

Q: Isn't it a fact that in a peak of rage, you took out a gun and chased your wife, shooting at her until you got to 8747 Bay Parkway, where you killed her?

A: No, sir.

Q: Mr. Bici, isn't it a fact that you called your father at 2:40 AM to tell him you had just killed your wife?

A: No, sir.

No further questions.

At 9:30 the next morning, Judge Lentol explained the charges to the jury.

At 4:48 p.m., the jury asked for clarification on the gun possession charge.

At 5:20 p.m., the jury returned to the courtroom.

I held my breath. I'd finally know why he only served eighteen months. Had he only been found guilty of gun possession?

COURT OFFICER: Is the verdict unanimous?

THE FORELADY: Yes.

COURT OFFICER: As to the first count of Criminal Possession of a Weapon in the Second Degree, what is your verdict?

THE FORELADY: Guilty.

COURT OFFICER: As to the second count of Murder in the Second Degree, what is your verdict?

THE FORELADY: Guilty.

Guilty on all counts. That had to mean a minimum of fifteen years.

So why only eighteen months?

And what happened in the apartment that night?

Chapter 73

Her Final Moments

* * *

Why did my sister argue with a man who once held a gun to her head and wrapped a phone cord around her neck? Was she too angry to care? Or was it because at the time Mehmet seemed harmless—the farthest thing from a killer.

Heroin had stripped away his ability to love, to hate, to feel. He wasn't capable of caring for anyone or anything, except his high. All Mehmet could feel was the drug's euphoria—not bliss, but indifference. People he'd once cherished had become objects, things. But the last thing heroin wanted was trouble. It did not want to kill. Not the brothers. Not the wife. No one. Killing meant police. Police meant running or jail—then where would he get his next hit?

But that night, in their apartment, something shifted.

They were arguing. Mehmet was still dressed, probably getting ready to go gambling. Jariyeh was in her slip, getting ready for bed. She had told Saranda, "This is it. I'm leaving Mehmet tonight," and after that infuriating family meeting, she must have been more determined than ever.

"I'm taking the kids and I'm leaving!" Jariyeh must have yelled.

"You're not taking the children," he said.

A woman's role was to serve her husband, bear his children—not have feelings, give opinions, or, God forbid, pursue happiness without him.

Their arguing woke Esat.

Mehmet grabbed his gun and aimed it at the woman he once loved. She wasn't a person; she was a possession—his Nuse. He was the King, and she was his subject, yet she wouldn't obey. Always picking on him. Always telling him what to do. Stop dealing. Stop using. Stop bringing home dirty money. Stop, stop, stop, like she was his boss. And now she was leaving?

No one left him.

———

Ever since reading the court transcripts, I've tried to piece together my sister's final moments. In the chase scene I used words like raced, bolted, and sprinted to describe her escape, as if she were a superhero—and could never understand how

Mehmet, who Esat said was drowsy, was able to keep up. Ten years later, I looked again at the medical examiner's cause of death and realized the bullet wounds must have slowed her down. All this time I had been avoiding the truth because I didn't want to face her suffering.

I entered the cause of death and list of bullet wound entries into AI. Then one by one I asked what damage each could have caused.

The wounds may not have happened in this exact order, or caused this exact damage—but they happened.

———

It was 2:30 a.m. on a chilly Tuesday in Gravesend, Brooklyn.

"Stay still or I'll shoot you!" Mehmet yelled.

Jariyeh dreamt that she would die and had welcomed the peacefulness of it— but that was then. This was now. She was terrified. She didn't want to die like this. Not in front of her children.

Hidden in the shadows, Esat saw his mother run into his sister's room.

Did Jariyeh think he wouldn't shoot her there?

The drowsy Mehmet stopped at the doorway, holding a gun.

Jariyeh raised her hands and moved toward him.

Was she worried for her daughter?

He pulled the trigger.

The bullet pierced through her left forearm and shattered Lata's window. White-hot pain shot up Jariyeh's arm. As blood dripped down her wrist, she forced herself past him and ran for the front door.

Mehmet sluggishly followed.

Relieved to see his mom run for help but scared, Esat hid in the closet.

With her left arm throbbing and nearly useless, Jariyeh struggled with the locks.

Mehmet fired again, hitting her in the right upper back—just missing her spinal cord. The bullet fractured her rib and punctured her lung. Blood flooded her chest as the lung collapsed. Each inhale scraped like glass.

But adrenaline shoved her forward.

Hunched over, she opened the metal door marked B4 and staggered into the hallway. Time slowed into frames—foot, breath, stairs, hallway—one after the other.

The drugged-up Mehmet followed, his steps unsteady but relentless. He had to finish what he started.

The corridor of their 148-unit building ran from Bay 31st to Bay Parkway. The block-long hallway of fluorescent light made Jariyeh an easy target. I imagined her long wavy brown hair swaying as she pushed forward, her bare feet slapping the marble floor. Each step slower than the last.

The glassy-eyed Mehmet pulled the trigger.

The shot echoed through the building as it struck her inner right thigh. Her leg gave way, but she caught herself and kept going, blood streaming down and smearing the floor.

"Oj Nanë! Oj Nanë!" she screamed for her mother.

Auxiliary Police Officer Michael Patino was arriving home from work when he heard a gunshot, followed by screams, coming from inside the building. A woman in a white nightgown pushed through the vestibule door toward him.

Shaking, Patino asked, "How can I help?"

Jariyeh didn't stop. She couldn't. She limped past him into the cool night air and turned left toward our building. The slap of her bare feet against the concrete was swallowed by the dark.

Patino turned to see who she was running from and came face-to-face with a five-foot-five white male, approximately thirty-two years of age and 150 pounds.

Mehmet pointed the gun at his stomach.

Patino froze, raised his hands, and backed away. "I—I didn't see anything. I— I don't want to get involved. I'm leaving," he stuttered, then bolted through the door toward his apartment.

Mehmet lowered his gun and continued the hunt.

At the corner of Bath Avenue and Bay Parkway, the empty B6 city bus was stopped at the light. Driver Paul Nissenson saw a woman in a white nightgown running toward him.

Jariyeh staggered alongside our bricked-in garden, past the rosebush where she and her children once posed in terrycloth outfits—a trail of blood marking her path. The castle-like archway of 8747 loomed ahead, its twin towers a silhouette against the night sky. Jariyeh pushed forward with scraping breaths, pressing her wounded arm to her side to dull the pain. With fight-or-flight locked in, her focus narrowed in on her salvation—her mother's house. Everything else was a blur.

At the corner, the traffic light flashed green. Nissenson made a wide right turn in Jariyeh's direction and heard a loud noise—like a gunshot—and slammed on the brakes. The bus screeched to a stop in front of 8747. He saw a man with a gun chasing the woman as she turned into the building entryway directly in front of him.

A wave of relief washed over Jariyeh as she passed beneath the gothic archway into our courtyard. A short walkway was all that separated her from the vestibule doors. The distance warped—short, then endless.

Mehmet cut into the courtyard right behind her.

"Oj Nanë! Oj Nanë!" Jariyeh called again for her mother, whose second-floor

window faced the street.

Upstairs, Vera and Zogu heard the screams.

"It's Jariyeh," Zogu said, and jumped out of bed.

The bus driver watched in horror as Jariyeh pushed into our brightly lit vestibule and reached for the bells. With her good hand, she slammed our buzzer—2I—again and again, then pumped the locked door. Her only escape.

Mehmet stopped ten feet behind her, took aim, and fired.

The bullet blew out the vestibule glass, passed beneath her armpit, and tore into her side, puncturing the thoracic artery. Blood surged out in pulses as the impact spun her around to face her killer.

A sob of defeat escaped her.

Mehmet fired.

Once.

Twice.

Jariyeh clutched her body as it twisted—one way as a bullet pierced her left breast, the other way as a second tore through her right breast.

Unable to stand, she fell backward onto the marble floor.

All hope of escape gone.

The blood trail from her daughter's room to her mother's vestibule—a final testament to her fight.

Mehmet looked down and fired one last time.

Was she looking up at him as the bullet entered her chest? Did it feel like a bomb going off inside, as other chest-wound victims reported? Was her last thought, I'm going to die? Or was she concerned for her children?

She lay there, eyes open. Staring into nothing. Her vision blurred. Her breathing a rasp. Her body ablaze with pain.

Upstairs, Zogu sprinted toward the apartment door.

Mehmet turned and walked rapidly toward the bus. At the curb, he aimed his gun at the driver. Frozen, Nissenson braced for death. Instead, Mehmet turned and trotted toward his building, slipping the gun into his waistband as he entered his vestibule.

Our Polish superintendent rushed into the hallway and saw the kind young woman from next door lying there in a blood-covered slip. He clutched his chest and dropped. His wife ran out after him.

Zogu found the super dead on the floor, his wife crying over him, and turned to the shattered vestibule. He rushed through the double doors and saw his favorite sister lying in a pool of blood and glass.

Blood gurgled from her mouth.

From above, Jariyeh watched as her brother checked the pulse of the body below—as if it weren't hers. The scene was a total mess. He was devastated. She was peaceful. In an instant, she was in her daughter's bedroom, watching her sleep. Her boys lay in their beds.

—

As I imagined my sister's final moments, I sought meaning beyond this world. Some believe that before birth, we gather with kindred spirits and choose the experiences we need to grow—each agreeing to play roles we do not yet fully understand. There, it's intellectual. Here, emotions take over.

Did Nana agree to manipulate? Bekim to break tradition? Baba to abandon? Filanza to fan the flames? And Mehmet to brutally murder? After death, in a "life review," they would relive every emotion they made others feel: the joy, the sadness, the pain. That was heaven and hell.

Had Jariyeh agreed to it all? Was her dream of flying on a winged horse the universe's way of telling her she was about to complete her mission and "come back home"?

If so, what growth could justify this tragedy? Was it necessary for someone else's evolution—like mine? Had she chosen her life, and the way it would end—in a vestibule, at twenty-six, with three children at home? Was Nana's decision to send them to the Bicis part of the plan?

If all of it had been preplanned by us—not God—did the reason for the murder even matter?

It did to me.

Chapter 74

The Confession

* * *

Four decades had passed since Jariyeh's murder. The memories were everlasting, yet distant—almost untouchable. For fifteen years, I wrote and rewrote. Wanting to get it right. Wanting to be exact. As some questions got answered, others appeared. Conflicting stories, shifting timelines, and new discoveries kept sending me to square one. Things weren't as black and white as I had hoped. The more I learned, the more I realized it was up to me to figure out what happened. If anyone knew it was Mehmet, and luckily, I had access through his children.

In 1991, I learned that they were living with their aunt in Queens. At first I hesitated, afraid of reigniting the blood feud. When I learned Mehmet was in prison on drug-related charges, I told my family I had access to the children.

"Stay away from the Bicis. All they are is trouble," Nana said.

But I couldn't. I had to repay my sister for everything she had done for me—for us—and remind her children who she was, in case they had forgotten. In case the Bicis had tarnished her memory.

It took a year to get the aunt's number. She promised to tell them I called, but never did. One night she admitted that twenty-one-year-old Esat and another boy were being charged with murder. The policeman's son, who had done the killing, took a plea and implicated his friends. She promised to give me Esat's trial information, but never did. I called several courthouses until I reached the right number. After a tearful plea for information about my murdered sister's son, a court employee broke the rules and gave me the time and date.

I showed up, sat in the last row, and stared at the two young men from behind, trying to figure out which was Esat. When a short recess was called, my heart pounded as I watched them stand and turn. When I saw little Esat all grown up— looking like Luan—I lowered my head and wept.

Not wanting to upset the Bicis and risk being cut off, I didn't approach him in the hallway. The aunt and Filanza invited me to lunch, and said Esat's lawyer needed another five thousand dollars—four months' salary for me. I borrowed it from Zogu, not saying what it was for.

Eventually I got to meet the kids. Lata had grown into a beautiful, fiery sixteen-year-old. Perparim, at nineteen, was a runway model and professional skateboarder. When I brought them to see Nana, the pain in her eyes was devastating. Did seeing how much they embodied their mother's joyful spirit make her wish we'd kept them? Or would their presence have been a constant reminder of the daughter she had lost—and that their father was still alive?

I visited Esat in Rikers. We began writing letters. He told me about the time he saw me in court—how he didn't recognize me, how he wondered if I was "an admirer or an enemy," how when his aunt told him I was his mom's sister come to see him, he said, *"What is she waiting for I don't bite."* When she said, "Sometimes you do," he bit her and she screamed.

It reminded me of how Jariyeh and I used to bite each other when Lata was a baby. I was happy the Bicis had a playful side. Then Esat wrote that they had lied about the money and kept it.

"If you think I would ever grow to like your family. It will never happen!…Just keep it one on one, then I'll give you a chance. …if you betray me and bring other people into our relationship you would become my enemy!"

I didn't understand why he hated my family. Still, I did all I could to keep him, Perparim and Lata in my life. They were all I had left of my sister.

Esat read the books I sent. He loved *The Prophet* and asked me to send Gibran's *The Madman.* He wasn't just his father's son, he was also a thinker. He sent a poem "Lockdown."

> *Don't ask me no more questions*
> *Just get out of my face*
> *I'm not a rat*
> *I'm leaving this fucked up place…*

In 1996 Esat won his appeal, went to the safety deposit box, swapped a sock full of loose change for his grandfather's gold, and jumped bail. He did not trust the system. Six years later, he was found dead in Tijuana, Mexico—a drug deal gone wrong.

Was this what Jariyeh had warned Mehmet about when she said, "All the curses that mothers put on you for supplying their children with drugs could one day hurt our children." Or was Esat's childhood to blame?

Over the decades, I kept returning to Jariyeh's children for insight and they, without knowing it, kept nudging me toward answers that were just out of reach.

In 2021, Lata was eager to learn about the mother she never got to know and asked to read a draft. Some chapters she found hard to get through. I asked her to find out if her dad, who she lived with, would agree to an interview. He said no. Lata offered to be my intermediary. I emailed her a list of questions, hoping some might stir good memories. She never said whether she asked him any of them, and I didn't push. But over time, the answers came.

After a picnic in Central Park and a few drinks, she said, "Pop was devastated after he killed my mom."

"I think he killed her because he was high," I replied, having learned that heroin addicts could also be violent.

"No. He said he wasn't high when he shot her."

Interesting. That hadn't been one of my questions, I thought. Lata must have asked him after reading my draft.

"How could that be?" I asked. "Esat said Mehmet was drowsy and found his small red pills. And the bus driver saw him walk and trot, never run, like someone on downers."

"I guess you're right. Addicts don't always know when they're high," Lata chuckled.

Seeing that she was open to talking, I continued, "Esat heard them arguing that night, but I always thought of your dad as passive."

"Pop is passive, but he has a temper," Lata explained. "In front of my boys, he's quiet as a mouse, but with me he loses his shit over nothing. One time I asked why he drank my milk, and he popped off. Another time I turned the AC on, and he pushed me. He has a problem with women. He tells me I remind him of my mom." She smiled at the comparison.

"Do you think Mehmet was angry at Jariyeh and snapped?" I asked.

"Yeah, he reached a boiling point. He doesn't know how to communicate. He doesn't know how to argue. He was probably listening to my mom and taking it all in. And if he was withdrawing, he would've been aggravated. Otherwise, he's very docile. But when he pops off, his face turns evil.

One time little Pop went off on six-foot-two Agim. He pointed his finger up at him and screamed, 'You motherfucker!' Let me tell you—Agim was scared." Lata laughed. "I don't think he would've killed my mom, but being around the drug dealers and all the violence made him violent. It was nothing to gamble. Nothing to do drugs. Nothing to kill someone."

I paused, taking it in. "That makes sense," I said, then wondered if I should bring up the affair. Though never proven, it haunted me in whispers behind my back, especially during my married years. The affair accusation was also why my family didn't want me to write the book, or even mention Sam. To some Albanians, just saying Jariyeh had fallen in love with his photograph was proof enough of adultery. If there was ever a time to ask, this was it.

"Mehmet said he killed her because of an affair. But he told Jariyeh, 'I don't care who you sleep with as long as you don't leave me.' So even if there was an affair, that can't be why he killed her."

"Right," Lata said. "Pop said he killed her because she was going to leave."

My niece broke the news like it was a given.

I stared at her.

Had she known all along, or had my questions prompted her to find out? I should have felt relieved to finally have confirmation that it wasn't an affair. But I wasn't. Was it because the answer came too easily? Because this search had reconnected me to my sister, and I wasn't ready for it to end? Or because the "confession" felt incomplete.

"So, why was he upset about the affair rumors?" I asked.

"Those rumors didn't bother Pop. He was mad at your brothers."

"What do you mean—*my brothers*?"

"He heard a rumor that your brothers knew about the affair and were laughing behind his back."

What?

So *this* was why Mehmet wanted to kill Bekim and Zogu? Not because he planned to kill Jariyeh and feared they'd take revenge?

"If my brothers knew about an affair, the last thing they would do is laugh," I said. But I didn't think she believed me. Was this lie about my brothers one of the reasons Esat hated my family, saying things like: "You know who are innocent and who are guilty"?

Years passed, and I kept coming back to this lie about my brothers. Whoever started that rumor knew what they were doing. "Laughing behind someone's back" was a grave offense. There was only one way to "fix" such a disrespect.

> Law §595: "If a person's honor is offended, there is no legal recourse for such an offense. Forgive, if you see fit, but if you prefer, wash your dirty face."

The only way for Mehmet to wash his dirty face was with the offender's blood. *S'ka djal nane si lun me mu*--there's not a man born of woman who can play with me—were the brave words of thin-skinned Albanian men everywhere.

"They were making me out to look like a sucker," Mehmet had told Lata. "A punk. Everyone was saying she was having an affair, and her brothers were playing me."

If Mehmet never heard that lie, would my sister still be alive?

Jariyeh was going to tell Mehmet she was leaving anyway, but that rumor had set everything off. It was why Mehmet threatened to kill the brothers. It was why the family meeting was called. Why Bekim said those terrible things, hoping to defuse the situation. Did his words make Jariyeh argue more fiercely when she got home? Was that why Mehmet lost his temper—a temper I never knew he had.

That rumor wasn't just gossip. It was a deadly spark. Maybe Mehmet would have killed her for leaving him on another night—but it happened that night because of rumors. Rumors kill, especially when one's honor is at stake. Rumors were why elders gave my mother's uncle permission to throw her off the mountain. Rumors were why Nana went to the edge of the cliff to kill herself— luckily, Baba saved her. But no one saved Jariyeh.

Who started this lethal lie?

Petty people gossiped about Jariyeh, but this lie required more of a mastermind. Was it the Bici spies? Or the Bicis themselves?

The closer Jariyeh lived to us, the more frantic Filanza's rumors became. It meant we were winning. Worse still, that my mother was winning. Did Filanza up the ante when Mehmet didn't act on the affair rumors? Killing the brothers was better than killing a wife anyway. Was she hoping there would be blood? Hoping her son would kill my brothers and finally put Nana in her place? Hoping it would restore the Bici name? A name tainted when Filanza's husband broke off their daughter's engagement, then again when her son listened to his wife and moved out. Two dead brothers would set the record straight.

I let this theory sit for months before I found the courage to share it with Lata.

"I think your grandparents started the rumors that set everything off and got your mom killed."

"It wasn't my grandfather—he was a good man," Lata said.

I expected her to defend her grandfather. But I didn't expect what came next.

"Pop blamed Filanza. He didn't like her. Filanza was always gossiping. Always bitching. Always on a rampage."

No one liked this woman. When Selman died, people went in droves. When she died, Perparim refused to attend.

Mehmet had blamed Filanza? Why hadn't this come up before?

Was it true? Had Filanza instigated my sister's murder? The idea that women could do this to each other was disturbing.

My sister had been given to the Bicis, and thanks to the patriarchal Kanun, the only way out was through bloodshed.

Had *Albanism* killed my sister? Was honor to blame? Honor was why my mother couldn't support Jariyeh. Why Mehmet couldn't let her leave. Why Filanza spread rumors. This was harder to accept than an affair or drug dealers. Had the deadly force been our traditions—the ones I idolized? The ones that made me feel special. Safe. The ones I never questioned.

After forty-five years of wanting to know, the answers had been there all along—waiting. I imagined they would come from an earth-shattering interview, where I got Mehmet to finally confess. Instead, the answers came quietly. All I had to do was write this book and place it in his children's hands.

They would be the ones to draw the truth out of their father—and in doing so, perhaps begin to see who their mother really was. I hoped it would begin their healing, and his too.

Chapter 75

February 19, 1981

* * *

Fourteen days after the trial began, and two days before what would have been Jariyeh's twenty-eighth birthday, Zogu came home with the news.

"Mehmet was found guilty."

Jail was only jail. Six feet under was where he belonged. Still, the relief was overwhelming. My sister had gotten some justice. My brother could stop hunting him. Life could go on.

"The DA said they won because of Esat," Zogu told us.

I felt bad that my little nephew had seen his father jump out the window, but was happy Mehmet's own son put him away.

We didn't know it then, but the verdict wouldn't hold.

Years later, the appellate court deemed Esat's statement hearsay and threw out the DA's "change of clothes" evidence. Instead of fifteen to twenty-five years, Mehmet did time served—*eighteen months.*

My family didn't fight it. Prison was not how blood was repaid.

When Zogu mentioned the drug-dealing, murdering Albanians of the Kosova Connection, I was surprised. "My" Albanians were good, honest, and kind—like my father. They welcomed you, gave you their last morsel of food, and put your life above their own. They shook your hand and kept their word, without the need for lawyers or contracts. It took me a long time to realize my *Shqiptar*--People of the Eagle were flawed—like everyone else.

We Albanians were an ancient people living in the New World, trying to reconcile our differences. America had virtually done away with honor and shame. Power and greed seemed to be their gods. The biggest criminals were men in suits who sat safely behind desks, incited wars, controlled the money, passed the laws, and pushed pharmaceuticals.

Where did Albanians and our ancient traditions fit in? Maybe we no longer needed our patriarchal codes, but without them, would we forget to be honorable, to have integrity, to put others before ourselves.

We were trapped between broken systems. Albanian honor codes kept my sister captive. American courts allowed Barse to manipulate. Both systems allowed

Mehmet to lie. American witnesses took an oath, Albanians gave their besa.

In Albania, a lie carried greater consequences than perjury in court. In Brooklyn, where people were distracted by success and bills, lies could go unnoticed. But in tight-knit villages, where every relationship depends on trust, lies couldn't be tolerated. If villagers doubted Mehmet's word, the Bici name would be ruined. Their gold would mean nothing, and their marriage prospects gone. Then the Bicis would be forced to steal wives, as Filanza once threatened to do to Jariyeh, or move somewhere no one knew them.

If Mehmet had been honorable, he would have confessed to killing Jariyeh and accepted our family's right to his blood.

His one noble act—not trying to kill us—was a silent admission of his debt.

Instead, jail would have to stand in for justice.

Chapter 76

The Exhale

* * *

It had been one year and five months since Jariyeh died, and my family could finally breathe again. Nana started making plans for the future, and the first order of business was Luan's engagement. Not moving on would mean the Bicis had killed Jariyeh and destroyed our ability to be happy. Luan's engagement would give us a way back. Getting back to our old selves was imperative, even if it felt too soon. Was the rush Nana's way of showing the Bicis we were invincible? Her way of saying that though her son had not killed Mehmet, he was behind bars—and we would celebrate.

My twenty-year-old brother had many American girls wanting to marry him, but he preferred Albanian. Why wouldn't he? If I were a boy, I'd prefer an Albanian girl who'd let me go where I wanted and do as I pleased.

Just days after the trial, Nana brought Luan a photo of Behare, a sixteen-year-old northern Albanian. She'd gotten it from a fellow cleaning lady at 1 New York Plaza—the girl's mother. Luan had several options, but Nana told him Behare was his best choice. My fifth-degree black belt brother agreed.

News of Luan's engagement spread swiftly—surely even the Bicis heard. People came with chocolates, eager to bring joy back into our home. This would be the first time since Jariyeh's death that we'd show that "the living were for the living." The first time that we'd sing and dance. Jariyeh would've wanted us to, and surely her spirit would be there.

Our living room couches quickly filled with guests ready to see us in our glory. We were dressed to party, but no one knew where to begin. Thank God for rituals. Sodas and chocolates were served, a sign that sweetness was making its way back. Our days of bitter were coffee long behind us. As more guests filed in, the women drifted onto the carpets and eventually into the family room—ready to celebrate.

But who had the heart to begin?

Nana eyed Kamile—it was time. Waiting wouldn't make it easier. Kamile picked up the sheepskin tambourine. Roza whispered a song in her ear and grabbed the other tambourine. They would do this together. The two musical sisters, who once were three, began to sing. It was hard not hearing Jariyeh sing with them, but it was nice to see my family happy—not too happy. Nana warned, "Don't be too happy, because then you'll cry." One had to be neutral: sad but strong, cheerful but composed, because you never knew what awaited.

Celebrating felt awkward at first. But then, like muscle memory, the joy returned. The pain beneath it somehow made the celebration more potent. Roza and Kamile were surprised to hear me sing along. They didn't know I had asked Jariyeh to write the lyrics to wedding songs.

Roza offered to teach me the dance to "Moj Hatixhe" (My Ha-tee-jeh), a song about a girl's life journey. It begins with Hatixhe's Nuse transformation on *Nata Kanës*--Henna Night. The night she dyes her hair and nails with henna and cries to get her sadness out.

Kamile played the tambourine. Roza stood before me and I prepared to follow her every move. We stepped to the beat toward each other, then back, our hands moving like belly dancers.

♪ *Moj Hatixhe,*	♪ My Hatixhe
moj n'shami t'kuqe	with the red headscarf
Ti ngjyn nana	Your mother will dye
moj flokt a kuqe	your hair red.
Ti ngjyn nona	Your mother will dye
moj flokt a kuqe	your hair red

Roza and I raised our hands to our heads, as if dyeing our hair. Then danced in a half-circle and traded places.

♪ *Flokt e kuqe*	♪ Spirits will charm
ti shitoft zana	your red hair
A po t'dhimen	Will you miss
o baba e nana	your father and mother
A po t'dhimen	Will you miss your
o baba e nana	father and mother

To echo the ache of leaving our parents, we swept our hands over our hearts and traded places once again.

Baba, nana,	Father, mother
dy vllaznija	and two brothers
Shkoj te burri	I'll go to my husband
m'rrok pleqnija	and get old
Shkoj te burri	I'll go to my husband
m'rrok pleqnija ♪	and get old ♪

We bent over, one hand on the small of our backs, symbolizing the weight of getting older.

As the song continued, Roza and I pulled at our skirts as if children were tugging at our aprons. We imitated kneading dough to feed the farmhands. The song ended with an old Hatixhe missing her fancy Nuse clothes.

This was the life I had to look forward to. The life I was programmed to crave. I was almost eighteen and would soon be making this journey.

We sent a mediator to ask the Bicis if Jariyeh's children could attend Luan's wedding. The answer was an emphatic no. Not just for this celebration, but for every celebration to come. The Bicis never told the kids they were invited, so they thought we had abandoned them completely.

Luan's fiancé turned out to be a beautiful Nuse with a kind heart. But no one warned us about Behare's psoriasis, and no one warned them about Luan's temper. Marriage was the act of discovery.

At the wedding I wore a polyester pink gown. Unlike when Zogu got married, I was now a grown-up. Eyes would be on me. Weddings were where families went Nuse hunting. I knew not to dance with all my heart the way Jariyeh would have. That kind of dancing could be seen as too wild and imply I didn't know my place. It would deter matchmakers.

I wondered if Jariyeh was watching.

After school one day, Vera said, "A matchmaker came to ask for you."

"For who?" I asked nervously, meaning which boy. I hoped it was Rich, not some random kid whose family had seen me at the wedding.

"For Sami," she said.

Sami? There was no way I could marry Rich's brother.

"What did Zogu say?" I asked, afraid he hadn't been able to turn down his friend.

"He said, 'No. Sami is my blood-brother.'"

I thought "blood-brother" was a nice way of turning down a friend involved in illegal activities, since we'd already suffered from one criminal in-law. I didn't know Sami earned that status because he tried to help Zogu kill Mehmet. I was relieved my brother said no, but was upset that maybe now Rich couldn't ask for me. It wasn't a rule, but it just wasn't done.

I immediately called Arta.

She said Rich had no idea his brother was sending a matchmaker. A few weeks later, the handsome Sami exchanged pictures with an Albanian girl in France and got engaged.

"A matchmaker came for you today," Vera reported eagerly not long after.

"For who?"

"For Rich."

"Really...*and?*" Vera's words couldn't come fast enough.

"Zogu said no."

"Why did he say no?" I asked, tears filling my eyes.

"Because Sami asked first."

"But I wanted to marry Rich."

Vera knew Nana hadn't let Jariyeh marry the man she loved, so she bypassed her first in command and went straight to her husband. I was so embarrassed that he would now know that I liked a boy. Sitting on my bed, I nervously awaited Vera's return. When Zogu walked in, I wished the floor would open so I could disappear.

"Hane, you can't marry Rich," he said sweetly. "It would have been different if he had asked first. You don't want Sami looking at you and thinking you should've been his. That can cause problems between the brothers."

Zogu had the right to say no to any suitor. I was grateful he cared enough to explain. It made me feel acknowledged, and his reasoning made sense. What kind of Nuse would I be if I put my happiness before the sanctity of brothers?

Arta mailed me a poem:

> *Hane Hane, I'm sad too*
> *But Hane Hane, you should get your man soon.*
> *God should make your fantasy come true.*

It became painful to see Rich, so when I slept over Arta's we no longer went upstairs.

"It's going to be real funny when I get married," Arta said as we embroidered her dowry. "The second I start crying, I know you, Zenepe, and Aferdita are going to cry too. God Hane, it will be one big flood."

I laughed. Arta could always make me laugh. I was going to miss her.

"Besides, all us girls will go away someday. Right?" she said.

"Right," I agreed, taking a deep breath.

With her wedding day fast approaching, Arta wrote me a letter in code, with direction to hold it up to the mirror:

> DEAR HANE,
> I am not crazy but, I'm trying. Izzy hasn't called, and I miss him...
> It's really nice when you can love someone without getting killed.
> Love is something beautiful if you love the right person...

"Dear Hane, I am not crazy, but I'm trying. Izzy hasn't called, and I miss him...It's really nice when you can love someone without getting killed...Love is beautiful if you love the right person."

Before Jariyeh died, we never associated marriage with murder. This was our new reality. I was happy my niece had found "the right person" and wouldn't get killed.

Izzy is my life.
_ _ _ _ _ _ is your life.

Call Me...

From secret agent
Commander-in-chief
Retiring in August

I hoped I would also find my S.O.S.—Some One Special—but wasn't counting on it. What were the chances I'd fall in love with the boy Zogu and Nana chose?

Chapter 77

Dancing with Myself

* * *

Unlike some Albanian girls, I didn't climb out of my bedroom window to go to discos. Dancing in front of my mirror when no one was around was good enough. Music was my escape, like it had been for Jariyeh.

I sang about "a very kinky girl" with Rick James, though I didn't know what it meant. I made sex noises with Donna Summer while "Love to Love You Baby" played. Hall and Oates told me I made their dreams come true. And when Peter Brown sang "Dance with Me," I imagined Jariyeh looking down at me and added moves I thought she'd love. I wasn't dancing with myself—I was dancing with Jariyeh.

I was eighteen and still couldn't own records, so when my favorite songs came on, I'd rush to hit record on the tape recorder, trying to avoid the DJ's voice. Then I'd spend hours rewinding, playing, rewinding, playing, trying to capture all the lyrics, like Jariyeh taught me.

When MTV aired "Video Killed the Radio Star," I was hooked on music videos. Jariyeh would've loved watching her favorite songs come to life. I couldn't get enough of Michael Jackson.

"We're going to the Paramount," Saranda told me. It was an old movie theater turned New Wave dance club. Bekim and Zogu had played soccer with one of the owners. "Wanna come?" she asked, knowing how much I loved to dance.

"Yes," I said, unable to believe the offer.

She went to ask Bekim, who once caught me "dancing like an idiot" in front of the mirror.

"He said you can come," she reported, her eyes wide.

Oh my God! What do I wear? I rushed to my closet and put on my pink cashmere turtleneck and gray corduroy pants—pink and gray were the latest fad. In the bathroom, I clipped back my long chestnut-brown hair and swiped on a little mascara, hoping my brothers wouldn't notice.

We walked into the Paramount to the sounds of David Bowie and Queen. "Under Pressure" coursed through my body, and I felt like I was flying. I couldn't believe I was there. The old movie house was filled with rockers in leather jackets and pink and purple mohawks. I looked out of place in my good-girl outfit—but I didn't care. They were them; I was me. There was music—and I knew all the words.

Bekim and Zogu stood between the theater seats drinking beers with one of the owners, their former teammate. Saranda and I sat watching the dancers on stage—the official dance floor. I pointed out the better ones, aching to join them.

Billy Idol's "Dancing with Myself" came on, and I was fiending to get up. This was the closest I'd ever come to understanding Mehmet's need for a hit. Nothing was more important than losing myself in the oblivion of sound—but I needed my brothers' permission. I glanced up at them, hoping for a go-ahead nod. They paid me no mind.

"I *love* this song," I said, turning to Saranda.

Seeing my frustration, she tapped Bekim's leg and nodded toward me.

"Go dance," my modern brother said.

I got up and walked toward the stage as calmly as I could without running. The punk rockers stared at me—the girl in the frilly pink turtleneck who looked like she belonged on *Little House on the Prairie*. But I couldn't let that stop me. As Billy Idol asked the world to dance, I broke out the punk moves I'd learned from music videos.

During Jariyeh's nights at Il Galletto, she soared like an eagle around the dance floor to "Shote Galica," the song about a Sworn Virgin who wore pants and fought valiantly in wars. I was no warrior. I didn't want to shoot guns. I was a good girl, awaiting my fate, dancing with punk rockers who refused to be "normal." They craved freedom and self-expression—the very things Jariyeh had fought for before her tragic end. My sister had dared to be different, but she was surrounded by narcissistic men and accommodating women.

She never stood a chance.

Would I?

As I floated across the stage under the strobe lights, I felt Jariyeh smiling down at me—so proud. Her little sister was holding her own with these crazy kids. One by one they moved closer, syncing their moves with mine. Dancing with others was better than dancing alone in front of my mirror—this must be what heaven felt like. I wanted to dance with them, but kept my distance, careful not to embarrass my brothers in front of their friend. Then they'd never bring me again. *Would they bring me again?*

As Billy Idol and I sang the last verse, I squinted toward my brothers, praying they weren't signaling for me to stop. Saranda looked up at Bekim, who was deep in conversation, and waved for me to keep going. I was so grateful to have brothers who trusted me and took me dancing. If only they would take me to clubs ıll the time. I would never drink alcohol, do drugs, or date boys.

The pulsing beat of "Whip It" from Devo's *Freedom of Choice* album filled the air. They wore upside-down flowerpots to show the "de-evolution" of mankind. It wasn't just Albanians who were backward.

Bopping to the hypnotic beat, I sang about whipping my problems away. Still oblivious to how my family was keeping me down—not maliciously, but because it was all they knew. My only chance at survival was to be like Bekim and stop living for everyone else. But I was still determined to be Nana's "good girl," not yet brave enough to break the rules.

Those days were coming.

For now, I lost myself in the music. When I danced, I forgot how much I missed my sister. When I danced, I forgot the pressure of being eighteen and not engaged. When I danced, I could just be. If only I could dance all the time.

The song ended.

Saranda gave me the dreaded come-back wave. I walked off stage, sweating beneath my cashmere sweater.

"You're a good dancer," the club owner said as I sat beside Saranda.

My brothers smiled proudly.

I blushed, surprised they'd been watching.

"You dance just like Jariyeh," Saranda whispered.

Me? Like Jariyeh? Had I done it? Had I finally become like my hero?

I got home with the music still coursing through my veins. In the dark, I quietly put my pajamas on over my sweat, not to wake Nana.

"Did you have fun?" she asked.

"Yes," I said, surprised she was awake. "I had a lot of fun."

I wished she could have seen me in my glory. She would've been so proud, the way she had been with Jariyeh. I would do anything to make my mother love me, and it was possible if I met her one condition: perfection. I was desperately working on it, unaware there was no such thing.

"Zogu and I were talking," she said.

I went on high alert. Talking? About me?

Was I engaged?

"We decided that you can choose your husband."

My family was more modern than most, thanks to Baba, but I never expected this. Having a choice in who I'd marry was empowering—yet scary. A big decision for me, the youngest of eight, who had all her decisions made for her. If I picked an abusive husband, I'd feel alone in my misery. If Nana picked him, at least I could feel like a martyr who lived for the family. I was starting to see the appeal of letting others choose and calling it destiny. Was I ready to decide for myself? I took comfort in knowing that Nana and Zogu would take the lead, while God controlled things from above—and boy did He had some making up to do.

Choosing my husband meant choosing the man I'd have sex with, which was embarrassing. I didn't know how to reply to Nana, not that a reply was necessary.

"*Natën e mire*"--good night, I said.

"Natën e mire," she replied. "*Couca Nanës.*"

Mommy's girl?

I pulled the blanket over me and smiled. Jariyeh came to mind. The ability to choose my husband felt like a final gift from my sister. She hadn't been allowed to choose, and Nana was making up for that. Big changes came through great suffering.

I didn't know why she'd said no to Sam, but all of that was over with. Things were different. Nana was different. I was different.

The seed of questioning had taken root in my restless head. It would fester. Grow. Demand that I awaken to the workings of life, death, and God.

Fate played a part, but we still had a choice. If we kept doing today what we did yesterday—or 500 years ago—we'd get the same results. We'd blame fate when the fault lay in our refusal to change, or admit that the Kanun wasn't more important than human life. Baba knew that.

In the years to come, I'd search for the truth and realize that to know God I first had to know *myself*. The self who didn't see color, religion, or nationality—the self who knew we were one. In this place, there was no question of good or bad, fate or free will—or even God.

There was only being.

In this place everything was perfection.

Even the tragedies.

Jariyeh's murder was the worst thing that ever happened to me. Yet, if I hadn't loved my sister so deeply and she hadn't died so violently, I never would've had the courage to question a world riddled with female oppression—a world I once called "perfect." I never would've embraced my femininity. I never would've realized women mattered.

That I mattered.

I turned toward Nana, closed my eyes, and began to wonder how this *choosing my husband thing* was going to work. Of course, I wouldn't be allowed to date or anything crazy like that, but I hoped Nana wouldn't expect me to decide after one coffee-serving situation. Would I get to talk to the boy on the phone? Could I meet him in person? With a chaperone, of course. The thought of it was exhilarating.

What kind of man do I want to marry? For starters, a man who would protect me—not kill me. A kind man like my father, who laughed a hearty laugh and sang after dinner. *Wouldn't that be nice?* An honorable man who made me feel respected. A smart man who wouldn't mind that I was smart. Were there boys like that in this pool of "macho men" that surrounded me? *God, I hoped so.*

There was Ilmi, Saranda's youngest brother—the only Albanian I knew who went to college. I liked that. He wasn't as handsome as Sam, but still good-looking. I could fall for someone like him. I desperately wanted to love the man I'd marry. In this way, I was American.

Maybe I won't be a sad Nuse on my wedding day after all. I'll act sad, of course, so my family won't be disgraced. But when Jariyeh looks down at me in my wedding dress, possibly one I chose myself, she'd know the truth. She'd be so happy for me.

It had been two years since I lay in this bed while Jariyeh lay downstairs, bleeding between the double doors. Life would never be the same without her.

But now, for the first time, the future belonged to me.

Afterword

The illusion that Jariyeh's death had hurt me most was shattered on a hot summer day in Staten Island, while Nana and I were drinking Turkish coffee. She was seventy-nine. I was forty-one. Nana had recently retired from her cleaning job only because we had insisted. My mother began praying five times a day, not because she was religious, but because it gave her peace of mind. She often turned to me, the daughter who spent decades on a spiritual search, when she had questions about God or the unexplainable.

"I wish I could see Jariyeh in my dreams," Nana said. "But she never comes."

"Maybe she does, and you just don't remember. You know, you can call on Jariyeh anytime, and she will come. Would you like to try?" I asked, expecting her to say no. Visualizations weren't part of our upbringing. My siblings were sure I had joined a cult and joked that one day I'd levitate.

"Yes, I'd like to try," Nana said.

"Great. Close your eyes and relax," I said, as I closed mine.

"I can't keep them closed," she said.

I looked at her, confused. I'd never heard of such a thing. If her eyes couldn't stay closed, how did she fall asleep?

"So, hold them closed," I said, knowing how ridiculous that sounded and not expecting her to do it.

Watching her raise her heavy cleaning-lady hands with enlarged knuckles and gently press three fingers to each eyelid felt like a dagger to my heart. I realized then how desperate she was to see her daughter again, yet couldn't close her eyes. My invincible mother was somehow broken.

Eager to bring Nana some relief, I began again.

"In your mind, ask Jariyeh to come to you… Do you see her?"

"No. I can't see her."

What? How could she not see her? It was her daughter, for God's sake. Surely Nana remembered what she looked like. I felt my impatience. So much for all those years of meditation.

"All I can see is Jariyeh going to buy milk," Nana said, resting her thick hands on her lap. "I will never forget that day. I was looking out the window and saw her going to the store. You remember, the store across the street."

I instantly pictured my beautiful sister in a flowing summer dress, her long, wavy brown hair bouncing behind her. "Yes. I remember," I said, doing my best not to let Nana see my tears.

"I saw Jariyeh walking," she continued. "And said to myself, *my dear daughter, you are better off dead than alive like this*...I can't stop wondering if my words killed her."

"Your words didn't kill her," I said. "Too many other things happened." But I knew what she meant. Baba had warned us, "Words have power. Never curse someone or wish them ill, because if something happens, you only have yourself to blame."

"Now, when I close my eyes, all I see is that day," Nana said.

So *that* was why she couldn't keep her eyes closed. My mother had countless reasons to feel guilty about Jariyeh, but she blamed everything on that one day and those twelve words. If that moment was all she saw when she closed her eyes, no wonder they refused to stay closed. *The body was a wonder. How did her brain know to send signals to the exact muscles that kept her eyelids open—just so she wouldn't see that day, recall those words, and feel that guilt?* That survival mechanism, which began after Jariyeh died, stayed with her for thirty years.

How selfish of me to think that Jariyeh's death had hurt me most. What must it have been like for Nana to lie in bed all those years, waiting for sleep while replaying that moment?

If I hadn't been writing this book, I wouldn't have known this about Nana. I wouldn't have known why Jariyeh died—nor would my family. Whether or not they agree with my conclusions, these stories are here for them to consider.

In writing this book, I realized that healing doesn't come from shutting away the past, but from understanding it. By learning my history and listening to stories, I began to see what shaped me, what hurt me, and what I no longer needed to carry. The more I understood my sister's life, the more I understood myself. To my surprise, I began to see how much of Jariyeh lives on in me.

I married in 1983, at nineteen, old by our standards. I did my best to be a submissive Nuse, but the rebel in me wouldn't listen. Like Jariyeh, I stood up for myself. Unlike her, I had brothers who stood behind me. The rest is a story for another book.

Like Jariyeh, I was ecstatic when my daughter was born. I let her do what I couldn't growing up: wear shorts, have American friends, date boys, go to her prom. More importantly, I encouraged her to be smart. She became the first in our family to graduate college. Watching her excel quietly healed parts of my younger self. When she married an American, Zogu refused to attend because she was "diluting our superior race." Some things don't change.

Albanians are much more modern now, but I see how many of the same old beliefs still shape our lives. The men in my family continue to insist that we live by their rules and bully those who don't comply. I often feel alone in wanting change. The women support me quietly, still too afraid of "the almighty men." As much as the women try to adapt, some still blame the "new divorce epidemic" on women who "just don't listen."

I recently heard that a male relative learned Jariyeh had been seen entering the building with Sam and said, "You mean Mehmet was innocent?" But under the Kanun, a man was innocent only if he caught his wife in the act. Seeing her enter a building with another man did not make murder blameless. Was it easier for men to call women whores than admit they were not man enough to avenge their blood?

Aside from me, I know of no woman who dares stand up to these men. It's times like these that I miss Jariyeh most. If she were alive, I know she'd not only have my back—she'd be leading the way.

May *A Country Called Brooklyn* give voice to the silenced.

May it rally support for those facing domestic violence.

May it inspire us all to question our beliefs.

May it remind us that "words have power."

Above all, may it honor *Xharije's*--Jariyeh's life and bring joy to her spirit, as she brought joy to us.

If you feel moved, please send her a blessing.

With much love and respect,

Jariyeh's baby sister.

Hane

"Today I have given you the choice between life and death, between blessings and curses. Now I call on heaven and earth to witness the choice you make. Oh, that you would choose life, so that you and your descendants might live!"

—Deuteronomy 30:19

"Indeed, Allah does not change the condition of a people until they change what is within themselves."

—Surah Ar-Ra'd 13:11

Faleminderit

Thanks to my family. Without your stories, the book would have no life. Thank you to Kamile, my genius sister with the impeccable memory who tries her best to support me; Bekim, the brother who challenges Albanian traditions and strives to be his own person; Zogu, the brother who remains the ultimate Albanian and forces me to try and understand my people; Perparim, the nephew who encouraged me to tell his mother's story even when it was too painful; Dhurata (Lata), Jariyeh's gift from God, whose stories helped uncover the "why" of her mother's murder; and Saranda and Vera, who filled in what their husbands left out and shared touching memories of their best friend.

Thank you to the people who helped put Mehmet away: Judge Lentol, who had a big heart; District Attorney Wayne Roth; the police officers, especially Detective Cataneo, who stayed with my sister till 7 a.m.; and witnesses Michael Patino and Paul Nissenson. Paul, I left messages with HR at the MTA to no avail. I'm sorry you had to witness such horror, but I am grateful for your testimony.

Thank you to the Albanians who helped me become a writer: Isuf Hajrizi, who published my first article, "Plight of the Albanian Woman"; Shqipe Malushi, who encouraged me to go to college and read my drafts; and Shqipe Biba, who founded the American Woman's Organization, "Motrat Qiriazi," to empower women.

My friend Lillian Firestone, an honorary Albanian and cutthroat editor, taught me to show, don't tell; that less is more; and kept asking, "What do you really mean?" even when I couldn't bear knowing the answer. Xavier Trevino, who helped me better understand addiction. Thanks to my many readers who helped make the book what it is today: Edit Shkreli, Alida Malushi, Peri Basil, Todd Gross, Kaye Peters, Becky Curtis, and Geri Brin. Thanks to my wonderful beta readers.

I am grateful to my writing teachers, and classmates who believed in me even when my writing was terrible. And of course to my children, who answered my endless "How do you say this?" questions and teased me about English being my second language. I know my writing took time that should have been yours, and I hope this book makes you proud.

Finally, to my readers, thanks for helping bring my sister's story to life.

ABOUT THE AUTHOR

Hane Selmani was born in Kosova and raised in Brooklyn—inside a culture where obedience was prized and questions weren't encouraged. She was once comforted by captivity, but ultimately followed in her sister Jariyeh's footsteps and fought for her own liberation.

In 1997, she became the president of the Albanian American Women's Organization, which was founded to empower women. Under her leadership, the organization helped raise awareness of the genocide of Albanians in Kosova, efforts later recognized by the White House.

Alongside her activism, Hane embarked on a lifelong journey of self-discovery. She studied the Gurdjieff Work, whirled with Mevlevi Dervishes, and sat in silent retreats inspired by Gautama Buddha.

A Country Called Brooklyn is the first book in her memoir series.

For bonus content, book club resources, and more, visit haneselmani.com
For exclusive photos and stories beyond this book, scan below.

ENDNOTES

[i] N.S. Gill, *Albania—The Ancient Illyrians* (Library of Congress Article on the Ancient Illyrians), January 29, 2019, *https://www.thoughtco.com*

[ii] Quinn Hargitai, *"The Country that's Famous for Tolerance,"* February 22, 2022, BBC.com

[iii] Jane Jurgens, "Albanian American's," September 21, 2019, Gale Encyclopedia of Multicultural America. *Encyclopedia.com,*

[iv] Johanna McGeary, *"The Ethnic Cleanser: Slobodan Milosevic has lost almost every battle he's fought-except the one to stay in power,"* March 29, 1999, *Time,* Volume 153, No. 12, March 1999, page 99.

[v] U.S. Department of State, *"Justice for Uncompensated Survivors Today (JUST) Act Report: Albania,"* *https://www.state.gov*

[vi] Traditional Albanian folk song: "Halil Gashi"

[vii] Prof. Bernd Fischer, *"Politicizing History: The Second World War in Albania,"* April 12, 2021, https://tiranaobservatory.com

[viii] Peter S. Green, *"The Ever-changing Logistics of Drug Smuggling,"* Wall Street Journal, https://www.wsj.com

[ix] Anthony M. DeStefano, *"Kosovo Albanian Mafia and KLA Reports From USA and Other Countries,"* Wall Street Journal, pages 1 and 18, September 9, 1985.

[x] Luke Lewis, *"700 Words That Explain Exactly What It Feels Like To Do Heroin,"* February 5, 2014, https://www.buzzfeed.com,

Michelle Horton, *"What It's REALLY Like To Be Married To A Drug Addict"* yourtango.com. December 4, 2014, https://www.yahoo.com/news/

Stacia Nicholson, *"Heroin Chic: The Art of Imitating Life,"* September 22, 2016, https://aliquotthesciencespot.com

[xi] Munich Re, *"Heroin—the Other Opioid,"* November, 16, 2017, www.munichre.com

[xii] Maia Szalavitz, *"A Brief History of New York City's Heroin Scene,"* December 14, 2015, https://www.vice.com,

Cait Etherington, *"Looking back at New York's 'Summer of Love' and the birth of the East Village,"* June 14, 2017, https://www.6sqft.com

[xiii] Walter H. Bowart, "How the CIA Planned the Drugging of America: Did Timothy Leary and the CIA work hand in hand to create the "turn-on, tune-in, drop-out" drug culture of the Sixties? Or was Leary a pawn in the CIA's attempt to deceive America's youth," *CIA Gallery,* September 1979, pages 51 and 99, *https://www.cia.gov*

[xiv] Raymond H. Anderson, "Rejected Albanian Suitor Seized in Shooting of Father of Girl, 14," *New York Times*, May 27, 1965, pages 1 and 26

Rejected Albanian Suitor Seized In Shooting of Father of Girl, 14

By RAYMOND H. ANDERSON

In the isolated mountain communities of Albania the breach of a man's word is regarded as one of the most serious of offenses—an offense that demands revenge.

Early yesterday morning on the Lower East Side, the Albanian immigrant father of a 14-year-old girl was seriously wounded in what was reported to be a feud resulting from the girl's refusal to carry out a marriage arrangement.

Two other men, one an Albanian and the other a bystander, also were wounded as the three stepped off a bus at the corner of Allen and Stanton Streets at about 2 A.M.

According to the police, two men emerged from a doorway as the bus left the curb and began shooting, one with a .32-caliber revolver and the other with a .32-caliber automatic.

The weapons were found nearby.

The reluctant fiancée's father, Selman Bici, 40, of 132 Ludlow Street, fell to the sidewalk, shot in the back.

The other Albanian, Maliq Kulemani, 36, of 145 Orchard Street, was struck in the upper right-arm and chest.

The third man, Joseph Avolglione, 54, of 151 Allen Street, was wounded in the thigh.

The wounded men were taken to the Beekman-Downtown Hospital, which reported last night that Mr. Bici and Mr. Kulemani were in fair condition. Mr. Avolglione was listed in satisfactory condition.

The police put out an alarm for two Albanian brothers, one the rejected suitor for the hand of auburn-haired Drita Bici. The suitor, Xhevat Abdyli, 27,

Continued on Page 26, Column 4

VICTIM OF FEUD: Selman Bici in recent photo with his wife Filaz. His daughter's rejected suitor shot him.

xv John J. Cardillo, *"I Used To Come For Your Guns—Now I Support Your Right to Defend Yourself."* Blaze Media, June 26, 2014, https://www.theblaze.com

xvi Maggie O'Kane, *"Kosovo drug mafia supply heroin to Europe,"* March 13, 2000, www.theguardian.com
O'Kane writes: "International agencies fighting the drug trade are warning that Kosovo has become a "smugglers' paradise" supplying up to 40% of the heroin sold in Europe and North America."

xvii Dan Bilefsky, *"In Albanian Feuds, Isolation Engulfs Families"* New York Times- Europe, July 10, 2008
Bilefsky writes: "The National Reconciliation Committee, an Albanian nonprofit organization that works to eliminate the practice of blood feuds, estimates that 20,000 people have been ensnared by blood feuds since they resurfaced after the collapse of Communism in 1991, with 9,500 people killed and nearly 1,000 children deprived of schooling because they are locked indoors."

Jonathan Finer, *"Albania confronts its Hatfields and McCoys"* SeattleTimes.com, Nation & World. August 24, 2007
Finer writes: "Where there is no respectable order, Kanun has always filled the vacuum," said Ismet Elezi, 87, a law professor at Tirana University who has studied Kanun for more than 50 years. He said the version that emerged after Hoxha is particularly devastating for Albania because it permits retaliation against any family member of a killer, "even the baby in the cradle…"

xviii Henry Kamm, "Firefight on Albania Coast Stirs Speculation in Internal Woes," *New York Times,* October 16, 1982, Section 1, page 3

Mustafa Band, *Wikipedia,* https://en.wikipedia.org/wiki/Mustafa_Band, accessed February 4, 2026.

xix Larry Celona, Richard Rosen with Mel Greene, "Knifer ambushes, slays B'klyn mom" Daily News, March 15, 1983, page C3

xx Dan Bilefsky, *"Albanian Custom Fades: Woman as Family Man"* The New York Times, June 25, 2008
Bilefsky writes: "About 40 sworn virgins in the northern Albanian countryside. Pashe Keqi, 78, said she decided to become the man of the house at age 20 when her father was murdered in a blood feud. Kamile Stema, 88, was the eldest of nine sisters and took the oath to remain a virgin at age 20, after her father died."

xxi Female-initiated divorce:

Qur'an 2:229: Wife may seek release (khula), often returning dowry.

Torah, Deuteronomy 24:1: Husband initiates with bill of divorce.

New Testament, Matthew 19:9: Divorce only for sexual immorality.